Endorsements

Through this book, Joan Lipis provides biblical followers of Jesus with a visionary new resource for worship and instruction. Her integrated approach provides a strikingly fresh stance toward the biblical feasts that are so faithfully chronicled throughout the Bible. *Celebrate Jesus!* puts new light on how and why to use biblical feasts in the context of a local congregation or fellowship. This book reminds us that these feasts embody God's covenant with all persons, in all cultures, for all of creation. The author draws generously on her Jewish upbringing and American experience. After reading this book, you will never think about eating chocolate chip cookies in the same way again.

Timothy C. Morgan,
Deputy Managing Editor
Christianity Today

Many see the teachings of the Old Testament as antiquated and passé. Joan Lipis reminds us they're God-breathed and relevant.

Several times in Hebrew Scriptures we see the phrase "feasts of the Lord." If they're "of the Lord," there's a good reason to celebrate them with joy—and Joan Lipis shows us how.

Joan has written a clear and compelling book. It's simple enough for the young believer to grasp but goes deep enough to invite further investigation. She speaks from her rich experience as a seasoned Jewish believer in Jesus. I have had the privilege of being her pastor in Jerusalem. She's the real deal. Enjoy the celebration.

Wayne Hilsden
Senior Pastor, King of Kings Community
Jerusalem

There is an increasing importance today for the body of Christ to understand the biblical calendar as we press in to hear God's voice.

Celebrate Jesus! will stimulate you to worship according to God's divine order and excite you as you stand with the rest of the Kingdom community celebrating Jesus.

Robert Stearns
Founder and Executive Director, Eagles' Wings Ministries
Clarence, NY

Joan Lipis, firebrand Messianic Jewish disciple of Yeshua (Jesus), has once again shown herself to think "outside the box" in her extremely helpful and greatly researched book on the God-ordained biblical holy days as found in Holy Writ and Jewish life.

Joan brings her spiritual intensity, her Kingdom devotion, her love of Yeshua, and her commitment to all that is honoring to God into her thorough investigation of the spiritual implications of each of the scriptural holy days and her practical recommendations for their respective celebrations.

Few products of this nature explore both the heavenly heights and earthly soundness of each of the *Chagim*, or holy days. Joan, herein, roundly sounds out all for the benefit of the biblical enthusiast so keen to grow in God and in more effective witness. I heartily recommend this labor of love to all sincere devotees of the Master, Jesus.

Ray Gannon, Ph.D.
Director of Messianic Jewish Studies, The King's Seminary
Van Nuys, CA

The New Testament is a completion of the preparatory work begun so wonderfully in the first Testament (Old Testament). Believers can understand the magnificent fullness of the Lord's work only when they know both Testaments and the connections between them. Joan brings deep roots in Jewish and Jesus communities to this wonderful study of the festivals. Her biblical and spiritual insights drawn from a life devoted to worship of the Lord will profoundly enrich your praise and love for our crucified, risen, and coming Messiah Jesus.

Gerry Breshears, Ph.D.
Professor of Theology, Western Seminary
Portland, OR

Joan Lipis has written one of the most informative, practical, and spiritual books I have ever read on the feasts. It is indeed obvious that God has given her insight and revelation for "such a time as this." I was particularly impressed with her in-depth knowledge of how each feast relates to the Kingdom. This is a must read for all serious students of the Bible.

Lana Heightley
Founder and President of Women With A Mission
Colorado Springs, CO

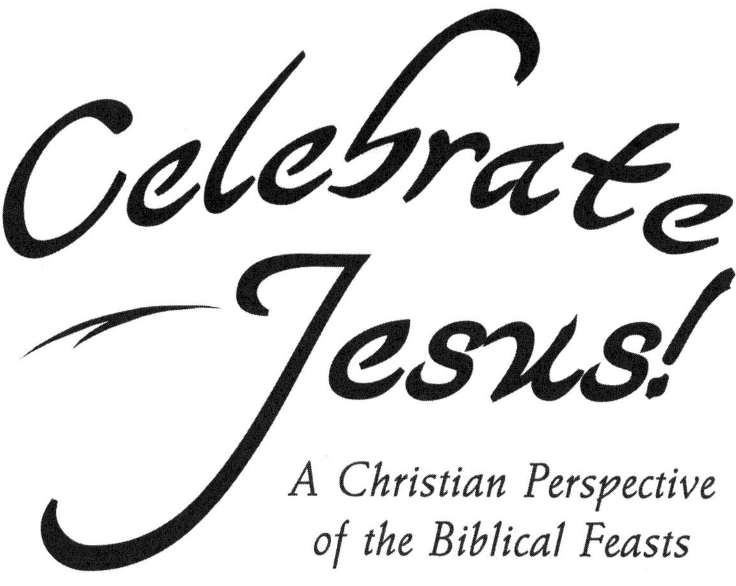

A Christian Perspective
of the Biblical Feasts

Explore the Significance of the Feasts
to the Community of the Kingdom

ISBN: 978-0-9817054-7-7
SECOND PRINTING, August 2009

Published by Palm Tree Publications
A Division of Palm Tree Productions
Keller, Texas, U.S.A.
Printed in The U.S.A.

www.palmtreeproductions.net

Cover Design & Interior Layout: Wendy K. Walters

To contact the author:

www.novea.org
www.CelebrateJesusTheBook.com
http://CelebrateJesus-TheBook.Blogspot.com/

Novea Ministries
P.O. Box 62592
Colorado Springs, CO
USA 80962

For...

My brothers and sisters in the
Community of the Kingdom
and to our King—
He alone is worthy.

Contents

Acknowledgments

With Thanks

Celebrate Jesus! is a love song to our blessed Savior. Many have sung solos, blending their voices into perfect harmony. I cannot fully express my gratitude but know that there is a storeroom of rewards waiting them:

Sonja Khan Hoekstra-Foss, for her tireless reading and gracious hospitality providing a desert refuge.

Avi and **Leah Brickner**, spiritual parents to many, for their endless prayers, wisdom, and love.

Lana Heightley, friend, missions team leader, and cheerleader whose love for the Word and the Kingdom encouraged me to write.

Tina, cherished friend and prayer partner.

Katy and **Brian**, for their patience, carrying my burdens when I had no more strength.

Kathy, whose idea to invite a few friends to Passover Seder led to thousands joining the celebration, and **Gwen**, who made it all possible!

Lynn, **Kari**, and **Brian**, for their advice.

My **intercessors**, known and unknown,
who prayed me through.

Tim, whose unflinching dedication
kept me on the computer.

Jan, who helped with the Hebrew, and **Noam**,
my "ram in the bush," God's last-minute provision.

Jamil and **Rae**, who made me beautiful.

My family: **Mom, Mark,** and **Lani**,
for their steadfast love.

Special thanks to **Palm Tree Productions**:
Wendy, **Todd,** and **John**, who were committed
to my success in word and deed.

Above all, I acknowledge the **Holy Spirit**,
who gave me the words and invited me to join in His
song of praise to **Jesus** to the glory of the **Father**.

Prologue

Enjoy the Journey

God is moving in and on the hearts of many Christians around the world, stirring a desire for a deeper understanding of the Old Testament and how it relates to the New Testament. A natural effect of this stirring is an increasing interest in God's ordained feasts and their relevance in the lives of both Jewish and Gentile Christians today.

In the early years of my walk of faith, I was a bit confounded that there were no opportunities within the church to celebrate Jesus in the so-called Jewish holidays. I thought that celebrating the holidays seemed to perfectly combine my two cultures, Jewish and Christian. But the holidays transcend any culture. Because they are fixed in God's character, His acts, and His plan of redemption, they belong to the Kingdom.

As with all of Scripture, the study of the feasts is a journey that will ultimately bring you into a deeper love of and intimacy with God. I pray you will enjoy and share your journey.

The book you now hold in your hand is meant to be a resource to introduce you to the holidays, laying a foundation upon which you can build. It will hopefully inspire you to adopt and adapt them into your lives and ministries.

Despite my minimal fluency of Hebrew, my love for the language has led me to share with you the pictures so many of the words evoke. I've tried to keep within the accepted principles of context and usage.

Finally, my intention is not to offer the practicalities of celebrating the holidays. The **who** and the **why** of the celebration is much more important than the **how**. To that end, herein I have focused on the scriptural basis and its personal application for each holiday.

For some practical suggestions and resources for further study, visit my blog: http://CelebrateJesus-TheBook.blogspot.com/

Lovingly offered to you, for the glory of Jesus.

Joanie

Jerusalem, 2008

Introduction

You Are Invited

"You are invited!" We eagerly read an invitation with excitement and anticipation of being in a party atmosphere, celebrating with family or friends.

Holidays, too, are wonderful reasons to celebrate. Whatever we are celebrating, holidays give us a sense of belonging. Often they define us as individuals, as a family, or as a people. They connect us to ourselves, to our communities, to our nation, and to our God. They help us remember where we've come from as we look forward to where we're going.

For those reasons and more, God gave Israel a calendar full of holiday celebrations. God designed them to establish and perpetuate a community who would abide in relationship with Him and with each other. God's holidays were times of remembering, rejoicing, and resting in His love and His goodness. Above all, they were opportunities to worship and to celebrate Him.

There was a holy day every week, every month, and eventually nine annual feasts! These celebrations were to be observed for all generations, and they are an integral part of Israel's identity to this day.

Even in their most challenging situations, many Jewish people gather, light candles, and forget their surroundings as they remember better times.

Growing up in a Jewish home, I was somewhat familiar with the feasts. Although I didn't know much about them, I knew they were an important part of our culture. At the beginning of every school year, all the Jewish children would be excused to attend the synagogue to observe the fall holidays. Later, I took a more serious interest in them. I was on a spiritual search and wanted to know more about my heritage and identity as a Jew. Yet, it wasn't until I became a follower of Jesus that the holidays became important to me. Suddenly they had life, purpose, and meaning for my own life as I discovered that Jesus is the heart and prophetic fulfillment of every one of God's holy days.

Although most of the celebrations commemorate events in Israel's history, God intended them to reveal His character and His plan of redemption through Jesus. Jesus is the heart of every celebration—it is He who is sending an invitation to all who know and love Him to come to His parties. For this reason, I submit that the feasts are neither Jewish nor Israeli, but rather celebrations of the Kingdom of God, created to be enjoyed and embraced by us all, both Jew and Gentile.

Please join me in a fascinating study of God's parties.

You are invited!

Chapter One

God's Purposes For the Feasts

Let's take a look at God's purposes for the feasts so we can glean their potential blessings in our lives: remembering, rejoicing, and resting in God.

God designed His feasts so that we would

- remember who He is and what He has done in the past;
- rejoice, knowing He is in control of our present;
- rest in Him as we face the uncertainty of the future.

Throughout Scripture, we hear the recurring principle that remembering the past gives us hope. The holidays are continual reminders of God's character and mighty acts of deliverance. As we focus on specific events in God's redemptive history, we can face whatever challenges confront us today or tomorrow.

By remembering who God is and what He had done in the past, Jeremiah had hope even as he lamented the destruction of Jerusalem:

This I recall to my mind, therefore I have hope.
—Lamentations 3:21

In James 1:2-4, James admonishes us to take joy in our trials, knowing they will produce fruit in our character.

As we remember God in our past and rejoice in Him in our present, we can rest in His promises for our future:

> *Surely goodness and mercy shall follow me all the days of my life; and I will dwell in the house of the LORD forever.*
> *—Psalm 23:6*[1]

Creating a Kingdom Community

Nothing draws people together as much as a shared experience. When people meet, they always look for commonality. Questions begin like, "Where are you from?" "Do you know...?" "Do you remember...?" "When did you…?" "Where were you when…?" Answers can bring an immediate sense of community as events, memories, experiences, and even mutual friends come alive between them. On a trip from Israel to Malawi, Africa, I met a man who lives on the same street where I grew up! We immediately began a lively conversation.

Nations share experiences by commemorating events, celebrating a historical personage, or honoring their fallen soldiers. People often celebrate their national holidays even when outside their native land. It makes them feel they are still part of the community that was significant to their past.

God's intention, however, was to create something more than a community. His goal was to create a Kingdom—a Kingdom over which He would have dominion. His Kingdom would share a history of events and memories; but more importantly, it would be a Kingdom community with whom He would enjoy a covenant relationship:

> *If you will indeed obey My voice and keep My covenant, then you shall be a special treasure to Me above all people; for all the earth is Mine. And you shall be to Me a kingdom of priests and a holy nation.*
> *—Exodus 19:5-6a*

God's Kingdom began with a man, a family, and a nation. Through that nation, Israel, God would reveal to the world

- His character and His ways;
- His promises to His Kingdom people;
- His expectations of His Kingdom people;
- His Kingdom principles.

Everything that God did in, for, to, and through Israel would bind them as a community to Himself and to each other. The feasts perpetuated that sense of community as the people celebrated and commemorated God's mighty acts of deliverance.

Despite differences in language, traditions, and even national culture, there is still an unmistakable sense of unity among the Jewish people through their shared heritage. No matter where we are in the world, almost every Jewish person will observe the major holidays of Passover and Yom Kippur (the Day of Atonement). We will eat different foods, but matzo (unleavened bread) will be found on every Passover table.

However, through Jesus Christ, God's Kingdom community was extended to the Gentiles:

But as many as received Him, to them He gave the right to become children of God, to those who believe in His name: who were born, not of blood, nor of the will of the flesh, nor of the will of man, but of God.
—John 1:12-13

The mystery hidden in ages past was revealed

...by the Spirit to His holy apostles and prophets: that the Gentiles should be fellow heirs, of the same body, and partakers of His promise in Christ through the gospel.
—Ephesians 3:5b-6

Grafted into the vine by God's grace through faith, Gentiles together with Jews comprise God's Kingdom community. Jews and Gentiles share the same redemptive history. Does not the Lord's Supper bind us together as a community? Through the sacrament, are we not inexorably bound to the past, the present, and the future?

When we remember who He is and what He has done in the past, we can rejoice in His sovereignty in the present, and we can rest in His faithfulness for the future. Remembering, rejoicing, and resting are what God intended through all His appointed times and feasts. In addition, we should consider the opportunities to extend God's Kingdom to those outside His community as we tell, teach, proclaim, declare, and celebrate who God is and what He has done for us:

One generation shall praise Your works to another, and shall declare Your mighty acts... They shall speak of the glory of Your kingdom, and talk of Your power, to make known to the sons of men His

mighty acts, and the glorious majesty of His kingdom.
—Psalm 145:4, 11-12

Meeting with God

In effect, God is saying to you, "My calendar has been marked from the beginning of time. Beloved child, please meet Me, I am waiting ... we have a date!"

Imagine an invitation to meet with God face to face!

In 1972 I worked on the American presidential campaign. My job was to schedule our candidate for meetings around New York City. Several days before the candidate arrived, the advance team would descend on our office to make last-minute arrangements. They needed to check every meeting site. They had to arrange for security. They had to organize protocol for dignitaries. They had to verify all schedules. They had to approve all press requests. They had ultimate responsibility and authority for the visit.

Needless to say, our office teemed with people and activity. Despite all the stress and pressure it put upon our little office, we considered it a privilege for our city to host the man who could be our next president. An even greater privilege awaited those who would meet with him face to face.

We have been given the greatest privilege of all—a meeting with God:

> The Lord, to whom belongs greatness, the power and the glory, the victory and the majesty; for all that is in heaven and in earth is His. His is the Kingdom: He is exalted as

head over all. In His hand is power and might, to make great and to give strength to all.[2]

- The Creator, who brought from nothing all that is into being by a breath, a word, an act of His will
- The Redeemer and King of Israel
- The Lord of Hosts, the King of Kings
- The First and the Last
- The Holy One

The God of all who live and breathe and have being has invited us to meet with Him. Who can really comprehend the magnitude of that privilege?

Let's consider just three blessings that flow from our times of meeting with God:

- We draw closer to Him.
- We grow in knowledge of Him.
- We abide in communion with Him and each other.

THE BLESSING OF DRAWING CLOSER TO GOD

Who among us hasn't been so busy that our relationship with God was affected? Despite our good intentions, our mornings (or evenings) are wasted away with little emergencies and emails. Our days are filled with demands of work, family, or ministry. Projects and people sap our time and energy and distract us from God. A day goes by without having spent time with our Beloved, the Lover and Overseer of our soul. One day becomes two, or three, or four. Without our noticing it, the flame of our passion begins to diminish. If not reignited, something within us will begin to die spiritually.

The psalmist said:

> *As the deer pants for the water brooks, so pants my soul for You O God. My soul thirsts for God, for the living God.*
> *—Psalm 42:1-2a*

He had tasted the sweetness of God's presence, yet a separation had made his soul downcast, discouraged, and depressed. His soul was drying up.

If separation from God means thirst unto death, so it follows that nearness to Him means satisfaction and life. In the Gospels we see how the crowds followed Jesus wherever He went. They kept pressing in closer and closer, reaching out just to touch His garment for healing, for wholeness—for life.

The holidays are designed to make us STOP, put the things of the world aside, and renew our relationship with Him and with each other.

THE BLESSING OF GROWING IN KNOWLEDGE OF GOD

Throughout the Old Testament, after He had done a mighty act, God made His purpose known. "I am doing this ... that you might know that I am the Lord your God" (see Exodus 6:7; Ezekiel 36:11, 36).

God wants us to know Him, not simply to know about Him. It's the difference between reading about someone, or even meeting that person, versus being a close friend.

I remember refusing to meet someone because of a negative impression of his work. Sadly, what I thought about what he did affected what I thought about him as a person. But as I grew in my knowledge of him as a person, I understood why he did the things he did. My respect for him and his work increased.

There are many people today who have a false understanding of God. They don't like some of the things He does or that He allows to happen. Perhaps you've questioned God's character because you've not understood His ways. Growing in knowledge of God is one of His purposes for the holidays and His command to celebrate them "for all generations."

A.W. Tozer calls it a paradox of the Christian life that the more we know God, the more we want to know Him. God's riches and love are unsearchable, unfathomable; yet His sweetness and goodness beckon all of us to dig deeper. After forty years of speaking with God face to face, Moses still said:

> *O Lord GOD, You have begun to show Your servant Your greatness and Your mighty hand.*
> *—Deuteronomy 3:24a*

The apostle Paul wrote his one ambition in life:

> *But what things were gain to me, these I have counted loss for Christ. Yet indeed I also count all things loss for the excellence of the knowledge of Christ Jesus my Lord ... that I may know Him and the power of His resurrection, and the fellowship of His sufferings, being conformed to His death.*
> *—Philippians 3:7-8, 10*

Jesus, in His final prayer, defined eternal life as coming to know

...the only true God, and Jesus Christ whom You have sent.
—John 17:3

THE BLESSING OF ABIDING IN COMMUNION WITH EACH OTHER

A common saying among the Jewish people is, "If a Jew in Tel Aviv gets hurt, a Jew in Paris will bleed." Despite our differing opinions, traditions, or lifestyles, there is an invisible and unbreakable bond among us. We might come to blows over some insignificant issue, but woe to an "outsider" who dares to speak against us!

The Jewish sense of unity is partly the result of observing and following the same calendar and holidays through the generations since they were given. While we may celebrate the holidays in different styles in disparate cultures, we celebrate them as a community. This is especially true in Israel. By 3:00 on Friday (or on any pre-holiday afternoon), most of the stores in Israel are closed, and family members are making their way home for dinner at Mom's house. It's fun to see the young people carrying huge bouquets of flowers along with their backpacks. Holidays are family times.

God commanded the Jewish men to come to Jerusalem for the three major festivals. Try to imagine the excitement as pilgrims came from all over the world to worship God. They filled the streets with the sounds, smells, and customs of their native countries. Each one came to meet with God and to be in communion with the "rest" of the family.

THE BLESSING OF ABIDING IN COMMUNION WITH GOD

To *abide* means *to sit down, to dwell, to live.* We live in a transient world—no one stays in one place very long. To abide has very little meaning. But God's Kingdom is all about abiding in communion with Him.

If drawing closer to God brings peace, satisfaction, safety, and wholeness, how much more will we experience as we abide in Him? As we abide in and with Him, we know by personal experience who He is. King David wrote of that intimate relationship with the One True God:

> *The secret [of the sweet, satisfying companionship] of the Lord have they who fear (revere and worship) Him, and He will show them His covenant and reveal to them its [deep, inner] meaning.* —*Psalm 25:14* (AB)[3]

Imagine the joy we could experience as God's family if we would celebrate His holidays as a community, putting aside our normal routine (the Bible defines it as "customary work") to abide with Him and each other without distraction or diversion. He could breathe new life, new vitality into His people who have become discouraged and depressed. Would not worship be the natural response?

Worship & Celebration

We were created to worship and to celebrate God.[4] From the beginning of time, God's plan was that His creation would respond to Him in loving worship. Celebration is the natural response to that which we enjoy.[5] Worship and celebration are the only possible responses to a revelation of God's glory.

FILLING THE EARTH WITH THE KNOWLEDGE OF GOD'S GLORY

To the Eastern mind, worship and celebration flow as naturally as the ebb and flow of the ocean. The holidays were and are opportunities to gather, to worship, and to celebrate. As we do so, the knowledge of God's glory (who He is and what He has done) is released throughout the world. And that is God's ultimate purpose for His holidays and for everything He does. Consider the ways God revealed His glory:

- Through creation[6]
- Through Israel[7]
- Through the incarnation of Jesus[8]
- Through the church

What is the most often repeated verse or phrase in Scripture? Would you be surprised to learn that it is "that they would know that I am God"?

To risk being simplistic, let's look at the Hebrew root for the word *know, [yāda']: to know, learn to know, to perceive, find out, discern, distinguish, know by experience, recognize, admit, acknowledge, confess.*

God has determined that one day all creation will know that He alone is God. He has promised that in that day

> *... the earth will be filled with the knowledge [yāda'] of the glory of the LORD, as the waters cover the sea.*
> *—Habakkuk 2:14*[9]

All creation was designed to give God worship and praise:

> *Let everything that has breath praise the LORD. Praise the LORD!* *—Psalm 150:6*

> *You alone are the LORD; You have made heaven, the heaven of heavens, with all their host, the earth and everything on it, the seas and all that is in them, and You preserve them all. The host of heaven worships You.*
> *—Nehemiah 9:6*

Nothing can prevent His creation from worshiping Him. No dungeon is dark enough. No hole is deep enough. No prison bars are thick enough to shut out His presence, His glory, or hinder our worship. Jesus said that if the people didn't worship Him, the stones would cry out. The psalmist writes:

> *How awesome are Your works! ... **All the earth shall worship** [emphasis added] You and sing praises to You; they shall sing praises to Your name.* *—Psalm 66:3-4*

There are three words that cannot be separated: feasts, worship, and Jerusalem. The heart of the feasts is worship, and the center for worship is Jerusalem. God has appointed Jerusalem to bear His name and feast times to glorify His name. Through the psalms that make up the Bible's book of prayer and worship, we can hear the joyous sounds of the people's songs as they went "up" to the mountain of the Lord:

> *I used to go with the multitude; I went with them to the house of God, with the voice of joy and praise, with a multitude that kept a pilgrim feast.* —*Psalm 42:4b*[10]

When King Jesus rules from His temple in Jerusalem, we will be worshipping Him as we celebrate the holidays:

> *In the first month, on the fourteenth day of the month, you shall observe the Passover, a feast of seven days; unleavened bread shall be eaten. And on that day the prince shall prepare for himself and for all the people of the land a bull for a sin offering. On the seven days of the feast he shall prepare a burnt offering to the* L*ORD* ...
>
> *In the seventh month, on the fifteenth day of the month, at the feast, he shall do likewise for seven days, according to the sin offering, the burnt offering, the grain offering, and the oil.* —*Ezekiel 45:21-23, 25*

Through the prophet Isaiah, God's Word seems to indicate that Sabbath and New Moon will be observed ***forever***:

> *"For as the new heavens and the new earth which I will make shall remain before Me," says the* L*ORD*, *"so shall your descendants and your name remain. And it shall come to pass that from one New Moon to another, and from one Sabbath to another, all flesh shall come to worship before Me," says the* L*ORD*.
> —*Isaiah 66:22-23*

Consider the potential impact in both the natural and spiritual realms should the entire Kingdom community celebrate the holidays. The earth would be filled with the knowledge of God's glory in the face of Christ Jesus. The earth would be filled with worship! Filling the earth with the knowledge of God's glory through His Kingdom community is the fulfillment of God's purposes in giving the holidays.

THE DEFILEMENT AND RESTORATION OF THE HOLIDAYS

Over the years Israel's worship became tainted. The prophet Hosea echoed God's lament as the people profaned God's Sabbaths and New Moons by worshipping the false gods of the nations.

The people observed the holidays, but they did so half-heartedly. They came at the appointed times, but not with pure and loving hearts. They couldn't wait until they returned home to their other gods.

God spoke to the prophet Isaiah:

> *These people honor Me with their lips, but have removed their hearts far from Me.* —*Isaiah 29:13*

God had warned the people:

> *Your New Moons and your appointed feasts My soul hates; they are a trouble to Me. I am weary of bearing them.*
> —*Isaiah 1:14*

Finally God had had enough:

> *I will also cause all her mirth to cease, her feast days, her New Moons, her Sabbaths—all her appointed feasts.*
> —*Hosea 2:11*

Jeremiah painted a sad picture:

> *The roads to Zion mourn because no one comes to the set feasts. All her gates are desolate; her priests sigh, her virgins are afflicted, and she is in bitterness ... He has done violence to His tabernacle, as if it were a garden; He has destroyed His place of assembly; the LORD has caused the appointed feasts and Sabbaths to be forgotten in Zion. In His burning indignation He has spurned the king and the priest.*
>
> *—Lamentations 1:4; 2:6*

God was serious about His holidays because He is serious about His relationship with His people. As long as the people would not worship Him with all their heart, all their soul, and all their mind and strength, their celebrations were unacceptable. But the people's sin did not alter God's purposes for the holidays. God's plan has always been to bring redemption to Israel's broken relationship with Him and restoration to His holiday celebrations.

There was a reason why God called these holidays "His feasts" in Leviticus 23:2. They were established by Him for His purposes. He established them for all times and for all people—for all those in His eternal Kingdom.

Now, let's lay a foundation for our study of each holiday. The following chapter is brief but crucial to the rest of our study.

Endnotes

1. Also Romans 8:28-30.
2. Taken in part from 1 Chronicles 29:11-12.
3. *The Amplified Bible.* (1987). Grand Rapids, MI: Zondervan.
4. I define worship as a response to and a declaration of God's worthiness, usually including an act of humbling oneself, as exemplified by Israel (Exodus 4:30), Isaiah (Isaiah 6:5), Daniel (Daniel 10:8), and the disciples (Matthew 17:6). I consider celebration an exuberant expression of joy and praise.
5. Piper, John. (1986). *Desiring God.* Multnomah Press, p. 37.
6. Psalm 19.
7. Isaiah 43.
8. John 1:14.
9. Also Numbers 14:21; Psalm 46:10; 72:19; Isaiah 6:3; et al.
10. Also Psalm 122:1-2; 84:5-7.

Chapter Two

Holiday Basics

And the LORD *spoke to Moses, saying, "Speak to the children of Israel, and say to them: 'The feasts of the* LORD, *which you shall proclaim to be holy convocations, these are My feasts.'"*

—Leviticus 23:1-2

The holidays separated Israel from the nations of the world. They became the framework upon which the people would build their lives.

The holidays divided Israel's calendar into times and seasons, regulating planting and harvesting. They also orchestrated and defined the people's worship on a cyclical basis. The holiday calendar was divided into weekly, monthly, and annual seasonal holidays.

Weekly Holiday[1]

The rising and setting of the sun determines days, and days determine weeks.

Each week ends with the holy day of Sabbath [*Shabbat*]. It is to be a day of rest. The Sabbath begins at sundown of the sixth day (Friday) and ends at sundown on the seventh day (Saturday). Thus the Sabbath is the last day of the week and determines weeks.

Monthly Holiday

Months are determined by the cycle of the moon. Each month begins with the appearance of the new moon; hence, the name of the monthly holiday is New Moon [*Rosh Chodesh*, which means *head of the month*].

The moon not only establishes our months but also our seasons. Isn't it interesting that despite the changes to God's calendar, the phases of the moon are still indicated on the Gregorian calendar?

Annual Seasonal Holidays

There are nine annual holidays, seven of which are listed in Leviticus (the third book of the Torah). The Levitical holidays reflect the three seasons of harvest—spring, summer, and fall. The modern calendar year begins in January; however, according to Exodus 12:2, God's year begins in the spring when life bursts through the cold winter ground.

Here is an overview of the annual holidays per season:

SPRING

- Passover [*Pesach* (*pay'-sah*)]
- Feast of Unleavened Bread [*Hag Matzot* (*hag mat-zoat'*)]
- Feast of Firstfruits [*Hag Bikkorim* (*hag bik-or-im'*)]

SUMMER

- Feast of Weeks [*Shavuot* (*sha-voo-oat'*)][2]

FALL

- Blowing of Trumpets [*Rosh Hashanah* (*rosh ha-sha-na'*)]
- Day of Atonement [*Yom Kippur* (*yom ki-poor'*)]
- Feast of Tabernacles [*Sukkot* (*su-coat'*)]

WINTER

The holidays of winter are not listed in Leviticus. They are included in this study because of their significance to Israel and to the Kingdom community:

- Purim (*poo-rim'*)
- Hanukkah (*hahn-nu-kah'*)

Purim is found in the book of Esther. Hanukkah's beginnings are found in the Apocrypha[3] and are chronicled by Josephus.[4]

Jesus used the history and celebration of Hanukkah as the setting of His last public declaration of His deity as recorded in John 10:22ff. The holiday also has great eschatological implications as described in the final chapters of Daniel (9:26–12:13).

To summarize, we have a weekly holiday (Sabbath), a monthly holiday (New Moon), and nine annual seasonal holidays. These holidays were to be distinct, holy, and set apart for the purpose of rest, celebration, and worship. Consider that the Hebrew word for *appointed* can be translated "rehearsal." Could it be that God intended these holidays as worship rehearsals for our eternity with Him?

A Five-Fold Approach

God's holidays can and should be considered from five different perspectives. I suggest that all of the following perspectives are vital. By focusing on one and eliminating others, we distort the fullness of God's intentions. I believe this distortion has prevented the church from embracing the holidays and adopting (and adapting) them as its own.

Our study of each holiday will be based on these five perspectives:

- **SEASONAL** (*time of the agricultural year*)
- **NATIONAL** (*historical event in Israel's history*)
- **SPIRITUAL** (*revelation of the character of God*)
- **REDEMPTIVE** (*relating to God's plan of redemption*)
- **KINGDOM** (*application to our lives*)

SEASONAL

The seasonal aspect of the holidays reflects the times and seasons of harvest. Perhaps no one knows better the importance of the seasons than a farmer. Being connected to the land, the farmer understands his dependence on the One who is in control of the seasons. The three harvest festivals are a continual reminder of God's sovereignty. Man may plant and water, but it is God who brings in the harvest.

NATIONAL

Often this is the only aspect of the holidays considered. Subsequently, the holidays are thought of as "Jewish holidays." While it is important that we remember that the holidays usually commemorate a specific event in Israel's history, if we look beyond this shortened perspective, we will see that Israel's history foreshadowed the greater redemption that applies to all in the Kingdom.

SPIRITUAL

God revealed Himself to Moses within the context of the Passover story in Exodus 34:5-6.[5] Nowhere else in the Old Testament is this revelation more complete. The Hebrew words form a symphony that crescendos in Jesus; we hear its refrain throughout all of Scripture.

Yet to fully understand or appreciate God's character this side of heaven is impossible. We simply get small glimpses. As Paul says in 1 Corinthians 13:12a, "For now we see in a mirror, dimly." However, each holiday seems to showcase particular facets of His being.

REDEMPTIVE

Clues and foreshadowing of God's plan of redemption can be found in each of the feasts. Jesus, the Holy Spirit, or the church are revealed in each holiday.

Most teachers agree that the holidays of the spring and summer have been fulfilled completely. Many will contend that the feasts of the fall will be fulfilled with the return of Christ. Could be, but I am not convinced. Regardless, there is a decided eschatological significance to the holidays of the Day of Atonement, Feast of Tabernacles, and Hanukkah that we'll examine in detail in those chapters.

KINGDOM

Like everything else in God's Kingdom, the holidays have personal application for each of us. Often the spirit of repentance and the spirit of grace and supplication fall during the teaching of the holidays as congregants come face to face with the love of God. I personally can testify of people whose lives have been dramatically changed through the message of Hanukkah. Imagine what God could do if we observed, and not just studied, the holidays!

I contend that if any one of these five aspects is ignored or elevated in a holiday, God's anointed purpose for the holiday cannot be fulfilled.

A Word of Caution

Paul tells us not to esteem one day above another (Romans 14:5), yet doing so remains a tendency among different expressions of faith. I recognize that to keep a Saturday Sabbath is easy in Israel. Most of the nation shuts down on Friday afternoon. Public transportation ceases to operate, almost all businesses are closed, and in most neighborhoods a sense of separation from the commotion of life reigns. Celebrating the resurrection of Jesus on Sunday with my brothers and sisters in Kingdom community is also very important to me.

How or if you observe God's holidays is a decision to be made personally. Please do not judge or criticize others for making a different decision.

Now, let us begin our study of the holidays with the weekly holiday of the Sabbath.

Endnotes

1. God's time included the movement of both the sun and the moon. Sadly, in the course of time, we have made changes to God's order. For instance, instead of the biblical accounting of the day—from sunset to sunset—our days go from midnight to midnight! Rather than following the phases of the moon, we've developed a complicated accounting of months. Is it therefore surprising that the occult and false religions actually worship these celestial bodies rather than the One who created them?
2. This holiday has many designations including "Firstfruits" and "Pentecost."
3. The books of the Maccabees.
4. Josephus, Flavius. *Antiquities of the Jews, Book XII.*
5. As we will study later, Passover is more than just an event. The term *Passover* relates not only to the specific holiday, but also encompasses the entire story, from bondage to freedom. Since it is the most significant of all the holidays, I will go into greater detail in presenting it.

Chapter Three

Sabbath

God's Special Day

Remember the Sabbath day, to keep it holy. Six days you shall labor and do all your work, but the seventh day is the Sabbath of the LORD your God. In it you shall do no work: you, nor your son, nor your daughter, nor your male servant, nor your female servant, nor your cattle, nor your stranger who is within your gates. For in six days the LORD made the heavens and the earth, the sea, and all that is in them, and rested the seventh day. Therefore the LORD blessed the Sabbath day and hallowed it. —*Exodus 20:8-11*

I didn't like the Sabbath. I didn't know its significance or importance to God. What I did know was that it was very inconvenient.

I'd only been in Israel a few days and wasn't prepared for Shabbat (its Hebrew name). My hostess had warned me to be on the 2:30 p.m. bus home. I'd planned to stop at the grocery store when I returned, but the market was closed. The streets were empty, and I had no food. Absolutely nothing in the small kitchen at the bed and breakfast.

- Not a snack.
- Not a drink.
- Not a pita.
- Not even a stick of gum.
- Nothing!

So I did the only thing I could—declare a fast and try to be very spiritual. It didn't work. I wasn't spiritual. I was just hungry.

I soon learned to prepare for Sabbath in Israel. Preparing for Sabbath means making sure the cupboards and refrigerator are stocked, and everything needed for the next twenty-four hours is on hand.

By 3:00 in the afternoon, Israel begins to shut down. Most shops are closed. Public transportation takes its last round, bringing students and soldiers back home to Mom's. Sabbath is a time for the family, and a special meal is prepared for Friday night. Often extended family and friends are invited.

To prepare for the Sabbath feast, markets are filled with frantic shoppers on Thursday evenings and Friday mornings. Many people don't work at all on Friday, so the malls and parks are crowded with people enjoying the beginning of their weekend. From its frenzied beginning, Sabbath becomes a festive occasion.

I was only unprepared that one time! I had learned my lesson. But once I settled into "real life" in Israel, I learned something else. I learned that I could use the quietness of the day to catch up in my office. I accomplished much without the distraction of phone calls and emails.

Eventually, however, I was convicted by the words in James 1:23 to be a doer of the Word and not just a hearer. God's Word is clear about His special day. The Sabbath is very important to Him and to the life of His Kingdom community.

Let us examine the seasonal, national, spiritual, redemptive, and Kingdom aspects of the Sabbath.

Seasonal

The Sabbath is designated to be the seventh day of God's week. It begins at sundown on Friday and concludes at sundown on Saturday.[1, 2]

The Sabbath is God's special day:

> *Six days shall work be done, but the seventh day is a Sabbath of solemn rest, a holy convocation. You shall do no work on it; it is the Sabbath of the LORD in all your dwellings.* —Leviticus 23:3

It was to be a day of rest, blessed and hallowed by God.

Let's begin our study by looking at four key Hebrew words from the above verse: *Sabbath*, *rest*, *bless*, and *hallow*.

SABBATH: [*shabbat*] is derived from the verb [*shabat*], which means *to cease, to put an end to, to come to an end.*

REST: [*nu'ach*] means *to rest or to cause to rest.* This word is exciting because of its usage denoting military victory:

> *The LORD your God is giving you rest and is giving you this land.* —Joshua 1:13b

> *The* L*ORD* *your God has given you rest from your enemies all around, in the land which the* L*ORD* *your God is giving you to possess as an inheritance.*
> *—Deuteronomy 25:19*

A well-known and favorite passage also uses a derivative of the word *rest*:

> *He leads me beside the still waters [or waters of rest].*
> *—Psalm 23:1*

BLESS: [*barakh*], the Hebrew concept of *bless*, includes *enduing with power for success, prosperity, longevity.* Whereas the majority of usage is of God bestowing His blessing upon His creatures, He also bestows it upon His creation.

HALLOW: [*qadas*] means *to be or to make holy, sanctified, sacred, separated from the common or ordinary.*

God cares so much for us, His children, that He gave us His day as a time of rest and victory. Besides the weekly Sabbath, most of the Levitical festivals were also considered Sabbaths, including:

- First day of Passover
- Final day of Passover
- First day of Feast of Weeks
- Blowing of Trumpets
- Day of Atonement
- First and eighth day of Feast of Tabernacles

God made only one command for the Sabbath: "**Do no work**." Sadly, there has been a plethora of inconclusive discussions on the definition of "work," hence the continual confrontation between the religious establishment and Jesus and between the religious and secular Jews today. Regardless, a celebration of the Sabbath can have a profound effect on a believer's relationship with God.[3]

National

There are at least six important relationship aspects of the Sabbath to the nation of Israel:

- Sign of the covenant
- Trusting God's provision
- God's concern for all of His creation
- Reckons other festivals
- Basis of God's judgment against Israel
- Restoration in the Kingdom

God's gift of the Sabbath was a sign of His covenant with Israel, making an everlasting separation between her and the other nations:

> *Surely My Sabbaths you shall keep, for it is a sign between Me and you throughout your generations, that you may know that I am the LORD who sanctifies you. You shall keep the Sabbath, therefore, for it is holy to you ... Therefore the children of Israel shall keep the Sabbath, to observe the Sabbath throughout their generations as a perpetual covenant. It is a sign between Me and the children of Israel forever.*
> —*Exodus 31:13-14a, 16-17a*

In Nehemiah's prayer and recitation of Israel's history, he specifically mentions God's gift of the Sabbath:

> *You came down also on Mount Sinai, and spoke with them from heaven, and gave them just ordinances and*

true laws, good statutes and commandments. You made known to them Your holy Sabbath, and commanded them precepts, statutes and laws, by the hand of Moses Your servant. —*Nehemiah 9:13-14*

TRUSTING GOD'S PROVISION

God's command to "do no work" on the Sabbath presented a challenge to Israel while on her journey from Egypt to Canaan. Obedience to God meant that the people could not gather manna on the Sabbath. They had to trust His faithfulness by gathering enough on the sixth day to last them through the Sabbath. They were to gather only what they needed, nothing more but nothing less. Failure to comply resulted in death:

Then he said to them, "This is what the LORD has said: 'Tomorrow is a Sabbath rest, a holy Sabbath to the LORD. Bake what you will bake today, and boil what you will boil; and lay up for yourselves all that remains, to be kept until morning.'"... Then Moses said, "Eat that today, for today is a Sabbath to the LORD; today you will not find it in the field. Six days you shall gather it, but on the seventh day, the Sabbath, there will be none ... Let every man remain in his place; let no man go out of his place on the seventh day." So the people rested on the seventh day. —*Exodus 16:23-30*

GOD'S CONCERN FOR ALL OF HIS CREATION

God's Sabbath applied to all His creatures and creation. Israel was to manifest His heart by allowing both servants and animals a day of rest:

> *The seventh day is the Sabbath of the LORD your God. In it you shall do no work: you, nor your son, nor your daughter, nor your male servant, nor your female servant, nor your ox, nor your donkey, nor any of your cattle, nor your stranger who is within your gates, that your male servant and your female servant may rest as well as you.*
>
> *—Deuteronomy 5:14*

Not surprisingly, He extended His Sabbath to the land:

> *And the LORD spoke to Moses on Mount Sinai, saying, "Speak to the children of Israel, and say to them: 'When you come into the land which I give you, then the land shall keep a Sabbath to the LORD. Six years you shall sow your field, and six years you shall prune your vineyard, and gather its fruit; but in the seventh year there shall be a sabbath of solemn rest for the land, a sabbath to the LORD. You shall neither sow your field nor prune your vineyard. What grows of its own accord of your harvest you shall not reap, nor gather the grapes of your untended vine, for it is a year of rest for the land. And the sabbath produce of the land shall be food for you: for you, your male and female servants, your hired man, and the stranger who dwells with you, for your livestock and the beasts that are in your land—all its produce shall be for food.'"*
>
> *—Leviticus 25:1-7*

RECKONS OTHER FESTIVALS

To determine the timing for the Feast of Firstfruits and the Feast of Weeks, the people counted from the Sabbath. You will see later the confusion and contention this created between the Pharisees and Sadducees, especially concerning the Firstfruits of Passover. Sabbath also determined the sabbatical year and the Year of Jubilee, as shown in Leviticus 25:8-9.

BASIS OF GOD'S JUDGMENT AGAINST ISRAEL

Not keeping the Sabbath affected God's blessing or judgment on Israel:

- Because Israel rebelled and defiled the Sabbath in the wilderness, she did not enter His rest.[4]
- Because Israel rebelled and did not keep the sabbatical year, she was exiled to Babylon. The length of exile was determined by the years the Land was denied its Sabbath.[5]
- Because Israel rebelled and worshipped God along with idols, He despised and took away her Sabbaths, New Moons, and feast days.[6]

RESTORATION IN THE KINGDOM

The restoration of the festivals manifested God's everlasting covenants with His Kingdom community. When Israel reentered the Land, she immediately began to celebrate the festivals.[7] Today, there are many Gentile believers embracing and celebrating the festivals. The ultimate restoration of the festivals will be in the

Kingdom when Jesus Himself presides in Jerusalem. In that day the roads to Zion will once again throng with the multitudes coming from every tribe, language, and nation to celebrate the festivals:

> *"For as the new heavens and the new earth which I will make shall remain before Me," says the LORD, "so shall your descendants and your name remain. And it shall come to pass that from one New Moon to another, and from one Sabbath to another, all flesh shall come to worship before Me," says the LORD.*
> *—Isaiah 66:22-23*

In that day, Jesus will serve as our High Priest offering the festival sacrifices![8]

> *And on the seventh day God ended His work which He had done, and He rested on the seventh day from all His work which He had done. Then God blessed the seventh day and sanctified it, because in it He rested from all His work which God had created and made.*
> *—Genesis 2:2-3*

Psalm 121 assures us, "He who keeps Israel shall neither slumber nor sleep." Psalm 46 assures us that God is "a very present help in trouble." Yet God, who is always actively and intimately involved in our lives, rested from all His labor.

So why did He rest? Was He weary? Was He tired? Or was there a higher purpose for His cessation of work?

The word for *rest* in the above verse is the Hebrew word [*shabat*] and not [*nu'ach*]. God's rest was more than a "settling down in quiet"; it was a complete and total cessation of His labor. He ended His work of creation, yet His creative miracles are still very much in evidence today! Let us consider what the Sabbath reveals about the character and ways of God.

GOD IS CREATOR

Sabbath is a weekly reminder that God is Creator. It was He who brought forth the sun and moon by an act of His will through a whisper. The Hebrew of Genesis 1:3 is simply translated:

God said, "Light live." Light lived.

By a single word, the sun came into being. No wonder that the worship in heaven ascribes glory, honor, and power to God as Creator.[9] The wonders of His creation surpass the ability of poets or artists to express.

Rightfully and understandably, God takes pleasure in His creation. Perhaps at the end of each day of the creation, He sat back, smiled, nudged a nearby angel, and said, "It is good!" What did He see? Giraffes and insects, birds and fish, trees and flowers, snow and dust, man and mountains, the visible and the invisible. Creation was the first revelation of His glory.[10]

GOD IS SOVEREIGN OVER HIS CREATION

God has complete control over His creation:

- He covers Himself with light as with a garment.[11]
- He makes the clouds His chariot and walks on the wings of the wind.[12]

- He sets the boundaries for the nations.[13]
- He says to the ocean, "Go this far and no farther."[14]
- He commands the rain, the snow, and the hail.[15]

GOD IS SUSTAINER

God made a promise to Noah that He would sustain His creation:

> *While the earth remains, seedtime and harvest, cold and heat, winter and summer, and day and night shall not cease.*
> *—Genesis 8:22*

David praised God for His sustaining constancy:

> *In them He has set a tabernacle for the sun, which is like a bridegroom coming out of his chamber, and rejoices like a strong man to run its race. Its rising is from one end of heaven, and its circuit to the other end; and there is nothing hidden from its heat.*
> *—Psalm 19:4b-6*

GOD IS PERFECT REST

As God's provision and blessings flow from His presence, so does His rest. By resting on the seventh day, He bids us to do the same; He commands us to do the same.

Daring to contemplate why God stopped and rested on the seventh day, I suggest that He knew the work He set before

Himself was done. It was finished. It was whole, complete, and perfect. Throughout Scripture, seven is regarded as the number of perfection. His creation was finished and perfect.

GOD IS SABBATH PEACE

Rest and peace are closely related to each other and to the Sabbath. The traditional Hebrew greeting on the Sabbath is "Shabbat Shalom"—Sabbath Peace.

As already noted, *rest* [*nu'ach*] connotes *victory* and *finality*. In that blissful state you have peace. You are probably quite familiar with the Hebrew word for *peace* [*shalom*]. However, you might not be familiar with the fullness of its meaning. Most people think of *peace* as the *absence of war*, but God's shalom goes well beyond the cessation of work or of war. *Shalom* means *the peace that comes from being complete, fulfilled, "of entering into a state of wholeness, unity and restoration of relationships.*"[16] "Shalom" was the good news proclaimed by the angels at Christ's birth:

> *Glory to God in the highest, and on earth peace, goodwill toward men!*
> —Luke 2:14

Shalom/peace is a characteristic of the Kingdom:

> *The Kingdom of God is not eating and drinking, but righteousness and peace and joy in the Holy Spirit.*
> —Romans 14:17

Through the prophet Isaiah, God conjoins peace, salvation, and His sovereignty:

> *How beautiful upon the mountains are the feet of him who brings good news, who proclaims peace, who brings glad tidings of good things, who proclaims salvation, who says to Zion, "Your God reigns!"*
> —Isaiah 52:7

God's rest is not from without but from within. Shalom/peace is the result of being whole in body, soul, and spirit. The word reflects a sense of quiet and tranquility and a feeling of contentment.

Do you see the relationship between rest and peace? When we have completed our task, the battle is over and the victory has been won. We come into our destiny and are at rest in *the shalom of God.* When we are praying for "the peace of Jerusalem," we are actually standing in agreement with God for Jerusalem to become complete—fulfilling her destiny as a diadem in the crown of God.[17]

God's ultimate blessing is His shalom/peace. God commanded Aaron to give this blessing over Israel (and by extension, over you):

> *The LORD bless you and keep you; the LORD make His face shine upon you, and be gracious to you; the LORD lift up His countenance upon you, and give you peace.*
> —*Numbers 6:24-26*[18]

It is only as we cease from our labor that we can find in the stillness the victory, the wholeness, and the fulfillment He promises.

GOD IS PROVIDER

> *And God said, "See, I have given you every herb that yields seed which is on the face of all the earth, and every tree whose fruit yields seed; to you it shall be for food. Also, to every beast of the earth, to every bird of the air, and to everything that creeps on the earth, in which there is life, I have given every green herb for food."*
> —*Genesis 1:29*

Beyond providing for our natural needs, the Sabbath reminds us that God provides for the needs of our soul:

He restores my soul. —Psalm 23:1

The Lord will guide you continually, and satisfy your soul in drought, and strengthen your bones; you shall be like a watered garden, and like a spring of water, whose waters do not fail. —Isaiah 58:11

God's ultimate provision is for the desperate need of our spirits—our redemption:

For God so loved the world that He gave His only begotten Son, that whoever believes in Him should not perish but have everlasting life. —John 3:16

He became their Savior. In all their affliction He was afflicted, and the Angel of His Presence saved them; in His love and in His pity He redeemed them; and He bore them and carried them all the days of old. —Isaiah 63:8b-9

Redemptive

The Sabbath finds its fulfillment in Jesus. Remember the constant confrontations between Jesus and the religious establishment about His activities on the Sabbath? I suggest to you that there might have been an element of honest concern in the hearts of the religious.

Israel had suffered the judgment of God for her defilement of the Sabbath. While in exile, the religious developed systems of behavior that would ensure obedience to God's laws. In effect, they made the Torah "God's garden" and then erected fences to keep trespassers off the "grass." Soon the fences, rather than the garden, became the focus.

The religious made demands on the people that God never intended: Sabbath became a burden rather than a blessing. Into this situation Jesus announced:

> *The Sabbath was made for man, and not man for the Sabbath. Therefore the Son of Man is also Lord of the Sabbath.* —*Mark 2:27-28*

Three redemptive aspects of Jesus are revealed through the Sabbath.

JESUS HAS AUTHORITY OVER CREATION

Creation is the result of the work of the triune Godhead. The Father commanded, the Son created, and the Spirit was the *agency* or *means* of creating:

> *For by Him all things were created that are in heaven and that are on earth, visible and invisible, whether thrones or dominions or principalities or powers. All things were created through Him and for Him. And He is before all things, and in Him all things consist.*
> —*Colossians 1:16-17*

> *In the beginning God created the heavens and the earth. The earth was without form, and void; and darkness was on the face of the deep. And the Spirit of God was hovering over the face of the waters.*
> —*Genesis 1:1-2*

As Creator, Jesus has sovereign authority over His creation:

- The wind and waves obey Him.[19]
- Walls cannot stop Him.[20]
- Death cannot hold Him.[21]
- He multiplies food to abundance.[22]
- He heals the sick and raises the dead.[23]
- He walks on the water.[24]

JESUS GIVES LIFE

Jesus came that we might have life, abundantly and eternally:

In Him was life, and the life was the light of men.
—John 1:4

The thief does not come except to steal, and to kill, and to destroy. I have come that they may have life, and that they may have it more abundantly. *—John 10:10*

My sheep hear My voice, and I know them, and they follow Me. And I give them eternal life.
—John 10:27-28

JESUS IS PERFECT PEACE AND REST

The world is longing and looking for peace and rest. All around us there are wars and rumors of wars; tribulation and pressure seem to come from every side. How often have you awakened with a sense of dread and heaviness of soul before you even got out of bed? We are all desperate for peace.

There is only one source of true and lasting peace—Jesus. There is no expiration for His invitation or His promises:

> *Peace I leave with you, My peace I give to you; not as the world gives do I give to you. Let not your heart be troubled, neither let it be afraid ... in Me you may have peace. In the world you will have tribulation; but be of good cheer, I have overcome the world.*
> —*John 14:27; 16:33*

> *Come to Me, all you who labor and are heavy laden, and I will give you rest.* —*Matthew 11:28*

The rest that Jesus gives is eternal. As discussed earlier, the words for *rest* and *shalom* include the sense of *finality, victory, wholeness, and completion*, which we can only taste now. Ultimate victory will be experienced in the new heavens and new earth when disease, dying, and death will be bound and banished forever. The good news of the gospel is that WE WIN!

The Sabbath is the time we can remember God's provision of our yesterdays, rejoice in His presence in our todays, and rest in His promises for our tomorrows. Following are some Kingdom principles that we can glean from the Sabbath.

REST IS ETERNAL

The Hebrew words related to the Sabbath point to a world beyond this world—a time beyond this time. It will be a world without war, disease, or tears. It will be a time without time—a time of finality, victory, and eternity.

ENTER BY FAITH

There is only one way to enter into God's rest—by grace through faith in Jesus.[25]

Ibrahim is a troubled man. He's experienced tragedy, betrayal, and hardship. He cannot find hope, peace, or rest. His religion and his concept of God tell him that he is being punished, yet he cannot understand why. I've often shared with him the promises and hope found in Jesus. His response is always, "If it were only true, it would be so good." He is bound by unbelief and fear, which are preventing him from entering into God's rest in Christ Jesus.

The words of Isaiah to Hezekiah are true for us today:

If you will not believe, surely you shall not be established.
—Isaiah 7:9

Lack of faith leaves us in the wilderness.[26] As with Israel's spies who refused to believe God's promise, unbelief is an act of disobedience. It is more than a rejection of God's Word; it is a rejection of His invitation to relationship. It is a rejection of Him!

Regardless of the circumstances of your life, make a decision to believe God:

Do not harden your hearts as in the rebellion, in the day of trial in the wilderness, where your fathers tested Me,

tried Me, and saw My works forty years. Therefore I was angry with that generation, and said, "They always go astray in their heart, and they have not known My ways." So I swore in My wrath, "They shall not enter My rest."
—Hebrews 3:8-11

FAITH IS A DECISION

Faith is always rooted and grounded in the knowledge of the love and the goodness of God. Psalm 116 is a prayer specifically for the Sabbath about God's loving-kindness and faithfulness. Perhaps written by David, this psalm has become part of the liturgy of Passover; consequently, it was probably sung by Jesus during His last supper just hours before being betrayed.

What might Jesus have felt, knowing what was before Him? Fear? Stress? Anxiety? Remember, He was fully human with all our frailties and weaknesses:

Return to your rest, O my soul, for the LORD has dealt bountifully with you. *—Psalm 116:7*

The psalmist used the root word [*nu'ach*], thus commanding his soul to find victory in God. Just as the psalmist had, Jesus made a decision to rest in God. It was actually a command to His soul.

- **WILL**: Seek God!
- **MIND**: Remember God!
- **HEART**: Settle down!

Faith is more a decision of the will than of the heart or the head. I meet many people who tell me they think Jesus is the Messiah, but they refuse to make a decision to follow Him. Others have their heart stirred a bit, but they never take the next step.

> *Now faith is the substance of things hoped for, the evidence of things not seen.* —*Hebrews 11:1*

Faith has substance. It sometimes requires a white-knuckled decision: I will believe; I will trust; I will remember. We will all find rest for our souls hidden with Christ in the heart of God. Let's redefine stress as: **S**eeking **T**he **R**efuge **E**ver **S**afe, **S**ecure.

AVAILABLE TO ALL

As God offers His new covenant to all people, so does He offer His Sabbath peace and rest:

> *Blessed is … the son of man … who keeps from defiling the Sabbath … to the eunuchs who keep My Sabbaths, and choose what pleases Me, and hold fast My covenant … Also the sons of the foreigner who join themselves to the LORD, to serve Him, and to love the name of the LORD, to be His servants—everyone who keeps from defiling the Sabbath, and holds fast My covenant—even them I will bring to My holy mountain.* —*Isaiah 56:2-7a*

TAKE A BREAK

God gives us the gift of Sabbath rest:

> *There remains therefore a rest for the people of God. For he who has entered His rest has himself also ceased from his works as God did from His.* —*Hebrews 4:9-10*

There is nothing we are doing (or need to do) that is more important than resting in God. Consider the admonition God gave to the church of Ephesus:

> *I have this against you, that you have left your first love.*
> *—Revelation 2:4*

Sabbath enables us to take a break from all our labors FOR Christ and return to our first love OF Christ. Jesus is our eternal Sabbath.

Let's move on to the much-neglected monthly celebration, New Moon.

Endnotes

1. Rabbinic reckoning is that the Sabbath begins when three stars are visible, or they base it on meteorological calculations.
2. It bears repeating that in Israel I can hallow the seventh day as the Sabbath and celebrate the Lord's resurrection on the first day of the week. The purpose of this book is only to encourage an observance of Sabbath, regardless of the "when" or "how."
3. There is no accepted tradition even among Messianic Jewish believers on the how the Sabbath should be celebrated, but common elements might include:
    - Kindling candles with prayers to Jesus, the Light of the world.
    - Blessing wine and bread, using an adaptation of Jewish traditional prayers to point to Jesus, thus linking the Sabbath with Communion.
    - Husbands blessing their wives, often reading Proverbs 31; parents blessing their children.
4. Ezekiel 20:12-16.
5. 2 Chronicles 36:21.
6. Lamentations 2:4-6; Hosea 2:11.
7. Ezra 3:5; Nehemiah 10:33.
8. Ezekiel 45:17.
9. Revelation 4:11.
10. Psalm 19:1-4.
11. Psalm 104:2.
12. Psalm 104:3.
13. Deuteronomy 32:8.
14. Job 38:11.
15. Job 37:6.
16. Theological Wordbook of the Old Testament, (TWOT). (1980). Chicago: The Moody Bible Institute, #2401.
17. Psalm 122:6; Isaiah 62:3.
18. Bless: [barakh]; peace: [shalom].
19. Matthew 8:26; Mark 4:39.
20. Luke 24:16.
21. John 20:1-18; Luke 24:5-7; Acts 2:24, et al.
22. Matthew 14:13ff.
23. Matthew 4:24; 9:18ff; Mark 1:34; John 11:43.
24. Matthew 14:22ff.
25. Ephesians 2:8.
26. Numbers 14.

Chapter Four

New Moon
New Beginnings

Make two silver trumpets for yourself; you shall make them of hammered work; you shall use them for calling the congregation and for directing the movement of the camps … at the beginning of your months, you shall blow the trumpets over your burnt offerings and over the sacrifices of your peace offerings; and they shall be a memorial for you before your God: I am the LORD your God.
—Numbers 10:2, 10

The monthly holiday of New Moon is first mentioned in Numbers 10:10, and its sacrifices and offerings are outlined in Numbers 28:11-15. Devoid of any further scriptural explanation, New Moon was nevertheless part of the cycle of Israel's celebratory calendar. By the end of King David's life, New Moon was well established:

For by the last words of David the Levites were numbered from twenty years old and above; because their duty was to help the sons of Aaron in the service of the house of the

LORD ... to stand every morning to thank and praise the LORD, and likewise at evening; and at every presentation of a burnt offering to the LORD on the Sabbaths and on the New Moons and on the set feasts, by number according to the ordinance governing them, regularly before the LORD.
—1 Chronicles 23:27-28, 30-31

New Moon was included with the other holy days during the revival under Ezra and Nehemiah.[1] The holiday has eschatological implications, as we will be celebrating it during the Millennial Kingdom.[2]

New Moon, along with the other holy days, was eventually suspended as a result of God's displeasure at the impurity of Israel's worship, as the people began to worship the creation rather than the Creator:

Bring no more futile sacrifices; incense is an abomination to Me. The New Moons, the Sabbaths, and the calling of assemblies—I cannot endure iniquity and the sacred meeting. Your New Moons and your appointed feasts My soul hates; they are a trouble to Me, I am weary of bearing them.
—Isaiah 1:13-14

I am encouraged that, as God restores all things, more believers are discovering New Moon as another opportunity to gather together as a family and as a community to worship Jesus. Excited to rediscover this jewel of a holiday, a small group of believers and I began to celebrate New Moon several years ago. At sundown on the first day of the lunar month we gather, blow silver trumpets, worship, and fellowship as we eagerly anticipate the return of Jesus.[3]

Seasonal

The holiday of New Moon designates the beginning of the lunar month and occurs when the moon is aligned between the earth and the sun. It is not a perfect alignment, for that would be an eclipse.

> At this time, the dark (non-illuminated) portion of the moon faces almost directly toward Earth, so that the moon is invisible to the naked eye, as seen from Earth.[4]

> In ancient times … the new months were determined by observation. Each month began when the first sliver of moon became visible after the dark of the moon. Observers would watch the sky at night for any sign of the moon. If they saw the moon, they would report their sightings to the Sanhedrin, which would interrogate them to make sure that they were not mistaken … If two independent, reliable eyewitnesses confirmed that the new moon had appeared and described it consistently, the Sanhedrin would declare the new month and send out messengers to tell people when the month began.

> The day after the moon appeared was a festival, announced with the sounding of the shofar, commemorated with solemn convocations, family festivities, and special sacrifices. The importance of this holiday in ancient times should not be underestimated. The entire calendar was dependent upon these declarations; without the declarations, there would be no way of knowing when holidays were supposed to occur.[5]

National

Biblically, the focus of New Moon is the blowing of the silver trumpets to announce the beginning of a new month according to the lunar calendar. God seems to love firsts, and there were many events in the life of Israel that occurred on the first day of the month and, therefore, on New Moon. This is just a sampling:

- The flood waters receded.[6]
- The flood waters dried up.[7]
- The tabernacle in the wilderness was set up.[8]
- The Israelites were first commanded to celebrate Passover, even in the wilderness.[9]
- Aaron died.[10]
- The altar was restored and sacrifices resumed.[11]
- The Law was read.[12]

We can discern many facets of God's character through New Moon as we consider God's precision in specifying important events to take place on the first of the month.

Spiritual

The spiritual aspect of New Moon reveals two important principles about God.

GOD IS ORDER

The precise movements of the sun, the moon, and the earth, which bring them into alignment on New Moon, reminds us that God brings order out of chaos:

> *The earth was without form, and void; and darkness was on the face of the deep.* —*Genesis 1:2*

Within six days, there was shape and structure. There was nothing random or left to chance in God's perfect creation. Every insect, every flower, every animal had its place and purpose. Each of the heavenly bodies was set in an orderly motion. The daily, monthly, and yearly rotation of the sun, the moon, and the earth are continual reminders of His perfect order. Only God knows how many more galaxies exist, but we can be sure they are in order.

GOD DEMANDS PURE WORSHIP

God is holy; He demands and is worthy of worship that is holy. Because Israel's worship became defiled and unacceptable, He rejected their celebration of New Moon.

Influenced by her neighbors' pagan worship, Israel eventually adopted and adapted their pagan rituals. New Moon became a celebration of the queen of heaven alongside the Creator of heaven. The moon, not its Creator, became the object of their worship, as noted in 2 Kings 23:4-5 and

Jeremiah 44:17-25. God rejected Israel's defiled and perverted worship, comparing it to harlotry:

> *For the spirit of harlotry has caused them to stray, and they have played the harlot against their God. They offer sacrifices on the mountaintops, and burn incense on the hills, under oaks, poplars, and terebinths, because their shade is good.*
> *—Hosea 4:12b-13a*

Impure worship was the evidence of Israel's breaking her covenant with God. God would not be mocked; what Israel sowed, she also reaped. There came a day when God stopped striving to regain what was rightfully His and silenced her harlotry:

> *I hate, I despise your feast days, and I do not savor your sacred assemblies. Though you offer Me burnt offerings and your grain offerings, I will not accept them, nor will I regard your fattened peace offerings. Take away from Me the noise of your songs, for I will not hear the melody of your stringed instruments … I will turn your feasts into mourning, and all your songs into lamentation.*
> *—Amos 5:21-23; 8:10a*

However, God's covenant love is steadfast; He has promised to heal, purify, and restore her feast days. In that day, the entire Kingdom community will celebrate:

> *"And it shall come to pass that from one New Moon to another, and from one Sabbath to another, all flesh shall come to worship before Me," says the* Lord.
> *—Isaiah 66:23*

Redemptive

There are three aspects of New Moon that reveal Jesus in God's redemptive plan.

JESUS ALIGNS ALL THINGS

Jesus will realign all things, restoring creation back to God.

When sin entered the world through the "first Adam," all of God's perfect order went out of alignment. Sin affected man, beast, and even the earth itself. Only through Jesus is creation brought back into God's order, as He restores man's relationship with God and sets creation free.[13]

Even beyond restoration, Jesus will make all things new:

> *Now I saw a new heaven and a new earth, for the first heaven and the first earth had passed away. Also there was no more sea. Then I, John, saw the holy city, New Jerusalem, coming down out of heaven from God, prepared as a bride adorned for her husband. And I heard a loud voice from heaven saying, "Behold, the tabernacle of God is with men, and He will dwell with them, and they shall be His people. God Himself will be with them and be their God. And God will wipe away every tear from their eyes; there shall be no more death, nor sorrow, nor crying. There shall be no more pain, for the former things have passed away."*
>
> *Then He who sat on the throne said, "Behold, I make all things new."* —*Revelation 21:1-5a*

Realignment and restoration is what we celebrate monthly on New Moon.

JESUS IS OUR HOLINESS

The sound of the silver trumpets on New Moon anticipates Jesus' return for a pure and holy Kingdom community, a community who worships Him in the beauty of holiness and in spirit and in truth, as indicated in 1 Chronicles 16:29 and John 4:23.

I meet many people today who are very sincere in their worship. Some have given away all their worldly possessions and live lives of great sacrifice. But like Israel, they are offering God something tainted and defiled by worshipping a god of their invention. Scripture is clear—there is only one God and only one way of approaching Him. Without the imputed righteousness of Jesus, worship, and indeed all of our sacrifices, are vanity.[14]

RETURN OF JESUS

As the silver trumpets usher in New Moon, we are reminded of that "final trump," announcing the return of Jesus:

> *For the Lord Himself will descend from heaven with a shout, with the voice of an archangel, and with the trumpet of God. And the dead in Christ will rise first. Then we who are alive and remain shall be caught up together with them in the clouds to meet the Lord in the air. And thus we shall always be with the Lord.*
> *—1 Thessalonians 4:16-17*

Kingdom

Just as the Sabbath gave us a new beginning each week, New Moon gives us a new beginning each month. There seems to be an instinctive, albeit unrecognized, need to gather as a business, community, or family once a month. I believe this is the result of God's ordained calendar, a time to reflect on our relationship with God.

WALKING IN ALIGNMENT

On New Moon, the moon's reflected light of the sun is hidden from our sight, thus challenging us to consider if our lives are reflecting Christ's light. Jesus said:

> *You are the light of the world. A city that is set on a hill cannot be hidden. Nor do they light a lamp and put it under a basket, but on a lampstand, and it gives light to all who are in the house. Let your light so shine before men, that they may see your good works and glorify your Father in heaven.*
>
> *—Matthew 5:14-16*

To receive and reflect His light, we must remain in alignment with both Him and the world, retaining our rightful position before both. We must abide in communion with Him.[15] We must be in the world but not part of it.[16] It is only as we are in such alignment that men will see our good works and glorify the Father. Staying in alignment requires continually choosing to walk the narrow road that leads to life:[17]

> *I beseech you therefore, brethren, by the mercies of God, that you present your bodies a living sacrifice, holy, acceptable to God, which is your reasonable service. And*

do not be conformed to this world, but be transformed by the renewing of your mind, that you may prove what is that good and acceptable and perfect will of God.
—Romans 12:1-2

The word translated as *conformed* is [*soos·khay·mat·id·zo*]. It has military overtones of soldiers marching in perfect rhythm. Paul is telling us to break rank by falling out of alignment with the world and marching in step with Christ Jesus.

HE IS OUR LIGHT

Until that glorious day when we are transformed into the likeness of Jesus, we are subject to the influences of darkness. There will be times of temptation and perhaps even struggle; times when the darkness threatens to hide His light. We do not have to let the darkness invade or separate us from His presence. Praise to God our Father that His grace always makes a way:[18]

This is the message which we have heard from Him and declare to you, that God is light and in Him is no darkness at all. If we say that we have fellowship with Him, and walk in darkness, we lie and do not practice the truth. But if we walk in the light as He is in the light, we have fellowship with one another, and the blood of Jesus Christ His Son cleanses us from all sin.
—1 John 1:5-7

WORSHIP IN HOLINESS

New Moon challenges us to give God only that which is pure. Today the Kingdom community faces the same challenges of tolerance as did Israel. If we are not discerning, we too can embrace traditions that are counter to the Word of God.

Defiled worship is idolatrous, deceptive, and insidious. It begins in the heart when we are pulled away, even by that which looks good. Soon we find that what we are bringing before God is imperfect.

Israel's worship was unacceptable to God because she brought imperfect sacrifices to Him. The imperfections and blemishes were not in the animal, but in the people. Just as Cain, they too came to God on their own terms. He wasn't pleased then, nor is He pleased now when we come to Him with that same attitude. God tells us to be holy because He is holy; He will not settle for less.

Our worship of God is not confined to a church service. Worship is a way of life and needs to overflow from a pure heart in response to a loving God.

Worship that doesn't come from a heart of love is not worship. That is the principle of the first and greatest commandment:

> *You shall love the LORD your God with all your heart, with all your soul, and with all your strength.*
> *—Deuteronomy 6:5*

Let's move on to the annual Levitical feasts to the Lord, beginning with the Passover.

Endnotes

1. Ezra 3:5; Nehemiah 10:33.
2. Isaiah 66:18-24; Ezekiel 45:17.
3. According to the Jewish university campus ministry, Hillel, *Rosh Chodesh* has blossomed into a celebration of women and femininity. While *Rosh Chodesh* exists as a women's holiday in traditional Jewish sources, the connection has been made much stronger with the emergence of the women's movement and the establishment of women's *Rosh Chodesh* groups. There is no one way to celebrate *Rosh Chodesh* (http://www.hillel.org/jewish/rituals/roshchodesh/default).
4. *Wikipedia, The Free Encyclopedia.* http://en.wikipedia.org/wiki/New_moon.
5. *Judaism 101.* http://www.jewfaq.org/chodesh.htm.
6. Genesis 8:5.
7. Genesis 8:13. Note also that this was the first day of the first month!
8. Exodus 40:2, 7.
9. Numbers 9:1.
10. Numbers 33:38.
11. Ezra 4:6.
12. Nehemiah 8:2.
13. Acts 3:21; Romans 5:10; 8:19-21.
14. Romans 3:21-26.
15. John 15:4.
16. James 4:4.
17. Matthew 7:13-14.
18. For that reason, your celebration of the feasts should be based on the Word of God and not merely on the traditions of men. Allow the Holy Spirit to instruct and guide your worship.

Chapter Five

Passover: An Overview

The Fulcrum of the Old Testament

Watching a lamb being slaughtered wasn't my idea. Pain and blood are not on my list of sought after experiences. Yet there I was, not only to watch the lamb's death but also to take its meat home and eat it!

I knew God wanted me to join my friends. Part of preparing for Passover was to find a lamb. We went to the lamb farm and watched a newborn being fed out of a bottle. Snuggled in the arms of the surrogate mother, it had no idea of its future. Then we walked beside the gates of the older lambs, some curious, others oblivious to everything but their food.

Finally, we came to the butcher. There on the platform, feet securely tied, was a lamb. A red stripe was painted on its back. It had been selected just for us. It was our lamb.

It stood motionless. Unable to move its feet to balance, it fell to the ground. Patiently, motionless, it waited.

A stream of water washed the throat area. A knife appeared. A stream of blood. A gush of blood. Water washed the blood toward the drain; water and blood mixed together. The work was swift and seemingly painless.

A few hours later, we were handed our packages of lamb meat. The others ate it with friends and family, continuing the tradition that began in Egypt. I couldn't. I needed to be alone with my Redeemer, the Lamb of God who took away all my sins. It was the most memorable Passover I'd ever observed.

The holiday of Passover is unlike any other holiday.

- Passover is an event—God's redemption of Israel from the destruction of death.
- Passover is a holy day—the fourteenth day of the first month of the year on the Hebrew calendar.
- Passover is a season, including two other Passover-related holidays: Unleavened Bread and Firstfruits.[1]
- Passover is a celebration, requiring specific observances and rejoicing.
- Passover is a foreshadowing of the death, burial, and resurrection of Jesus the Messiah.

My Hebrew professor, Dr. Ron Allen, used to say, "Passover is the fulcrum of the Hebrew Bible, as the crucifixion is the apex of the new covenant." In many ways, the Passover event lays a foundation for the rest of Scripture. Therefore, we will devote more time to this holiday than any other.

Exodus 2:23-24 and 34:5-6 form a libretto describing God's character, which reverberates throughout Israel's songs of praise on the lips of the psalmists and in Luke 2, the words of Mary, Simeon, and Zacharias. Because of the beauty of some of the Hebrew words, we'll look at them in detail in the coming chapters.

Some of the significant revelations that come from Passover are:

- God as Father
- God's memorial name
- God's character
- God's ways
- God's pattern of redemption
- God's model of faith unto personal salvation
- The uniqueness of Israel

Consider Jesus' command as He celebrated Passover with His disciples at their last supper: "When you do this . . . remember Me." Was He referring only to the taking of the bread and wine, or did He mean something more? I believe that Jesus was instructing them to continue to observe the Passover, but to do so in remembrance of Him!

Before we get into the details of Passover, here's an overview of Passover according to our five perspectives:

- **SEASONAL**: Passover celebrates the barley harvest, the first harvest of the year.
- **NATIONAL**: Passover commemorates God's redemption of Israel. Each of the holidays associated with Passover focuses on a particular aspect of that redemption. Passover focuses on God's protection from the judgment against Egypt: the plague of death to the firstborn.

- **SPIRITUAL**: Through the Passover event, God revealed His memorial name, His character, and His expectations of a covenant people.
- **REDEMPTIVE**: Jesus is called "The Lamb of God who takes away the sin of the world" (John 1:29). He fulfilled every requirement for the sacrificial lamb.[2] Through His sacrifice, He brings redemption to all who choose to accept His offer of grace by faith to come under the sign of His blood.
- **KINGDOM**: God offers redemption to the world. How we respond to that offer is only one of the many personal applications of Passover.

We will expand on these perspectives; but first, let's review the history of Passover.

The Setting

Psalm 105 gives a concise yet poetic account of the Passover story, which actually began when God made a covenant with Abraham. God warned Abraham that his descendants would be in bondage for over 400 years. However, with the warning came the promise that one day God would bring them out of bondage and into their own land. The compelling setting of Passover is that time of bondage in the land of Egypt, when God begins to fulfill His promise.

The book of Exodus begins with the family of Abraham's grandson. Jacob/Israel had come to Egypt at the invitation (and under the protection) of Pharaoh and his chief counselor Joseph, who was one of Jacob's sons. The people had flourished. Eventually a new Pharaoh came to power who neither knew nor acknowledged Joseph. Thus began Israel's trouble:

Now there arose a new king over Egypt, who did not know Joseph. And he said to his people, "Look, the people of the children of Israel are more and mightier than we; come, let us deal shrewdly with them, lest they multiply, and it happen, in the event of war, that they also join our enemies and fight against us, and so go up out of the land." Therefore they set taskmasters over them to afflict them with their burdens.

And they built for Pharaoh supply cities, Pithom and Raamses. But the more they afflicted them, the more they multiplied and grew. And they were in dread of the children of Israel. So the Egyptians made the children of Israel serve with rigor. And they made their lives bitter with hard bondage—in mortar, in brick, and in all manner of service in the field. All their service in which they made them serve was with rigor.
—Exodus 1:8-13

Under the hand of God, the people continued to multiply, increasing the anger and fear of Pharaoh. Desperate to stop Israel's fruitfulness, Pharoah imposed harder bondage and worse afflictions until the order came from him to kill all the male babies. Several thousand years later, the story would repeat itself when King Herod, afraid of the One who was born to be King of Kings, ordered all the male children under two years old to be killed. Both Moses and Jesus were delivered from untimely death.

The Story

Moses was God's man, through whom He would show Pharaoh and the world His glory. We don't know much about Moses' childhood other than he lived with his Hebrew mother until he was weaned. Probably at the age of three, Moses was taken to the courts of Egypt, where he was educated in their culture, philosophy, and religion. Perhaps from the time he was with his mother, Moses understood that the Hebrew slaves were his natural brethren:

> *Now it came to pass in those days, when Moses was grown, that he went out to his brethren and looked at their burdens. And he saw an Egyptian beating a Hebrew, one of his brethren. So he looked this way and that way, and when he saw no one, he killed the Egyptian and hid him in the sand. And when he went out the second day, behold, two Hebrew men were fighting, and he said to the one who did the wrong, "Why are you striking your companion?"*
>
> *Then he said, "Who made you a prince and a judge over us? Do you intend to kill me as you killed the Egyptian?"*
>
> *So Moses feared and said, "Surely this thing is known!" When Pharaoh heard of this matter, he sought to kill Moses. But Moses fled from the face of Pharaoh and dwelt in the land of Midian.*
>
> *—Exodus 2:11-15*

Moses remained in Midian forty years. One day he was arrested by the sight of a bush that was burning yet was not consumed. Drawing closer to see, he discovered that he was looking at a manifestation of the presence of God. The words God spoke out of the fire have echoed down through the pages of Scripture:

> *And the Lord said: "I have surely seen the oppression of My people who are in Egypt, and have heard their cry because of their taskmasters, for I know their sorrows. So I have come*

down to deliver them out of the hand of the Egyptians, and to bring them up from that land to a good and large land."
—Exodus 3:7-8

God sent Moses to confront Pharaoh with the message, "Let My son go that he may serve Me."[3] But God also warned Moses:

I am sure that the king of Egypt will not let you go, no, not even by a mighty hand. So I will stretch out My hand and strike Egypt with all My wonders which I will do in its midst; and after that he will let you go.
—Exodus 3:19-20

The king of Egypt did refuse to let the slaves go and actually taunted Moses and God:

And Pharaoh said, "Who is the LORD, that I should obey His voice to let Israel go? I do not know the LORD, nor will I let Israel go." *—Exodus 5:2*

Pharaoh's heart hardened. First he hardened it by his own choices, then God continued the hardening process. God had his reasons:

But indeed for this purpose I have raised you up, that I may show My power in you, and that My name may be declared in all the earth.
—Exodus 9:16

God went to war against the gods of Egypt. Each of the plagues specifically targeted one of their false deities. God was answering Pharaoh's taunt. Soon he and the world would know that only God is God.

Nine times Moses went before Pharaoh with the same message from the Lord, "Let My people go" or ... Moses warned Pharaoh that his refusal would bring plagues upon the land. Pharaoh refused, and the results were disastrous.

It is interesting to note that Moses brought God's warnings in a pattern of triplets.[4] The first three plagues brought discomfort:

- Water was turned to blood, and the people couldn't drink it.
- The land stank as it was covered with dead frogs.
- Lice were on man and beast.

The next triplet brought disease:

- The land was "corrupted" by swarms of flies.
- Livestock died from disease.
- Boils broke out on man and beast.

The third triplet brought destruction:

- Hail and fire struck throughout the land, breaking every herb and tree, man and beast.
- Locusts ate whatever was left from the hail.
- Darkness stopped all movement.

The tenth plague brought death.

Even before the first plague, God warned Pharaoh of the final plague. In His initial instructions to Moses, God said:

> *Then you shall say to Pharaoh, "Thus says the* Lord*: 'Israel is My son, My firstborn. So I say to you, let My son go that he may serve Me. But if you refuse to let him go, indeed I will kill your son, your firstborn.'"*
>
> —Exodus 4:22-23

And that's exactly what happened. God executed judgment against Pharaoh and his land:

> *And it came to pass at midnight that the LORD struck all the firstborn in the land of Egypt, from the firstborn of Pharaoh who sat on his throne to the firstborn of the captive who was in the dungeon, and all the firstborn of livestock. So Pharaoh rose in the night, he, all his servants, and all the Egyptians; and there was a great cry in Egypt, for there was not a house where there was not one dead.*
>
> —Exodus 12:29-30

In contrast, no harm came to Israel:

> *But against none of the children of Israel shall a dog move its tongue, against man or beast, that you may know that the LORD does make a difference between the Egyptians and Israel.* —Exodus 11:7

From the fourth plague onward, God made a distinction, protecting Israel from the devastation He inflicted on Egypt. It was His preservation of life that is the focus of the Passover celebration and the reason for the holiday's name:

> *Now the LORD spoke to Moses and Aaron in the land of Egypt, saying ...*
>
> *"Speak to all the congregation of Israel, saying: 'On the tenth of this month every man shall take for himself a lamb, according to the house of his father, a lamb for a household ...*
>
> *'Your lamb shall be without blemish, a male of the first year. You may take it from the sheep or from the goats. Now you shall keep it until the fourteenth day of the same*

month. Then the whole assembly of the congregation of Israel shall kill it at twilight …

'And you shall take a bunch of hyssop, dip it in the blood that is in the basin, and strike the lintel and the two doorposts with the blood that is in the basin. And none of you shall go out of the door of his house until morning …

'Now the blood shall be a sign for you on the houses where you are. And when I see the blood, I will pass over you; and the plague shall not be on you to destroy you when I strike the land of Egypt. So this day shall be to you a memorial; and you shall keep it as a feast to the LORD throughout your generations. You shall keep it as a feast by an everlasting ordinance.'"

—Exodus 12:1, 3, 5-6, 22, 13-14

Today many celebrate Passover as a holiday of freedom, but it is much more. Freedom was the end result, the effect of Israel's deliverance. The cause of freedom was the redemptive act of God:

It will come to pass when you come to the land which the LORD will give you, just as He promised, that you shall keep this service. And it shall be, when your children say to you, "What do you mean by this service?" that you shall say, "It is the Passover sacrifice of the LORD, who passed over the houses of the children of Israel in Egypt when He struck the Egyptians and delivered our households."

—Exodus 12:25-27a

God's focus was on the sacrifice.[5] The blood of the sacrificial lamb applied to their doors was a sign to God that the people believed and trusted Him to protect and preserve their lives. Because of that faith, the people were redeemed and delivered from their bondage. Later, we will discuss the meanings of the words *redemption* and *deliverance.*

Passover begins God's calendar in the spring, the season of new life.

> *This month shall be your beginning of months; it shall be the first month of the year to you.*
> *—Exodus 12:2*

I grew up in the northeastern part of North America, where winters are fairly cold. Snow often covers the ground for extended periods. As a skier, I loved the snow, but by March I longed to see the flowers. As the first flowers pushed through the hard winter crust of the earth, everyone was infected with spring fever. The daffodils were like trumpets, calling forth new life. Trees sprouted little buds. Everywhere the earth was returning to life.

In Israel there's limited snow and the winter is short, yet spring still shouts its arrival. Hills are covered with the white and pink blossoms of the almond trees. Calves and baby lambs frolic in the pastures. Barley, the first harvest of the year, is being prepared.

Passover is extremely important to the nation of Israel. A family entered Egypt, but a nation left—430 years later.

A CHOSEN NATION

God created a peculiar nation from Abraham's seed in accordance with His covenant promise. The choice of Israel was completely God's. It was not because the people were bigger or better than any other nation, but because He loved their fathers (Abraham, Isaac, and Jacob):

> *The LORD did not set His love on you nor choose you because you were more in number than any other people, for you were the least of all peoples; but because the LORD loves you, and because He would keep the oath which He swore to your fathers...*
>
> *—Deuteronomy 7:7-8*

My brother once asked me, "Where are God's miracles today?" The answer was obvious—Israel. Everything God promised has come true:

- Israel never ceased to be a nation.
- Israel is back in her own land and speaking her ancient language.
- Jewish people are recognizing Jesus as their Messiah.
- Jerusalem is being filled with worship and praise.

Knowing I'm God's witness to the world is a tremendous responsibility as well as a privilege. That God would stake His reputation on my life and that of my nation is astounding! Regardless of the highs and lows of the relationship, Israel remains the chosen witness of God.

FIRSTBORN SON

God's relationship with Israel is unique. He describes Israel to Pharaoh as His son. This passage is the first time God describes Himself in terms of being a father:

> *Thus says the LORD: "Israel is My son, My firstborn."*
> *—Exodus 4:22*

Years ago, I attended Bible study at a Jewish synagogue. We met in the library. We were studying a passage in 1 Samuel when the rabbi declared, "God is both good and bad."

"Rabbi, that cannot be!" I blurted out. "That's not what God says about Himself. He describes Himself as good. He is the very definition and standard of all that is good, merciful, kind. He is love."

I'd kept a guard on my tongue for the many weeks I'd attended the classes. I didn't want the group to know that I believed in Jesus until the time was right. Apparently this was the time!

The rabbi tried to control his anger as he said, "You sound like a Christian. They believe God is a Father."

"Rabbi," I argued, "open any one of these books and you will see that believing God is our loving Father is very Jewish."

Quietly but sternly, the rabbi asked me to leave the study. He rejected God's own words to His beloved "firstborn" son. Although he read this self-description of God every year at Passover, the rabbi did not believe it.

CHOSEN TO WITNESS

God had a specific purpose for delivering and redeeming Israel. She was to be His witness to reveal to the world His character and His ways:

> *"You are My witnesses," says the LORD, "And My servant whom I have chosen, that you may know and believe Me, and understand that I am He. Before Me there was no God formed, nor shall there be after Me. I, even I, am the LORD, and besides Me there is no savior. I have declared and saved, I have proclaimed, and there was no foreign god among you; therefore you are My witnesses," says the LORD, "that I am God."*
>
> *—Isaiah 43:10-12*

To that end, God established a law in Israel defining how Israel was to live as a nation of covenant people. The foundation for all their interaction was to be love:

> *Hear, O Israel: The LORD our God, the LORD is one! You shall love the LORD your God with all your heart, with all your soul, and with all your strength.*
>
> *—Deuteronomy 6:4-5*

My father was an atheist, yet he vehemently identified himself as a Jew. I once asked, "Why is being Jewish so important to you when you don't even believe there is a God?" He answered, "I'm proud to be part of a people who follow a code of ethics and morality. It's that code that defines us and separates us from all other nations."

His answer is not uncommon among the Jewish people. In fact, the introduction of many Jewish prayers reads, "Praised be Thou, O Lord our God, who has sanctified us by Thy commandments." The commandments given at Sinai did sanctify (separate) the Jewish people from all other nations. God's covenant commandments with Israel were meant to keep her separate and holy as His special treasure. Loving God was to be manifest in the people's relationship, not only to Him but also to each other and to the rest of the world.

God's desires and expectations have never changed for His Kingdom community. Passover is the commemoration and celebration of our redemption so that we are free to serve Him and live in covenant relationship as His witnesses to the world.

Spiritual

While we will go even further in depth in the next few chapters on the spiritual aspect of the holiday as well as its redemptive and kingdom aspects, there are some specific spiritual issues to be aware of as we continue our study of Passover.

God designed the Passover event to reveal His memorial name and to display His character. Each word He uses to describe Himself is like a facet of a precious jewel. The brilliance of His character breaks through Israel's dark hour just as it continues to break through into our darkness. Who God is, His character, is the foundation for what He does.

GOD'S MEMORIAL NAME

What's in a name? To the Hebrew people, a person's character is intrinsically connected to his name. That is why we see God often changing people's names, or telling parents what to name their children.[6] Knowing the reality behind His name, the psalmists consistently wrote, "Praise His name! Praise the name of the Lord":

> *And God spoke to Moses and said to him: "I am the* LORD. *I appeared to Abraham, to Isaac, and to Jacob, as God Almighty, but by My name* LORD *I was not known to them."*
> —*Exodus 6:2-3*

To understand the revelation of God's memorial name, we need to understand the context in which God revealed His name—Israel's bondage.

Israel's situation seemed hopeless. The people felt rejected, abandoned, and betrayed by God. They had heard stories about Abraham, the great man of faith. They had heard how God had commanded him to sacrifice his son Isaac. They held their breath waiting to hear what would happen, and they cheered when God sent a ram instead. They learned about Isaac, and Jacob, and then Joseph. Underlying all these stories was the promise of a land, their own land, where they would be free.

Yet hope in those promises faded as their bondage grew worse. All they could do was wonder, "Where is God?" "Has He forgotten us?" "What about His promises?" "Does He know what's happening?" "Does He see?" "Does He care?" Praying was impossible. They groaned:

> *Now it happened in the process of time that the king of Egypt died. Then the children of Israel groaned because of the bondage, and they cried out; and their cry came up to God because of the bondage. So God heard their groaning, and God remembered His covenant with Abraham, with Isaac, and with Jacob. And God looked upon the children of Israel, and God acknowledged them.*
> —*Exodus 2:23-25*

God heard their groaning. He hadn't forgotten His promises. It was time to put them into effect. Not only did He hear, but He also looked upon their grief and—importantly—understood.

Let's consider each of these verbs:

- God *heard* their groaning.

  Israel had no church building. There were no prayer meetings. Nor did the people have any written prayers they could recite. They weren't even praying. In fact, the Bible says that all they could do was groan. You've been in that place, haven't you? When you're too discouraged, too tired, too confused, or in too much pain to do anything else but groan. This passage says that God hears even the *groans* of His people.

- God *remembered* His covenant.

  God does not forget. The only thing He chooses not to remember is our sin. He knew when it was time to fulfill the rest of His covenant promise to His people.

- God *looked* upon the children.

  The Hebrew root [*ra'ah*] beyond simply *to see or to look at* means *to inspect, perceive, consider*. In other words, it means to ***really*** *see*. If God knows the number of hairs on our heads, do you think there is anything in our lives He cannot or does not see?

- God *acknowledged* them.

  Again we turn to the Hebrew for a better understanding of the word [*yada'*]. It means *to know by experience, to recognize, admit, acknowledge, and confess*. Further definitions include: *to consider,*

> *to know, be acquainted with.* God is thoroughly acquainted with our troubles and sorrows. Jesus was "a man of sorrows and acquainted with grief." He is able to sympathize with our weaknesses and suffering.

Have you ever tried to explain your feelings to people only to have them respond in a way that reveals either that they hadn't heard a word you said or didn't have a clue what you were feeling? Or worse, that they didn't care or even ridiculed your feelings? Such a response is often true when we share our feelings with people, but God never responds that way. He hears, remembers, sees, understands, and acknowledges what we are going through. Affirmation of our feelings, however, isn't enough—not nearly enough. We need God to help us in our misery:

> *So I have come down to deliver them out of the hand of the Egyptians, and to bring them up from that land to a good and large land.*
> *—Exodus 3:8*

This verse is the key to God's name and why He chose Passover to reveal it. God came down to deliver Israel, redeem her, and rescue her out of bondage. This verse is also a picture of God's love for us. This love came to its fulfillment with Jesus, God the Son:

> *... who, being in the form of God, did not consider it robbery to be equal with God, but made Himself of no reputation, taking the form of a bondservant, and coming in the likeness of men. And being found in appearance as a man, He humbled Himself and became obedient to the point of death, even the death of the cross.*
> *—Philippians 2:6-8*

These five actions of God—hearing, remembering, seeing, understanding, and coming down to deliver—are reflected in His name:

> *And God said to Moses, "I AM WHO I AM." And He said, "Thus you shall say to the children of Israel, 'I AM has sent me to you.' " Moreover God said to Moses, "Thus you shall say to the children of Israel: 'The LORD God of your fathers, the God of Abraham, the God of Isaac, and the God of Jacob, has sent me to you. This is My name forever, and this is My memorial to all generations.'"*
>
> *—Exodus 3:14-15*

I AM[8] is actively and intimately involved in our lives. He is the One who is uncreated, eternal, self-sufficient, and completely sufficient for all our needs.

One of the greatest tragedies of modern Judaism is the loss of the knowledge of the sound of YHWH because of the reverential fear of using His name in vain. Nevertheless, it is this name God wanted us to remember for all time.

GOD'S PROMISES

Throughout Scripture, and especially in the Psalms, we hear the echo of these themes from Exodus:

- Man's trouble
- Man's seeking
- Man's crying
- God's hearing
- God's deliverance

After revealing His memorial name, God gave five promises to Israel that reveal His covenantal relationship with His people. The first four promises are recited as part of the Passover ritual. God said to Moses:

> *And I have also heard the groaning of the children of Israel whom the Egyptians keep in bondage, and I have remembered My covenant.*
>
> *Therefore say to the children of Israel: "I am the LORD; I will bring you out from under the burdens of the Egyptians, I will rescue you from their bondage, and I will redeem you with an outstretched arm and with great judgments. I will take you as My people, and I will be your God. Then you shall know that I am the LORD your God who brings you out from under the burdens of the Egyptians. And I will bring you into the land which I swore to give to Abraham, Isaac, and Jacob; and I will give it to you as a heritage: I am the LORD."*
>
> *—Exodus 6:5-8*

Again, let's consider the Hebrew of four action words:

- I will ***bring*** you out.

  [*Yatza'*] means *to cause to go or come out, bring out, lead out.* Who among us doesn't understand being under burdens? Israel's burdens were physical. She was in slavery to hard labor. Bondage and burdens come in many different forms: physical, emotional, relational, mental, financial, and of course, the ultimate bondage, spiritual. Each of us has experienced at least one of those burdens or bondages. God still promises to "bring [us] out from under the burdens."

ꕥ I will ***rescue*** you.

[*Natzal*] means *to snatch away, deliver, rescue, save, strip, plunder.* I love this Hebrew word that connotes strength and a violent ripping and tearing away. The Hebrew sounds like two Velcro strips being pulled apart. God went into Egypt and snatched Israel away quickly and violently. In the Hebrew translation of the New Testament, it is the same word translated as *delivered* in Colossians 1:13:

He has delivered us from the power of darkness and conveyed us into the kingdom of the Son of His love.

ꕥ I will ***redeem*** you.

[*Gā'al*] means *to redeem, act as kinsman-redeemer, avenge, revenge, ransom, do the part of a kinsman.* This promise is the essence of the Passover story. In fact, it is the essence of the entirety of Scripture—God's redeeming love. Redemption means *the paying of a ransom to achieve the transfer of ownership.* The modern understanding of paying a ransom is of the weaker capitulating to the stronger. But this is not the biblical concept of redemption. God did not capitulate; Egypt could not hold Israel against God's will! No one and no thing can stand against the power of God.

Actually, there are two Hebrew words often translated as *rescue* or *redeem*; [*pada*] is the *actual ransom payment.* The other, [*gā'al*], focuses on the kinsman or closest relative, who pays the ransom. By using the word [*gā'al*] in this passage, God is promising that it will be He who ransoms Israel. God was giving us a picture of what was necessary to bring His people out of their bondage to sin. We will talk more about this later as we discuss the redemptive significance of Passover.

- I will ***take*** you as My people.[9]

God reiterates His choice of Israel as a peculiar people, a special treasure unto Himself. This is a promise He makes to individuals but never to another nation. This promise reveals God's everlasting heart for a personal and intimate relationship with Israel, "the apple of [His] eye" (Deuteronomy 32:10). No wonder He has sustained Israel to this very day!

GOD'S PROTECTION

God was and remains Israel's protector. He protects anyone who comes under the blood of the Passover sacrifice, as He said:

> *And it shall be, when your children say to you, "What do you mean by this service?" that you shall say, "It is the Passover sacrifice of the LORD, who passed over the houses of the children of Israel in Egypt when He struck the Egyptians and delivered our households."*
>
> *—Exodus 12:26-27*

The Hebrew word for *pass over* [*pasach*] is better translated as *spring or leap over*, yet it has the connotation of hovering over, as a bird hovers over its nest. Actually I prefer this meaning because of the picture it evokes. Whenever God saw the blood of the lamb upon a doorpost, He would hover over it, giving protection to those inside as the plague would spring over.

Before we continue, please note where the blood was applied. The lamb was killed on the threshold and its blood applied to the lintel on the top and to the two sides of the door. Top, bottom, side, side—the sign of the cross hidden within Passover.[10]

There is security and refuge under God's outstretched wings:

> *How precious is Your lovingkindness, O God! Therefore the children of men put their trust under the shadow of Your wings.*
> —*Psalm 36:7*

> *He who dwells in the secret place of the Most High shall abide under the shadow of the Almighty. I will say of the LORD, "He is my refuge and my fortress; my God, in Him I will trust." Surely He shall deliver you from the snare of the fowler and from the perilous pestilence. He shall cover you with His feathers, and under His wings you shall take refuge.*
> —*Psalm 91:1-4*

Jesus applies the picture of a protective bird to Himself:

> *O Jerusalem, Jerusalem ... How often I wanted to gather your children together, as a hen gathers her brood under her wings.*
> —*Luke 13:34*

Consider the design of the mercy seat, arguably the most important piece of furniture in the tabernacle and the temple:

> *You shall make a mercy seat of pure gold; two and a half cubits shall be its length and a cubit and a half its width. And you shall make two cherubim of gold; of hammered work you shall make them at the two ends of the mercy seat. Make one cherub at one end, and the other cherub at the other end ... And the cherubim shall stretch out their wings above, covering the mercy seat with their wings, and they shall face one another.*
> —*Exodus 25:17-20*

GOD'S PROVISION

God, who sees, also provides what His people need.

He saw that it was not good for Adam to be alone, so He provided him a helpmate.

When He sent Adam and Eve out of the Garden, He provided a covering for their nakedness.[11]

We are all familiar with the prophetic words of Abraham. Abraham knew that God would provide the sacrifice for the burnt offering:

> *Abraham said, "My son, God will provide for Himself the lamb for a burnt offering."* —*Genesis 22:8*

The Hebrew word used here for *provide* [*ra'ah*] is better translated as *see, to look at, perceive.* Do you remember who first called God "the-God-Who-Sees"? It was Hagar, concubine of Abraham and mother of Ishmael:

> *Then she called the name of the LORD who spoke to her, You-Are-the-God-Who-Sees; for she said, "Have I also here seen Him who sees me?"*
> —*Genesis 16:13*

Although in English we translate these two names of God differently (the One Who Sees, cf the One Who Provides), the Hebrew words come from the same root; God can see AND provide for all our needs.

The God who sees and acts on behalf of His children provided the lamb for the burnt offering:

> *And Abraham called the name of the place, The-LORD-Will-Provide; as it is said to this day, "In the Mount of the LORD it shall be provided."*
> *—Genesis 22:14*[12]

In like manner, God provided the Lamb for the Passover sacrifice and the redemption of all mankind. I AM (YHWH) continually protects and provides for all who will come under the blood of the Passover Lamb.

Let's begin an in-depth study of three of the spiritual facets of this extremely significant holiday.

Endnotes

1. There is actually a fourth holiday, Feast of Tabernacles, which is associated with the Passover/Exodus event. See chapter 14.

2. For a fuller list of how Jesus fulfilled the requirements of the Passover lamb, see blog: celebratejesus-thebook.blogspot.com/.

3. Exodus 4:23.

4. Warnings of plagues 1, 4, and 7 came as Moses met Pharaoh at the water. Warnings 2, 5, and 8 came as the Lord simply said, "Go to Pharaoh." Plagues 3, 6, and 9 came without any message or warning.

5. Exodus 12:27.

6. Abraham, Sarah, Jacob, and Jesus, to name a few.

7. Isaiah 53; Hebrews 4:15.

8. TWOT, #491. The English YHWH, usually pronounced today as Yah-veh or Yah-weh, comes from the root [*hayah*].

9. There is no unique aspect of the Hebrew word translated as "take."

10. God gave another picture of the cross as Israel marched out of Egypt. Numbers 2 gives a precise description of where each tribe should camp and how they should march. We have the details of the numbers in each camp. The camps on the north and south were of the same approximate number: 150,000. The western camp had a lesser number: 108,000. The eastern camp was the largest with 186,000. Seen from above, it would appear that Israel was marching in the shape of a cross!

11. Genesis 3:21.

12. "Mount Moriah" became the location of the Temple of Solomon. Today the Temple Mount is the most highly contested piece of real estate in the world.

Chapter Six

Passover: Spiritual

The Character of God Revealed

God extended His offer of salvation to both Israel and Egypt. Anyone who wanted to put his faith in Him could come into a home where a sacrifice had been made and be protected under the sign of blood. But not all of Egypt chose to accept that offer. Their decision determined their fate.

God had given Moses a frightening task. He'd already proven Himself to be faithful during Moses' confrontation with Pharaoh. But a more daunting task lay ahead—to bring Israel not only out of Egypt but also across the desert and into the Promised Land. Moses understandably refused to go into the desert unless YHWH accompanied him, but first he wanted to see God's glory. I doubt Moses didn't believe that God could or would help them. I believe he simply wanted to really know Him. See God's response:

> *Now the LORD descended in the cloud and stood with him there, and proclaimed the name of the LORD. And the LORD passed before him and proclaimed, "The LORD, the LORD*

God, merciful and gracious, longsuffering, and abounding in goodness and truth, keeping mercy for thousands."
—Exodus 34:5-7a

Each of the Hebrew words in this passage that describe God's character is a delicacy of God's love. Let us take our time to "taste and see that the LORD is good" (Psalm 34:8).

Merciful

[*Rachum*] means *compassionate, benevolent.*[1] The root [*racham*] refers to a *deep love (usually of a superior for an inferior) rooted in some natural bond.* "It expresses intensive or intentional and repeated action. It is also the root for 'womb,' thus reflecting the deep feeling people have toward babies or helpless animals."[2]

I've never conceived or lived with a child, but I vividly remember a wonderful day when I was taking care of the young daughter of a friend. Kirstie was about two and extremely active. Getting her to take a nap necessitated great creativity. Her parents had discovered a secret weapon—the car. Put Kirstie into a car seat, and she would be asleep within seconds.

We drove many miles that week!

One day in particular had been rather stressful. She was into everything, and my patience was wearing thin. "To the car," I suggested. "Let's have an adventure!" Of course, by the time we arrived at the promised little creek, she was sleeping soundly.

I parked the car and watched her. Her eyes were shut tight, but there was a smile on her lips. Her face was serene and practically glowed with an innocence that belied her actions earlier in the day.

As I watched her, my heart began to swell with love. Love grew and grew until my heart ached. I thought it would burst into a thousand pieces. Gone was the frustration of the morning. Gone was my impatience. There was only a rising sense of contentment and joy. Nothing could mar or stain the moment.

She looked so fragile. For a few more days she'd be dependent on me. Feelings previously unknown rose up from the very core of my being. I wanted to defend, protect, and provide for her needs. I wanted to nurture and nourish her in the love of God and then stand back and watch her blossom into the flower He created her to be.

Then it occurred to me that my love for this child was based on absolutely nothing. She wasn't my flesh and blood. She wasn't *doing* anything to win my approval. She was a precious child—bright, attentive, loving, and kind. But none of those qualities were the reasons I loved her. I loved her because I loved her!

In that moment I realized what God feels about us. He loves us not because of anything we are or do, but because He's a merciful, loving God. This deep-seated love, which comes from the heart of God, is the first word He uses to describe Himself in Exodus 34:5-6.

Gracious

[*Chanun*] means *merciful*[3] from the root [*chanan*], which means *to be gracious, show favor, pity, seek, or implore favor.*[4] "The verb depicts a heartfelt response by someone who has something to give to one who has a need. Overwhelmingly in the Old Testament, YHWH is the subject."[5]

God's graciousness, or grace, can be seen constantly when we recognize our almost helpless state. We dare not take for granted even our ability to breathe.

I was confronted by the reality of my dependence on God's grace while swimming in the Mediterranean Sea. Foolishly, like many others, I ignored the black flags warning swimmers to stay out of the water. Jumping the waves and standing against the undertow was fun for a while. But suddenly I realized that I was being carried farther and farther out to sea. I was held powerless in the grip of the water.

There was no time to panic, only to pray. God's grace came in the shape of three powerful swimmers who were able to push and pull me out of the water.

One cry from you, and He is ready to rescue you. He has committed the life of His Son to love, protect, and provide for you:

> *For when we were still without strength, in due time Christ died for the ungodly. For scarcely for a righteous man will one die; yet perhaps for a good man someone would even dare to die. But God demonstrates His own love toward us, in that while we were still sinners, Christ died for us.*
> *—Romans 5:6-8*

We are all caught in the grip of powerful forces of darkness and sin and are in desperate need. Only God can and will satisfy that need. His nature is grace.

Longsuffering

The root [*'anaf*] "is used to express the Lord's attitude of anger toward the covenant people when they have sinned."[6] The derivative that is used here [*'af*] refers to the nose and, by extension, to the face.

Imagine someone who is very angry; his nose gets red and his nostrils might flare. Certainly we see one of these manifestations in horses, whose nostrils are quite large and flare easily when they are aroused to anger.

The application of this term to God in the passage below means that it takes a long time before His nostrils flare in anger or that His face gets red. But in His stage of anger

> *... the earth shook and trembled; the foundations of the hills also quaked and were shaken, because He was angry. Smoke went up from His nostrils, and devouring fire from His mouth; coals were kindled by it.*
> *—Psalm 18:7-8*

Adam's nose became the seat of life as God breathed His life into Adam:

> *And the LORD God formed man of the dust of the ground, and breathed into his nostrils the breath of life; and man became a living being.* *—Genesis 2:7*

To breathe into Adam's nose, God had to be up close—literally in Adam's face. How lovingly intimate. God's face was Adam's first sight. Imagine looking that closely into God's face! There is only one other who has that close intimacy with the Father:

> *In the beginning was the Word, and the Word was with God, and the Word was God. He was in the beginning with God.* *—John 1:1-2*

"With God" is literally "face to face" with God.

God's face [*paneh*] is extremely important in the Hebrew Bible. God's face is equal to His blessings. When God's face (countenance) is looking upon His children, His blessings follow:

For they did not gain possession of the land by their own sword, nor did their own arm save them; but it was Your right hand, Your arm, and the light of Your countenance, because You favored them.
—Psalm 44:3

God commanded Aaron to put this "face" blessing upon the people of Israel:

And the LORD *spoke to Moses, saying: "Speak to Aaron and his sons, saying, 'This is the way you shall bless the children of Israel. Say to them:*

"The LORD *bless you and keep you; the* LORD *make His face shine upon you, and be gracious [chanun] to you; the* LORD *lift up His countenance upon you, and give you peace.'"*

"So they shall put My name on the children of Israel, and I will bless them." *—Numbers 6:22-27*

Lovers can bear to be separated but not to be rejected. Great is the pain when a lover turns away, refusing to show her face to her beloved. Imagine the horror of God turning His face away. From the deepest part of his hart, the psalmist cried:

How long, O LORD*? Will You forget me forever? How long will You hide Your face from me? How long shall I take counsel in my soul, having sorrow in my heart daily?*
—Psalm 13:1-2a

It is not surprising that the psalmist also wrote:

> *When You said, "Seek My face," my heart said to You, "Your face, LORD, I will seek." Do not hide Your face from me; do not turn Your servant away in anger.*
> *—Psalm 27:8-9a*

There is one time that God does turn His face from His children. His love, not His anger, makes Him turn away. If He looked at us while we are in sin, He would consume us in His holy wrath:

> *Behold, the LORD's hand is not shortened, that it cannot save; nor His ear heavy, that it cannot hear. But your iniquities have separated you from your God; and your sins have hidden His face from you, so that He will not hear.*
> *—Isaiah 59:1-2*

Praise to God for His salvation! God the Father makes provision for our sins to be forgiven so that He can turn His face back to His beloved:

> *For He has not despised nor abhorred the affliction of the afflicted; nor has He hidden His face from Him; but when He cried to Him, He heard.*
> *—Psalm 22:24*

> *Restore us, O God; cause Your face to shine, and we shall be saved!*
> *—Psalm 80:3*

Goodness and Truth

Scripture often uses these two words together; first, let us study them separately.

GOODNESS

[*Chesed*] is translated as *kindness*, *mercy*, and *love*. None of these definitions really captures the word's depth and breadth. Even our Hebrew lexicons have difficulty in defining this incredible word. In my opinion, the best definition is *faithful, covenant-keeping love.*

The word is used in relationships between people, as seen so beautifully in the story of Ruth:

> *And Naomi said to her two daughters-in-law, "Go, return each to her mother's house. The LORD deal kindly with you, as you have dealt with the dead and with me."*
> *—Ruth 1:8*

> *Then Naomi said to her daughter-in-law, "Blessed be he of the LORD, who has not forsaken His kindness to the living and the dead!"* *—Ruth 2:20*

> *Then he said, "Blessed are you of the LORD, my daughter! For you have shown more kindness at the end than at the beginning, in that you did not go after young men, whether poor or rich."* *—Ruth 3:10*

This word also reflects God's passionate (bridal) love for us in the story of Esther. God uses several love words in the following passage:

> *The king loved Esther more than all the other women, and she obtained grace and favor in his sight more than all the virgins; so he set the royal crown upon her head and made her queen instead of Vashti.*
> *—Esther 2:17*[7]

However, [*chesed*] is best seen in God's covenant relationship with Israel. I AM bound Himself in covenant relationship with Abraham, Isaac, and Jacob *knowing* the faithlessness of the people in their loins! It was an unconditional, eternal, and everlasting promise. God cannot break His unconditional promises.[8]

God is forever loyal to His Word, which is based on love. God made other covenants with Israel. Some of these were conditional upon Israel's response, but the foundation of their relationship was God's covenant-keeping faithfulness.

Knowing the pain of divorce and broken promises, I am so glad that God's [*chesed*] isn't influenced or affected by His emotions, but it is rooted in His sovereign will and omnipotent love. God promised:

> *My mercy I will keep for him forever, and My covenant shall stand firm with him. His seed also I will make to endure forever, and his throne as the days of heaven.*
>
> *If his sons forsake My law and do not walk in My judgments, if they break My statutes and do not keep My commandments, then I will punish their transgression with the rod, and their iniquity with stripes. Nevertheless My lovingkindness I will not utterly take from him, nor allow My faithfulness to fail.*
> *—Psalm 89:28-33*

God's love is the platform of our prayers and supplications. It is one of God's motivations to save and redeem us:

> *Have mercy upon me, O God, according to Your lovingkindness; according to the multitude of Your tender mercies, blot out my transgressions. —Psalm 51:1*[9]

TRUTH

[*'Emet*] comes from the root [*'aman*], which means *to confirm, support, uphold, to be established, be faithful.*[10]

Did you know that you speak Hebrew? Every time you say "Amen" you are speaking Hebrew! We end our prayers with this precious word as an exclamation point. We're saying, "It is so!" We often use the derivatives of this word:

- [*'Emet*], which is translated as *truth*
- [*'Emunah*], which is translated as *faithful* and *faith*

Whichever word is used, it carries the meaning of *certainty, solidarity, firmness regardless of circumstance, constant, or consistent.* It evokes the picture of the strong arms of a parent holding a helpless infant:

> *The eternal God is your refuge, and underneath are the everlasting arms ... The LORD your God, who goes before you, He will fight for you, according to all He did for you in Egypt before your eyes, and in the wilderness where you saw how the LORD your God carried you, as a man carries his son, in all the way that you went until you came to this place.* —*Deuteronomy 33:27; 1:30-31*

Truth is not relative or personal. You don't have one truth and I have another truth. Truth is absolute. Jesus the Christ is the standard of truth:

> *Jesus said to him, "I am the way, the truth, and the life. No one comes to the Father except through me."* —*John 14:6*

GOODNESS AND TRUTH TOGETHER

['*emet v*ᵉ*chesed*][11]

Let's put these words together. I said earlier that this expression, which appears many times throughout the Hebrew Bible, is extremely important. It is foundational to the character of God. It is an absolute link to His triune character. Jesus is the absolute image (likeness) of the Father.[12]

Understanding the truth of this expression ends the horrible distortion that God in the Old Testament is different from God in the New Testament. In this simple expression is the reality that God is One and His character (Name) is one.

Compassion

Although not in God's self-description, there is another important word describing God's character that comes from the Passover story: compassion.

[*Chamal*] is defined as *to spare, have compassion, be responsible for*.[13] "Basically this word connotes the emotional response that results (or may result) in action to remove its object (and/or subject) from impending difficulty":[14]

> *Then the daughter of Pharaoh came down to bathe at the river. And her maidens walked along the riverside; and when she saw the ark among the reeds, she sent her maid to get it. And when she opened it, she saw the child, and behold, the baby wept. So she had compassion on him, and said, "This is one of the Hebrews' children."*
>
> *—Exodus 2:5-6*[15]

How much more compassion does God have for Israel and for you!

Forgiving

God reveals His forgiveness as another aspect of His love. God's self-revelation continues in Exodus 34:7, revealing this facet of His character. We need to remember that love is not love, and grace is not grace, unless we see them in the context of forgiveness:

> *[The* LORD *God] keeping mercy [chesed] for thousands, forgiving iniquity and transgression and sin.*
> *—Exodus 34:7a*

[*Nasa'*] is primarily defined as *to lift, carry, take.*[16]

What is forgiveness? Forgiveness is the lifting up and carrying away of our sins, bringing them to the cross and onto the back of Jesus.

The word [*nasa'*] for forgiveness is not used in Israel; we use the same word for *excuse me* and *I'm sorry.* Many times we say, "I'm sorry," when in reality we're not sorry at all. Sometimes we say, "I'm sorry," when we really have nothing to be sorry for. As a result, the response to "I'm sorry" is often a casual, "En baya," which means *no problem!* Consequently, *forgiveness* isn't a concept readily understood.

We *do* need to say "I'm sorry" to God, because with Him there *is* a problem! God tells us the problem: iniquity, transgression, and sin.

The love and forgiveness of God is abundantly available to all who will ask. He has and never will turn away the broken, the needy, or the helpless. Remember that everyone, including the Egyptians, had the offer to be protected by anointing their doorposts with the blood of a lamb.

INIQUITY

['*Avon*] the "noun occurs with only the derived, abstract theological notion of the root: *infraction, crooked behavior, perversion, iniquity.*"[17]

Today there is an aversion to the concept of absolute truth and morality. This aversion is iniquity. As I speak to young people around the world, they argue with me that truth and morality are relative. They believe that each person can decide what he wants to declare as truth or use his own method to determine right and wrong.

This argument fades when I ask about the Holocaust. "Are you telling me that the Holocaust, which systematically murdered six million Jews plus another six million people, was morally right? Obviously it was morally acceptable to some people because they accepted as *truth* that the Jewish people were no more than rats and vermin."

At this point my young friends become uncomfortable, silent, or even retract their arguments against absolute truth and morality.

All humanity instinctively knows that there is a standard of morality and truth. Regardless of how we want it to read or how we try to reinterpret simple words, the Bible is clear about what God considers deviations from His standard:

The acts of the sinful nature are obvious: sexual immorality, impurity and debauchery; idolatry and witchcraft; hatred, discord, jealousy, fits of rage, selfish ambition, dissensions, factions and envy; drunkenness, orgies, and the like.
—Galatians 5:19-21 (NIV)

In the book of Revelation, we're told God refuses admission into heaven to

... the cowardly, unbelieving, abominable, murderers, sexually immoral, sorcerers, idolators, and all liars ...
—Revelation 21:8

TRANSGRESSION

[*Pesha'*] means *a rebellion, breach of relationship (covenant) with God, revolt against God's moral and righteous standard, casting off allegiance, which creates a gulf between man and God.*[18]

When I was a young girl, there was an advertisement that captured the attitude of transgression. With a clenched fist, a stomp of the foot, and a toss of the head, the child said, "I'd rather do it myself!"

While I don't remember what the issue was or the product that was being sold, I remember those words vividly. I remember because that was the attitude that described my life. I didn't care if my mother was right (and she usually was). I refused to do things her way.

God is the highest authority, so we are ultimately transgressing against Him. Adam and Eve's desire to be like God was a rebellion against His authority. They chose to change their alliance from God to Satan. They replaced God's righteous and moral standards with their own.

SIN

[*Chatta'ah*] from the root [*chata'*] means *to miss the mark (standard), failure to meet expectations, err, be mistaken, to miss or wander from the path of uprightness and honor, to do or go wrong, to wander from the law of God, violate God's law.*[19]

Sin implies and assumes that there is an absolute standard. Anything less than that standard, anything less than 100 percent, God considers sin. God doesn't look at the outward appearance, or even at the sincerity of our hearts; He looks at us and judges us by His standard—His Word.

This standard is especially true in the area of worship. If we are not worshipping God in spirit and in truth, our sincerity doesn't matter; we're not worshipping God as He deserves and demands to be worshipped. If we are not worshipping the God of the Bible in the way that He has prescribed—by grace through faith in Christ Jesus—we are worshipping wrongly. In fact, we may be worshipping an idol—a god we have created in our own likeness!

Every year I accompanied my parents to the synagogue during the holiday of the Day of Atonement. When I was old enough, I joined the adults praying all day. We fasted and confessed our sins according to the prayer book. The prayer book listed every conceivable sin, so I was sure that I was covered. In fact, I knew that I had committed every one on the list.

I was really sincere. I prayed and prayed and prayed. But at the end of the twenty-four hours of fasting and "affliction of soul,"[20] I left the synagogue wondering if my sins had been forgiven. I wondered if my prayers had been heard.

How God's heart must break at the determination for people to continue to worship and serve Him, even with sincerity, yet remain in their sin. God simply cannot forgive sin in any other manner than the one He has provided:

> *Jesus said to him, "I am the way, the truth, and the life. No one comes to the Father except through Me."*
> *—John 14:6*

It is easier to be "a little pregnant" than to ask God to bless us or to experience the fullness of His love while we remain in our sin. Herein is the other side of God's love—His justice, as God revealed to Moses.

> *[The LORD God] by no means clearing the guilty, visiting the iniquity of the fathers upon the children and the children's children to the third and the fourth generation.*
> *—Exodus 34:7b*

We have seen the love and the grace of God, which constantly extends the opportunity for a loving relationship. But as we see through the Passover story, there also comes a time when His patience is over—when His nose finally becomes red. Because of the continued stubborn refusal of Pharaoh, God's anger "visited" through the plagues to punish all of Egypt.

Visiting

[*Paqad*] means *to number, visit, punish, to attend to, muster, number, reckon after, care for, to pay attention to, observe, to pass in review, be called to account.*[21]

Through the prophet Ezekiel, God reminded Israel of the potential of the sins of the fathers being passed down to her descendants.

> *The word of the LORD came to me again, saying, "What do you mean when you use this proverb concerning the land of Israel, saying: 'The fathers have eaten sour grapes, and the children's teeth are set on edge'? —Ezekiel 18:1-2*

Even today, it is not unusual to see similarities of the lives of parents and children. Counselor offices are filled with clients trying to blame their unacceptable behavior on their families saying, "I'm just like my father (or mother)."

One day, we will all pass before God Most High for a thorough inspection. At that time, He will pay close attention, and we will be called to account for all we have done in our lives without regard to the sins of others.

> *"As I live," says the Lord GOD, "you shall no longer use this proverb in Israel. Behold, all souls are Mine; the soul of the father as well as the soul of the son is Mine; the soul who sins shall die... The son shall not bear the guilt of the father, nor the father bear the guilt of the son. The righteousness of the righteous shall be upon himself, and the wickedness of the wicked shall be upon himself."*
> *—Ezekiel 18:3-4, 20*

The justice of God demands that God visits with punishment the soul who sins, whether father or son, mother or daughter. But the love of God provides shelter and forgiveness. The two sides of God's character, love and justice, meet in the Person of Jesus. Is there a better time to find shelter under the blood of the Passover Lamb?

Next, let us take a closer look at how Jesus fulfilled the redemptive aspect of Passover.

Endnotes

1. Koehler, L. & Baumgartner, W. (Eds.). (1999). *The Hebrew and Aramaic Lexicon of the Old Testament* (HALOT) [Electronic form], #8747. Leiden, Netherlands: Brill.
2. TWOT, #2146a.
3. HALOT, #3019.
4. *The New Brown-Driver-Briggs-Gesenius Hebrew and English Lexicon*, (BDB). (1979). Peabody, MA: Brown, Francis, Hendrickson, pp. 335–336.
5. TWOT, #694.
6. TWOT, #133a.
7. Loved: [*'ahab*]; grace: [*chanan*]; favor: [*chesed*].
8. The personal experience of God's covenant blessings is based completely on our faith and trust and willingness to enter fully into that relationship.
9. Mercy: [*chanan*]; unfailing love: [*chesed*]; compassion: [*rachum*].
10. TWOT, #116k.
11. The English reads "goodness and truth," but the Hebrew reads "truth and goodness."
12. Colossians 1:15; John 14:9.
13. BDB, p. 328.
14. TWOT, #676.
15. Also Ezekiel 16:1-8; Ephesians 2:1-5.
16. BDB, p. 669.
17. TWOT, #1577a.
18. TWOT, #1846a.
19. Strong, J. (1996). *The Exhaustive Concordance of the Bible* [Electronic form], Ontario: Woodside Bible Fellowship.
20. Leviticus 23:26.
21. TWOT, #1802.

Chapter Seven

Passover: Redemptive

Jesus Is Our Passover Lamb

The rose is a marvelous picture of the progression of God's revelation.

The rose is only a bud at its first stage of development; yet everything the rose will become is contained in its womb. Slowly the rose opens. We begin to see its beauty and perhaps smell traces of its fragrance. The next stage is called the perfect bloom. At that point, the magnificence of the rose displays the glory of its Creator. Every part of the flower is in perfect alignment. Finally, the rose opens completely, and it's almost hard to see the totality of the rose as our focus is drawn to the individual petals.

The progression of the rose reflects the progression of God's plan of salvation as revealed in His Word:

- The bud stage is the **Torah**—the first five books of the Bible. The Torah is the bud of God's plan of redemption. Everything God wants to tell us is hidden in its pages.
- The next stage is the **Tenach**, comprising the Prophets and the Writings, which gives us further clarity of God's plan.
- The perfect bloom of Scripture is the revelation of Jesus the Messiah as presented in the **Gospels**. Nothing can improve that which is perfect!
- Lastly, the petals can be likened to the **Epistles,** which focus on the specifics of walking in the Spirit as we follow the Master.

Within a week after my salvation decision, I attended a messianic observance of Passover. The service combined elements of the traditional Jewish and the biblically historical Passover. I was amazed. How could I have performed the ritual and heard the story for forty years and never once asked, "Where is the lamb?"

As I grew in my knowledge of Scripture and in my relationship with Jesus, the bud of the Torah opened. I recognized the prophetic significance of Passover in Jesus; He fulfilled every detail.

God's Plan of Redemption

Before we can recognize God's plan of redemption throughout the holidays, let's affirm what we're looking for.

From the moment our ancestors Adam and Eve chose their own pleasure over God's, sin entered His perfect world. Sin broke their intimate relationship with God, as it continues to separate mankind from His presence today:

> *Your iniquities have separated you from your God; and your sins have hidden His face from you, so that He will not hear.*
> —*Isaiah 59:2*

Separation from God's face is a poetic way of saying that we are separated from experiencing God's love, His provision, His protection, and, most of all, His fellowship. As we saw through the Passover story, God must punish sin, and the punishment for sin is death—eternal separation from God. In Ezekiel 18:4, God warned Israel, "The soul who sins shall die." As Paul wrote in Romans 6:23, "The wages of sin is death." The redemption promise is in the end of that verse: "but the gift of God is eternal life in Christ Jesus our Lord."

God's justice demanded the death of anything or anyone defiled by sin. But His love extended a free gift—a provisional sacrifice—through the blood of animals:

> *For the life of the flesh is in the blood, and I have given it to you upon the altar to make atonement for your souls; for it is the blood that makes atonement for the soul.*
> —*Leviticus 17:11*

ATONEMENT

The word *atonement* is better translated as *reconciliation.* The blood of the sacrifice was the ransom price that brought reconciliation between the sinner and his holy God. But no matter how many animals were sacrificed, no matter how penitent the sinner, mankind could never be fully delivered because his sin was in his heart. From the first sin of Adam and Eve, sin became part of our spiritual DNA. Redemption would require a heart transplant, with God's love engraved upon it. The blood of bulls and goats was insufficient:

> *For it is not possible that the blood of bulls and goats could take away sins.* —Hebrews 10:4

Hidden deep within the rose bud was God's promise to become the sacrifice, coming down to deliver us, to redeem us by His body and blood:

> *I will put enmity between you and the woman, and between your seed and her Seed; He shall bruise your head, and you shall bruise His heel.* —Genesis 3:15

More clearly, we find in the Prophets:

> *For He said, "Surely they are My people, children who will not lie." So He became their Savior. In all their affliction He was afflicted, and the Angel of His Presence saved them; in His love and in His pity He redeemed them.* —Isaiah 63:8-9[1]

Who can explain the mystery of God, who is Spirit, becoming a man? If we could comprehend God's mind, we would be the greater. But nothing is impossible with the One who does understand! What was a foreshadowing during the Passover event became a reality several thousand years later:

> *[Christ Jesus], who, being in the form of God, did not consider it robbery to be equal with God, but made Himself of no reputation, taking the form of a bondservant, and coming in the likeness of men. And being found in appearance as a man, He humbled Himself and became obedient to the point of death, even the death of the Cross.* —Philippians 2:5-8

What could be a more astounding act of love than God taking on the form of His creature and then taking on Himself the punishment for the creature's sin!

God's holiness separated Him from our sin. His justice required blood atonement; His love took our punishment that enabled Him to restore the broken relationship.

WHAT'S IN A NAME?

Earlier we said that the connotation of God's memorial name I AM [*YHWH*] is His intimate and active involvement in the lives of His people.

Would He give His Anointed Son a name that is any less meaningful? Through an angelic messenger, God named Mary's baby:

> *. . . Joseph, son of David, do not be afraid to take to you Mary your wife, for that which is conceived in her is of the Holy Spirit. And she will bring forth a Son, and you shall call His name Jesus, for He will save His people from their sins.*
> *—Matthew 1:20b-21*

Yeshua [*yeshua'*] is the Hebrew name translated as Jesus. It comes from the root [*yasha'*], which means *to receive help, to be victorious, to accept help, also to save, help, to come to assist.*[2] Since I am primarily an English speaker, it has taken me time to get used to the Hebrew name for Jesus. But now Yeshua has become part of my very being. I was shocked to discover the root of His name throughout all of the Old Testament.[3]

Consider the many ways we need assistance, help, or rescue:

> *Then they said to one another, "We are truly guilty concerning our brother, for we saw the anguish of*

his soul when he pleaded with us, and we would not hear; therefore this distress has come upon us."
—Genesis 42:21

Alas! For that day is great, so that none is like it; and it is the time of Jacob's trouble, but he shall be saved out of it.
—Jeremiah 30:7

God is our refuge and strength, a very present help in trouble. Therefore we will not fear, even though the earth be removed, and though the mountains be carried into the midst of the sea. *—Psalm 46:1-2*

In each verse, the writer is facing severe trouble, anguish, distress, and affliction. The same root word is used in each of these verses: [*tsarar*], which means *to bind, be distressed, be cramped, be narrow, be scant.*[4] We use words like *uptight, anxious, stressed,* or *bound up.*

Who hasn't felt as if the weight of the entire world were sitting on his shoulders while he climbed up a very steep hill? Who hasn't felt as though caught in a vise, with his life being squeezed so hard he cannot breathe? We have all cried out along with the psalmist:

Save now, I pray, O LORD. *—Psalm 118:25a*

In this verse, the psalmist uses the word [*hoshi'ah*], which comes from the same root we saw above: [*yasha'*]. The people are crying out for God's salvation from their troubles, to be released from the narrow place of their distress, and to be brought into a wide place where they can breathe! In the following verses, [*tsarar*] is used along with a derivative of our root word [*yasha'*].

This poor man cried out, and the LORD heard him, and saved him out of all his troubles. *—Psalm 34:6*

Though I walk in the midst of trouble, You will revive me; You will stretch out Your hand against the wrath of my enemies, and Your right hand will save me.
—Psalm 138:7

Being released (saved, delivered) results in having freedom or, in other words, having room to take a deep breath. The psalmist writes:

I called on the LORD in distress; the LORD answered me and set me in a broad place. —Psalm 118:5

Jesus saves, delivers, releases, and rescues us from trouble, distress, anxiety, anguish—whatever is pressing in upon us—in body, soul, or spirit. He is our salvation, bringing us out of our bondage and bringing us to a place where we can take a deep breath:

Therefore if the Son makes you free, you shall be free indeed. —John 8:36

Jesus: The Passover Lamb

Every aspect of God's promises and character that He revealed to Moses was fulfilled by Jesus:

- He understands our bondage and burdens.

  Amazingly, God, who knows all and understands all, still considered it necessary to experience all! By becoming a man, Jesus experienced everything known to man—except sin:

In all their affliction He was afflicted, and the Angel of His Presence saved them. —Isaiah 63:9a[6]

For we do not have a High Priest who cannot sympathize with our weaknesses, but was in all points tempted as we are, yet without sin... that we may obtain mercy and find grace to help in time of need.
—Hebrews 4:15-16

You will never experience a troubling situation that is unknown to Jesus or from which He cannot save you.

☙ He came down to deliver His people out of bondage.

But now the righteousness of God apart from the law is revealed, being witnessed by the Law and the Prophets, even the righteousness of God, through faith in Jesus Christ, to all and on all who believe. For there is no difference; for all have sinned and fall short of the glory of God, being justified freely by His grace through the redemption that is in Christ Jesus, whom God set forth as a propitiation by His blood, through faith, to demonstrate His righteousness, because in His forbearance God had passed over the sins that were previously committed, to demonstrate at the present time His righteousness, that He might be just and the justifier of the one who has faith in Jesus.
—Romans 3:21-26

☙ He is the ransom price.

The Son of Man did not come to be served, but to serve, and to give His life a ransom for many.
—Matthew 20:28

Conduct yourselves throughout the time of your stay here in fear; knowing that you were not redeemed with corruptible things, like silver or gold, from your aimless conduct received by tradition from your fathers, but with the precious blood of Christ, as of a lamb without blemish and without spot.
—1 Peter 1:17b-19

৺ He is the Kinsman Redeemer.

But when the fullness of the time had come, God sent forth His Son, born of a woman, born under the law, to redeem those who were under the law.
—Galatians 4:4-5

Therefore, in all things He had to be made like His brethren, that He might be a merciful and faithful High Priest in things pertaining to God, to make propitiation for the sins of the people. For in that He Himself has suffered, being tempted, He is able to aid those who are tempted.
—Hebrews 2:17-18

৺ He brings us into the Kingdom of God's love.

But as many as received Him, to them He gave the right to become children of God, to those who believe in His name ... Jesus answered, "Most assuredly, I say to you, unless one is born of water and the Spirit, he cannot enter the kingdom of God."
—John 1:12; 3:5

৺ He is the incarnation of grace, mercy, and truth.

Over the years, a terrible misunderstanding of John 1:17 has created a seeming division in the indivisible I AM. He cannot be divided or separated, yet people have made a distinction between God of the Old Testament and God of the New Testament. The seed of this lie planted within the church grew into a disdain for the Jewish people and, worse, perverted the understanding of God's character. Look at this verse and ask what or who is being contrasted:

And of His fullness we have all received, and grace for grace. For the law was given through Moses, but grace and truth came through Jesus Christ. No one has seen God at any time. The only begotten Son, who is in the bosom of the Father, He has declared Him.
—John 1:16-18

Verse 16 tells us that we have received from God "grace upon grace." Can I AM, God of Passover, give His children anything other than grace?

Earlier, we explored the character of God with all the magnificent Hebrew words translated as *compassion, mercy, lovingkindness, and grace.* In the Hebrew translation of the New Testament, the word used for *grace* is not [*chanan*] but [*chesed*], which is *covenant-keeping love.*[7] Grace is an integral part of God's character.

If God revealed Himself as "love and truth" at Mt. Sinai, did He change over the ensuing years? Of course not! Repeatedly we hear, especially though the Psalms, the echo of God's character as revealed at Sinai: [*'emet v^e chesed*] love/grace and truth:

He shall send from heaven and save me; He reproaches the one who would swallow me up. Selah. God shall send forth His mercy and His truth. —Psalm 57:3

For the Lord *is good; His mercy is everlasting, and His truth endures to all generations.*
—Psalm 100:5

Righteousness and justice are the foundation of Your throne; mercy and truth go before Your face ... My faithfulness and My mercy shall be with him ... My lovingkindness I will not utterly take from him, nor allow My faithfulness to fail.
—Psalm 89:14, 24, 33

The God of Calvary is the God of Sinai. He is God. He is law, love/grace, and truth. What John is comparing is the way God mediated His precious mercy and truth. Moses could only carry God's covenant on tablets of stone. Jesus became the covenant and wrote His love upon our hearts! Hallelujah!

Jesus is "the Lamb of God who takes away the sins of the world."[8]

God gave Moses very specific instructions about the lamb to be sacrificed on that first Passover. Not surprisingly, Jesus fulfilled every detail:

On the tenth of this month every man shall take for himself a lamb, according to the house of his father, a lamb for a household ... Your lamb shall be without blemish, a male of the first year ... Now you shall keep it until the fourteenth day of the same month. Then the whole assembly of the congregation of Israel shall kill it at twilight. And they shall take some of the blood and put it on the two doorposts and on the lintel of the houses where they eat it ... Now the

> *blood shall be a sign for you on the houses where you are. And when I see the blood, I will pass over you; and the plague shall not be on you to destroy you when I strike the land of Egypt.*
>
> —Exodus 12:3-7, 13

Take a look at a few of these biblical elements and discover the revelation of Jesus as the Passover Lamb contained in God's Torah:

- He was chosen before the foundation of the world to be the Passover sacrifice.[9]
- He was chosen out of the flock—the house of Israel, the tribe of Judah.[10]
- He was offered to the world.[11]
- He was separated on the tenth of the month, tested, declared blameless, and sacrificed on the fourteenth.[12]
- Not one of His bones was broken.[13]
- His blood provides protection and redemption to all who will come under its sign.

Communion

Let's take a look at communion in light of what we've learned about Passover.

Jesus and His disciples were in the upper room on the night He was betrayed, observing the ancient Passover dinner. From John 13 and 1 Corinthians 11:23-25, we have hints of some of the ritual elements they might have included in their celebration.

A cup of wine was traditionally taken after the meal. Over this cup, Psalm 116 was sung. Listen to the libretto written by David to be sung at this most auspicious time by the Greater David:

> *What shall I render to the LORD for all His benefits toward me? I will take up the cup of salvation, and call upon the name of the LORD.* —Psalm 116:12-13

Rabbis today call this cup the Cup of Redemption. But David did not use those words. The Holy Spirit dictated "salvation," hence [*yeshu'ot*] from the same root [*yasha'*]. Isn't that what communion is all about? It is about our Passover Lamb who came down to redeem us by His blood, freeing us from our burdens and bondage to sin!

I AM heard the groaning of Israel. He remembered His covenant with the fathers. He looked, and He understood the situation. So He came down to deliver them. Because He is alive, He continues to deliver, rescue, and save all who will lift up the cup of His blood and trust Him enough to call upon His name.

Now let's begin an in-depth study of the Kingdom aspect of Passover.

Endnotes

1. Savior, saved: [*moshia*'], from the root [*yasha*'].
2. HALOT, #4074.
3. "In the world of Abraham, David, and Isaiah, names were common nouns and verbs from the living language, and their meanings were transparent. The meaning of a name was in fact the reason for that name being used" (Allen, R., "What's in a Name?"). Therefore, it should be no surprise that the Hebrew word for *salvation* is based on the same root as the personal name of the Savior.
4. Strong, J. (1996). *The Exhaustive Concordance of the Bible* [Electronic form]. Ontario: Woodside Bible Fellowship.
5. Troubles: [*tsarotav*]; saved: [*hoshi'ah*].
6. Affliction: [*tsaratam*]; saved: [*hoshi'am*].
7. Note: Hebrew translations of the New Testament are not inspired; they are translations, just like NIV, NASB, etc.
8. John 1:29.
9. Exodus 12:6; cf. 1 Peter 1:19-20; Revelation 13:8.
10. Exodus 12:5-6; cf. Hebrews 2:17; Matthew 1:3-16; Luke 3:23-33.
11. Exodus 12:3; cf. John 3:16; 1:12.
12. Exodus 12:6.
13. Exodus 12:46; Psalm 34:20.
14. To ransom: [*padah*]; to redeem: [*gā'al*].

Chapter Eight

Passover: Kingdom

Personal Application of the Passover

Kingdom application is always the most important aspect of the holidays. Several times Paul reminds us that Scripture is to be practical. Our lives are meant to be transformed by the washing of the Word.[1]

Below I suggest several ways for us to apply the lessons learned through the Passover event. My prayer is that the Holy Spirit will suggest other applications so that understanding Passover will have an impact that will affect and transform your relationship with God.

Recognizing Bondage

Earlier I mentioned that burdens come in different manifestations. They can be categorized as *physical* (relating to the body) or *spiritual* (relating to the spirit of man). However, often the most crippling is bondage in the *soul.* I define the soul as *mind, emotions, and will.* In other words: *what we think, what we feel, and what we choose.* Passover reflects what bondage looks like and celebrates our deliverance, redemption, and salvation from bondage—all bondage.

Salvation is a choice regardless of the type of bondage. Deliverance, redemption, rescue, and salvation are all aspects of God's offer.

We'll start our discussion by considering spiritual bondage—bondage to sin, which results in our eternal separation from God. Deliverance from spiritual bondage is the ultimate freedom. Testimonies abound from men and women who are incarcerated in the worst circumstances yet enjoy true freedom in the spirit.

SALVATION FROM SPIRITUAL BONDAGE

The primary Kingdom application of Passover is God's invitation for all to enter His Kingdom community. The entryway to His salvation hasn't changed—it is the blood-stained door. Jesus even fulfills that detail as He said of Himself:

> *I am the door … No one comes to the Father except through Me.* —John 10:7, 14:6

The Bible tells us a "mixed multitude" left Egypt that night. A multitude of Jews and Gentiles chose to come under the sign of blood and were spared God's punishment. God continues to make the same offer to all who are oppressed. Jesus offers:

> *Come to Me, all you who labor and are heavy laden, and I will give you rest.* —Matthew 11:28

Just as the Egyptians needed to choose to come under the sign of the blood, every individual needs to make the same choice today:

He came to that which belonged to Him [to His own–His domain, creation, things, world], and they who were His own did not receive Him and did not welcome Him. But to as many as did receive and welcome Him, He gave the authority (power, privilege, right) to become the children of God, that is, to those who believe in (adhere to, trust in, and rely on) His name.
—John 1:11-12 (AB)[2]

Salvation is both an event and an ongoing process. Salvation in the Spirit occurs at the moment we accept God's offer of forgiveness through the sacrifice of Jesus. But that only begins the process of salvation:

For if when we were enemies we were reconciled to God through the death of His Son, much more, having been reconciled, we shall be saved by His life.
—Romans 5:10

Whatever your need, your salvation is near. If you have not already done so, apply the blood of Jesus to the door of your heart. God will see it as clearly as He saw the blood on the doors in Egypt. This is the only way to receive deliverance from your sins.

SALVATION FROM SOUL BONDAGE

King David knew many troubles. At least twice he had to run for his life as the people he loved sought to kill him. Notice his prayer:

Attend to my cry, for I am brought very low; deliver me from my persecutors, for they are stronger than I. Bring my soul out of prison, that I may praise Your name.
—Psalm 142:6-7

Most of us to some degree are in *soul bondage.* Our souls are in prison. This is too important to rush past, so let's spend a bit of time exploring this real, but unseen, prison.

Our souls are the favorite target of Satan:

> *For the enemy has persecuted my soul; he has crushed my life to the ground; he has made me dwell in darkness, like those who have long been dead. Therefore my spirit is overwhelmed within me; my heart within me is distressed.*
> *—Psalm 143:3-4*

When we experience a painful event (divorce, death, negative words, any kind of abuse, family alcoholism, or addictions) the enemy immediately attacks us with lies about ourselves:

- You're no good, a failure, stupid, unlovable.
- Everything is always your fault.
- You are responsible for my happiness (or unhappiness).
- You don't matter.

Lies in our minds break our hearts. To survive, we put these broken, wounded pieces of our hearts into a place hidden within our souls. This place becomes a prison, trapping the pain behind thick walls of self-protection. Eventually, the prison walls begin to close in on us, squeezing us from every side. Finally, trying to free itself from bondage, the captured soul releases its frustration through rebellion, transgression, and sin. Even our bodies can eventually be affected through sickness and disease flowing from the bondage of our souls.

Thanks be to God—there is healing, deliverance, and freedom through Jesus!

One day while teaching in the synagogue, Jesus read from the prophet Isaiah:

"The Spirit of the LORD is upon Me, because He has anointed Me
To preach the gospel to the poor;
He has sent Me to heal the brokenhearted,
To proclaim liberty to the captives
And recovery of sight to the blind,
To set at liberty those who are oppressed;
To proclaim the acceptable year of the LORD."

Then He closed the book, and gave it back to the attendant and sat down. And the eyes of all who were in the synagogue were fixed on Him. And He began to say to them, "Today this Scripture is fulfilled in your hearing."

—Luke 4:18-21; Isaiah 61:1

To understand Jesus' claim of being the fulfillment of this prophecy, let us look at four particularly poignant Hebrew words in this passage.

[*Basar*] translated as *preach* means *to bring news, to tell or announce, proclaim, bear (good tidings)*. The root meaning is to "*bring good news, especially pertaining to military encounters.*"[3] The word was used in the context of bringing what the messenger considered to be good news to the hearer.

When Jesus applied this word to Himself, He claimed to have won the victory in the battle against His enemies. By virtue of His success, He has been anointed by God with the best message of all—salvation!

[*'Anav*] from the root [*'anah*], translated *poor,* has also been translated as *afflict, humble.*

Sometimes our souls are afflicted because of our own choices or sin. Sometimes they are afflicted because of the sins of others. Sometimes we are afflicted because we live in a sinful world.

Regardless of the cause, the word refers to the one who recognizes his helplessness; then in piety, humility, and trust turns to Jesus.

[*Qara*] is translated *proclaim*. This word goes beyond a public and general proclamation. It denotes "*primarily the enunciation of a specific message. In the case of the latter usage it is customarily addressed to a specific recipient and is intended to elicit a specific response.*"[4]

A great example of this word is when Jesus called for Lazarus to come out of the grave. Jesus gave a specific demand and only Lazarus responded. Jesus also is specifically calling you!

[*Deror*] is translated *liberty*. Except for this time, the word is only used in reference to Israel's Year of Jubilee when all debts were cancelled, freeing all who were in bondage!

Jesus has paid in full your greatest debt and is your Jubilee.

Remember what we said about the cup after the Passover dinner? It was probably this cup, which Jesus used to announce the new covenant and which became the cup of our communion service. We said that as Jesus took the cup, He recited Psalm 116. Hear the cry of pain and darkness of the psalmist:

> *I love the LORD, because He has heard My voice and my supplications. Because He has inclined His ear to me, therefore I will call upon Him as long as I live. The pains of death surrounded me, and the pangs of Sheol laid hold of me; I found trouble and sorrw. Then I called upon the name of the LORD: "LORD, I implore You, deliver my soul!"*
>
> *—Psalm 116:1-4*

The revelation given to Moses becomes the banner over the psalmist:

> *Gracious is the LORD, and righteous; yes, our God is merciful. The LORD preserves the simple; I was brought low, and He saved me.* —Psalm 116:5-6

But, the psalmist remembers the result of his soul bondage:

> *I believed, therefore I spoke, "I am greatly afflicted." I said in my haste, "all men are liars."* —Psalm 116:10-11

Finally, we get to the answer to the bondage of our souls:

> *What shall I render to the LORD for all His benefits toward me? I will take up the cup of salvation, and call upon the name of the LORD.* —Psalm 116:12-13

Look again at what Paul wrote to the Romans:

> *For if when we were enemies we were reconciled to God through the death of His Son, much more, having been reconciled; we shall be saved by His life.* —Romans 5:10

The salvation of Passover is continual. Our Passover Lamb was sacrificed on the fourteenth day of Nisan, but three days later He rose. Forty days later, He ascended and is seated at the right hand of the Father

> *... to bring out prisoners from the prison, those who sit in darkness from the prison house.* —Isaiah 42:7b

As you consider the goodness of God for hearing your cries, remember that all God asks from us is to trust Him enough to lift up the cup of His blood, which contains all that we need for our deliverance and salvation from every problem.

Knowing God as Father

Family is important to God. He calls Himself Israel's Father. In his letter to the Ephesians, Paul refers to God as the source of "the whole family" of creation:

> *The Father of our Lord Jesus Christ, from whom the whole family in heaven and earth is named…*
> *—Ephesians 3:14b-15*

The relationship of God as Father and His followers as His children is unique. No other gods offered their followers a relationship of familial intimacy. Sadly, the image that *father* conjures in the minds of many today is a distortion of the Fatherhood of God. Because of sin, our earthly fathers (and mothers) are often in soul bondage to their own past wounds and experiences. They are unable to nurture, not because they are wicked or evil, but because they have not been nurtured. How can parents give what they have not received themselves? Unredeemed and untransformed, many parents have been absent through divorce, death, neglect, addiction to alcohol, drugs, work, or ministry; or they have been abusive verbally, physically, spiritually, sexually, or emotionally.

But this is not an accurate representation of God, our Father. Look at more descriptions of the Father we have in

God, and notice His compassion as He provides for and protects His children:

> *The LORD your God, who goes before you, He will fight for you, according to all He did for you in Egypt before your eyes, and in the wilderness where you saw how the LORD your God carried you, as a man carries his son, in all the way that you went until you came to this place.*
> —*Deuteronomy 1:30-31*

> *I was a father to the poor ... A father of the fatherless, a defender of widows, is God in His holy habitation ... As a father pities his children, so the LORD pities those who fear Him.* —*Job 29:16; Psalm 68:5; 103:13*

> *What man is there among you who, if his son asks for bread, will give him a stone? Or if he asks for a fish, will he give him a serpent? If you then, being evil, know how to give good gifts to your children, how much more will your Father in heaven give good things to those who ask Him!*
> —*Matthew 7:9-11*

Provision and protection are generally considered masculine traits, especially in our Western culture. But a discussion of the fatherhood of God would be incomplete and unbalanced if we did not also consider the gentle, nurturing (a.k.a., feminine) side of God:

> *O Jerusalem, Jerusalem, the one who kills the prophets and stones those who are sent to her! How often I wanted to gather your children together, as a hen gathers her brood under her wings, but you were not willing.*
> —*Luke 13:34*

In the following verse, the Hebrew words for *breath* [*neshamah*] and *spirit* [*ruach*] are both feminine:

> *But there is a spirit in man, and the breath of the Almighty gives him understanding.*
> *—Job 32:8*

Let me address the misunderstanding of the fatherhood of God as He is revealed in the Hebrew Bible. I cannot count the number of times I hear, "God of the Old Testament is vengeful and violent, while God of the New Testament is full of grace and mercy." I think we've already established that it's the same God with the same characteristics. But just in case there is still a doubt, listen to the words of Jesus:

> *Jesus said to him, "I am the way, the truth, and the life. No one comes to the Father except through Me. If you had known Me, you would have known My Father also; and from now on you know Him and have seen Him."*
>
> *Philip said to Him, "Lord, show us the Father, and it is sufficient for us."*
>
> *Jesus said to him: "Have I been with you so long, and yet you have not known me, Philip? He who has seen Me has seen the Father; so how can you say, 'Show us the Father'?"*
> *—John 14:6-9*

While praying one day, I referred to God as "the God of love." The Spirit corrected me gently, saying, "He is not 'the' God of love, He is the very definition of love." Passover reminds us of the privilege of becoming a child of God and experiencing the Father's love:

> *The LORD is merciful and gracious, slow to anger, and abounding in mercy... He has not dealt with us according to our sins, nor punished us according to*

our iniquities...As far as the east is from the west, so far has He removed our transgressions from us.
—Psalm 103:8, 10, 12[5]

Trust vs. Faith

Administrating details and logistics are not easy for me.

I was leading a city-wide event for an expected 500 people. Teams were in place, and everyone was doing a terrific job. But the afternoon before, I was told there were no chairs in the auditorium.

I made a quick call to a pastor friend and arranged to get some chairs.

After the event, as a friend and I stood in the then-quiet auditorium praising God for His presence during the event, we looked over a sea of chairs. "Joan," he asked, "what about the chairs?" I had forgotten the pastor's provision that the chairs be returned immediately after the event so they could be used the next day for the church service!

Twenty years later, I was once again coordinating an event. This time it was not simply one evening in my city involving 500 people but an event that would last almost three weeks and extend throughout all of Israel! Thousands of people were affected. The details were staggering.

While struggling to make a myriad of decisions, I kept humming the words of a song, "Jesus will make a way. Through all the trials and all the pain, Jesus will make a way." It took about twenty minutes before I actually heard the words I was singing! It dawned on me—why was I concerned? God breathed all of creation into existence and sustains it by His right hand; can He not take care of a few details that are so overwhelming to me?

By God's strength, Moses brought Israel out of Egypt in one night. Over one million men, women, and children plus their worldly possessions and livestock were assembled without the use of cell phones, faxes, or email! How was that possible? Moses trusted and had faith.

If you are like me, you may sometimes think trust and faith are the same. Once again, Hebrew comes to our rescue. While faith and trust are interrelated, they are two distinct words.

TRUST

There are two Hebrew words that have been translated as *trust.* The first word, [*chasah*], is the more active of the two. It expresses the action of *running for protection, especially to a high place.* To seek refuge stresses the insecurity and self-helplessness of even the strongest of men. "It emphasizes the defensive or external aspect of salvation in God, the unchanging one in whom we find shelter":[6]

> *The LORD is my rock and my fortress and my deliverer; my God, my strength, in whom I will trust; my shield and the horn of my salvation, my stronghold.*
> *—Psalm 18:2*

> *How precious is Your lovingkindness, O God! Therefore the children of men put their trust under the shadow of Your wings.* *—Psalm 36:7*

That Israel is filled with rocks and hills is reflected in the use of parallel words such as trust, rock, stronghold, refuge, and shield as the psalmist runs to God, his refuge:

> *Blessed be the LORD my Rock, Who trains my hands for war, and my fingers for battle—my lovingkindness and my fortress, my high tower and my deliverer, my shield and the One in whom I take refuge.*
> *—Psalm 144:1-2*

> *In God is my salvation and my glory; the rock of my strength, and my refuge, is in God.*
> *—Psalm 62:7*

The second word for *trust* is [*batach*]. Whereas [*chasah*] emphasizes the action of *seeking refuge*, [*batach*] emphasizes the sense of *feeling secure*. "It describes the sense of well-being and security, which results from having something or someone in whom to place confidence":[7]

> *You will keep him in perfect peace, whose mind is stayed on You, because he trusts in You ... In returning and rest you shall be saved; in quietness and confidence shall be your strength.* *—Isaiah 26:3; 30:15a*

> *Whenever I am afraid, I will trust in You ... In God I have put my trust; I will not fear. What can flesh do to me?* *—Psalm 56:3-4*

FAITH

Trusting is an act of the will. It precipitates action and then a sense of well-being. It's about feelings. This is not so with faith. How often have you heard the expression, "Faith is blind"? I disagree. Blind faith can lead you into trouble. Faith that is pleasing to God is based on your knowledge of Him. Let's look at this important verse in the Hebrew Bible:

> *But the just shall live by his faith.* —*Habakkuk 2:4*

The Hebrew word translated here as *faith* [*'emunah*] is better translated as *faithful*, or *faithfulness*. [*'Emunah*] comes from the root [*'aman*]. We saw in "Passover: Spiritual" that [*'aman*] is best translated as *sure, certain, truth.* Faith is focused on the unchanging character and Word of God.

I believe that the testimony God established through Israel is the testimony of His faithfulness despite our unfaithfulness:

> *If his sons forsake My law and do not walk in My judgments, if they break My statutes and do not keep My commandments, then I will punish their transgression with the rod, and their iniquity with stripes. Nevertheless My lovingkindness I will not utterly take from him, nor allow My faithfulness to fail. My covenant I will not break, nor alter the word that has gone out of My lips.*
> —*Psalm 89:30-34*

If God could break His promises to Israel, you would have no reason to put your faith in Him. Our God is not capricious! He binds His reputation to His word. Our God does whatever pleases Him and what pleases Him is being faithful![8] The New Testament calls God "immutable, unchanging."

Ponder the request God made of both Israel and Egypt that first Passover night—"Kill a lamb and put its blood on the doorposts of your house." The people were supposed to trust God enough to do what He asked. They were to have enough faith to get dressed, gather their personal belongings, and then sit down to the mutton feast while all around them death stalked every household without the sign of the blood. It took trust and faith in the One who could and did save them. May we all echo the words of the psalmist and experience the salvation of the Lord:

> *I will love You, O LORD, my strength. The LORD is my rock and my fortress and my deliverer; my God, my strength, in whom I will trust; my shield and the horn of my salvation, my stronghold. I will call upon the LORD, who is worthy to be praised; so shall I be saved from my enemies.*
>
> *—Psalm 18:1-3*

Choosing Kingdom Obedience

Trust and faith will lead to action. A friend of mine used to say, "It's not what you know that counts, but what you do with what you know."

Historically the book of James, with the emphasis on *doing* for God, has provoked a controversy between faith vs. works. Perhaps because I was raised in a Jewish home, there is no difference to me. Love is not simply a feeling; it is an action. Love requires a determination to do what pleases the one we love.

The first and greatest commandment tells us to "Love the Lord [our] God with all our hearts, souls, and minds." That passage of Scripture continues by telling us what we are to do as we express our love:

> *You shall teach them diligently to your children, and shall talk of them when you sit in your house, when you walk by the way, when you lie down, and when you rise up.*

You shall bind them as a sign on your hand, and they shall be as frontlets between your eyes. You shall write them on the doorposts of your house and on your gates
—Deuteronomy 6:7-9

God the Father and God the Son repeatedly command us to act out of our love. Jesus said,

If you love Me, keep My commandments. —John 14:15

Obedience to Christ is not only an act of love, it is evidence of His lordship:

He arose and rebuked the wind, and said to the sea, "Peace, be still!" ... And they feared exceedingly, and said to one another, "Who can this be, that even the wind and the sea obey Him."
—Mark 4:39, 41

... with authority He commands even the unclean spirits, and they obey Him.
—Mark 1:27

I wear a gold ring on my left hand. A diamond rises from the intersection of two circles. It is a testimony to my commitment of love. The diamond represents success. One circle represents God's will, and the other represents my behavior. Only when my obedience intersects with the will of God will I know and enjoy true success.

True obedience requires a great cost. You might have to sacrifice your reputation, acceptance of family and friends, your job, or even your life. But the obedience that leads to success in God's eyes obeys despite situations or circumstances! What would have happened if Israel had *not* put the blood on the doorposts and lintels? Consider the words of James:

But someone will say, "You have faith, and I have works." Show me your faith without your works, and

I will show you my faith by my works. You believe that there is one God. You do well. Even the demons believe—and tremble! But do you want to know, O foolish man, that faith without works is dead?
—James 2:18-20

EFFECT OF UNGODLY LEADERSHIP

Paul's instructions to Timothy about praying for leaders are still applicable to us today:

Therefore I exhort first of all that supplications, prayers, intercessions, and giving of thanks be made for all men, for kings and all who are in authority, that we may lead a quiet and peaceable life in all godliness and reverence.
—1 Timothy 2:1-2

The Passover story reflects the devastating influence a godless leader will have upon his people. Remember that the plagues against Egypt were not because of the sins of individual people but because of Pharaoh's rejection of God. Pharaoh's choice affected all the people. Of course, we know that every person must stand before God and be judged according to his own decision about Christ, but the decision of leaders like Pharaoh can bring destruction on an entire country.

We see the influence of Israel's leaders through just a cursory review of her history. Under the godly leadership of King David, Israel expanded her borders greatly. Although David was a man of war, the country began to know peace. David's successor to the throne was Solomon. Solomon was unlike his father. Whereas David was a man after God's heart, Solomon's heart was lured away. Solomon did everything God had warned Israel against, especially marrying foreign wives. Those wives lured Solomon to fill Israel with temples and places of sacrifice and worship to false gods. Many of those "high places" were never destroyed and eventually turned the heart of Solomon and many others away from Jerusalem and David's God.

By the next generation, the kingdom was divided. Rehoboam governed the southern portion known as Judah. Jeroboam ruled Israel in the north and refused to follow the commandments of the Lord. His influence on Israel was tremendous and extended down generations to his son and then on the whole house of Israel:

> *Now Nadab the son of Jeroboam became king over Israel in the second year of Asa king of Judah, and he reigned over Israel two years. And he did evil in the sight of the LORD, and walked in the way of his father, and in his sin by which he had made Israel sin.*
>
> *—1 Kings 15:25-26*

Continuously and consistently the refrain continues from father to son, throughout the following generations.[9] Even though the kings might have done some good in their lives, even receiving a commendation from the Lord, their epitaph still reads: "and he did evil in the sight of the Lord . . . and made Israel sin."

It is said, "We get the politicians we deserve." Perhaps this is true. But the Bible tells us that it is God who raises and places our kings. And it is God's hand that can turn the hearts of those kings. This doesn't, however, release us from our commanded responsibility to pray for our kings:

> *Therefore I exhort first of all that supplications, prayers, intercessions, and giving of thanks be made for all men, for kings and all who are in authority, that we may lead a quiet and peaceable life in all godliness and reverence. For this is good and acceptable in*

the sight of God our Savior, who desires all men to be saved and to come to the knowledge of the truth.
—1 Timothy 2:1-4

The day may come when each of us experiences devastation caused by those in authority who are ungodly and rule in unrighteousness. But we can find refuge in Jesus, the King of all Kings. We can persevere, knowing that our eternity is in His Kingdom:

The kingdoms of this world have become the kingdoms of our Lord and of His Christ, and He shall reign forever and ever! *—Revelation 11:15*

Then to Him was given dominion and glory and a kingdom, that all peoples, nations, and languages should serve Him. His dominion is an everlasting dominion, which shall not pass away, and His kingdom the one which shall not be destroyed. *—Daniel 7:14*

ATTACKING THE PEOPLE OF GOD

Israel's bondage in Egypt was the result of Pharaoh's fear and jealousy (Exodus 1:9-10). She did nothing to deserve the bitter and cruel punishment. There have been many more pharaohs in Israel's history, even to this very day. It appears as though Israel is a target for destruction rather than for blessing.

Actually, Israel and the kingdom community are targets for both blessing by God and destruction by the enemy. Do not be deceived. As we get closer to the return of Jesus, God's people will be subject to increased persecution. Let us not fear what is to come but find refuge in the Passover Lamb.

Some "How To's" for Passover[10]

Observing Passover can be an important addition to Resurrection celebrations, as it helps us remember what we have been delivered from. Passover reminds us not only of our deliverance from sin but also from the trials and troubles of this world. Passover is a celebration of God's protection in the midst of injustice and judgment. Whether He protects us from within or takes us from persecution, there is security and refuge under the blood of the Passover Lamb.

First and foremost, the celebration of Passover (usually referred to as *Seder*)[11] is a community event. This is a time for family, friends, and even relative strangers to gather around the table. I remember the first time I facilitated a community Seder. I watched through the open door as a friend invited a passerby into the dinner.[12]

Most of the traditional elements of a Passover Seder find fulfillment in Jesus, but they can be cumbersome and confusing to the novice. I suggest you begin with the biblical basics found in Exodus 12: unleavened bread, bitter herbs, and lamb.[13] We know from 1 Corinthians 11:25 that some form of wine was also on the table.

The traditional Seder is liturgical with passages of Scripture being read before and after the meal. Questions, comments, and songs are encouraged throughout, as everyone should have a chance to participate.

Choose Scripture passages that recount each of these:

- Bondage of slavery in Egypt (Exodus 1–3)
- God's mighty acts of deliverance (Exodus 4–11; Psalm 105)
- Jesus as the Passover Lamb (John 1:1-14, 29-34; 3:14-21)
- Jesus' Last Seder/Supper (John 13–17; 1 Corinthians 11:23-26)

Also include the Great Hallel, Psalms 113–118. As you read through these verses, pause to reflect on how Jesus and the disciples might have felt on that last and most memorable evening as they recited these same words.

Above all, make your celebration of Passover just that—*your* celebration of the Passover Lamb—Jesus.

Passover is only the beginning of our spring celebrations. We will now take a look at its fellow holidays: Unleavened Bread and Firstfruits.

Endnotes

1. 2 Timothy 3:16-17; Romans 15:4.
2. The Lockman Foundation. (1987). *The Amplified Bible.* Grand Rapids, MI: Zondervan.
3. TWOT, #291.
4. TWOT, #2063.
5. This is the same refrain from Deuteronomy 34:5-6. Merciful: [*rachum*]; gracious: [*channun*]; slow to anger: ['*appayim*]; mercy: [*chesed*].
6. Kidner, F.D. (1973). *The Psalms.* Ad. Loc., Ps 46:1: TWOT, #700.
7. TWOT, #233.
8. Psalm 115:3.
9. 1 Kings 22:51-53; 2 Kings 13:1-2; 10-11.
10. See http://CelebrateJesus-TheBook.blogspot.com/.
11. *Seder* means "order" and reflects the liturgical elements of the traditional Passover dinner.
12. What a night that was! A few friends and I invited 21 people, but 105 showed up, representing over 30 churches throughout the city. Everyone brought food to share, but the logistics were so overwhelming that from then on we had the event catered.
13. Feel free to embellish even these elements. For instance, tortillas were used for the unleavened bread at one of my most memorable Passover dinners! Pita works fine, as does the traditional matzo. For the bitter herbs, horseradish is usually used. I prefer the kind made from beets as it is less pungent and a reminder of the blood of the sacrifice. Of course, the lamb intensifies the significance of the evening.

Chapter Nine

Feast of Unleavened Bread

Holiday of Freedom

God gave very specific instructions about the three holidays of spring, as individually they remind us of a particular aspect of redemption. However, Passover, Unleavened Bread, and Firstfruits were eventually considered as one—the Feast of Passover.

Whereas Passover focuses on the sacrifice that enabled Israel's deliverance, the Feast of Unleavened Bread focuses on the event of their deliverance—the effect of the sacrifice.

Passover is observed for one day, the fourteenth day of the month of Abib/Nissan. Unleavened Bread is observed for seven days. Although unleavened bread is eaten during the entire Passover season, the Feast of Unleavened Bread begins on the fifteenth day:

On the fourteenth day of the first month at twilight is the LORD's Passover. And on the fifteenth day of the same month is the Feast of Unleavened Bread to the LORD; seven days you must eat unleavened bread.
—Leviticus 23:5-6

There are eleven salient points concerning this holiday gleaned from Exodus 12:1; 13:3-10, 15-20; and Deuteronomy 16:3-4, 8:[1]

- It is celebrated on the fifteenth of the month.
- The purpose of the holiday is to commemorate God's deliverance of Israel.
- God's deliverance was a manifestation of His power, holiness, and love.
- All leaven had to be removed from homes under penalty of excommunication.
- Only unleavened bread was to be eaten for seven days, from the fourteenth to the twenty-first of Abib.
- Unleavened bread is a reminder of the affliction in bondage and the haste of God's deliverance.
- The holiday began and ended with a holy convocation.
- The entire week was a Sabbath with no customary work permitted on the first and last days.
- Jewish males were required to go to Jerusalem either on this or one of the other two pilgrim feasts.
- The holiday was to be observed by both Israel and strangers in the land.
- Its celebration is an annual and everlasting ordinance, a sign and a memorial from one generation to another so that Israel would always remember what God had done for her.

Seasonal

Unleavened Bread is in the spring, starting the day following Passover. It was also the first of the three pilgrim feasts requiring Jewish males to go up to Jerusalem.[2] The other two are Feast of Weeks and Feast of Tabernacles.

National

What could be more significant to the nation of Israel than the day of her deliverance? God's deliverance of Israel set her apart from all other nations:

> *Did any people ever hear the voice of God speaking out of the midst of the fire, as you have heard, and live? Or did God ever try to go and take for Himself a nation from the midst of another nation, by trials, by signs, by wonders, by war, by a mighty hand and an outstretched arm, and by great terrors, according to all that the* Lord *your God did for you in Egypt before your eyes?*
>
> *—Deuteronomy 4:33-34*

After more than four hundred years, Israel's day of freedom had come. Unleavened Bread commemorates the day Israel actually left Egypt—on the fifteenth of the month.

Now let's look at some of the points concerning this holiday in detail.

ISRAEL'S DELIVERANCE

In his movie, *The Ten Commandments,* Cecil B. Demille captures the drama of that awesome day. If you haven't seen the movie, maybe this description will stimulate your imagination.

> Look! High on that rock. It's Joshua blowing the shofar! Way out in front . . . there . . . it's Moses with his shepherd's staff. Moses moves forward, alone yet not alone; he is led by the Hand of God.
>
> Listen! It is the sound of the shofar. Here come thousands and thousands of freed slaves carrying, pushing, or dragging their belongings. Children are driving the herds and men are carrying the aged and the infirm. A few are carrying the bones of Joseph, who will be buried in the land of promise.

What a sight it must have been! This was a day to be remembered and celebrated forever—especially after what happened the night before:

- Goshen had been filled with the smell and sound of lambs being slaughtered on the threshold of the houses of the Jews.
- Egypt had also been filled with the smells and sounds of death. All of Egypt's firstborn men, women, and children, as well as the firstborn of the herds, died as God inflicted His tenth plague upon Pharaoh.

With the morning sun came freedom! For 430 years Israel had waited for this day to come. Ever since Moses appeared on the scene, their lives had gotten worse; some had lost hope. But on this day, God's promise finally came true.

Israel's deliverance came at a high price. God promised to "redeem" His people. In the overview of Passover in chapter five, we discussed the different Hebrew words for redemption. The word that might describe this holiday is [*gā'al*], which emphasizes the One who does the redemption, the Kinsman Redeemer. There is another word that Scripture uses in relation to Unleavened Bread, [*kofer*], which means *a ransom*,[3] derived from the Hebrew verb [*kafar*] meaning *to appease, make amends, to make atonement*:[4]

> *For I am the LORD your God, the Holy One of Israel, your Savior; I gave Egypt for your ransom, Ethiopia and Seba in your place.* —Isaiah 43:3

I will not presume to understand God's use of this word in this context, but it does reveal to me God's indescribable commitment to Israel based in His covenant-keeping love.

EGYPT PLUNDERED

Israel's ransom price was the death of the firstborn of Egypt, God's severe punishment for the sins of Pharaoh. God then allowed Israel to plunder Egypt's wealth:

> *Now the children of Israel had done according to the word of Moses, and they had asked from the Egyptians articles of silver, articles of gold, and clothing. And the LORD had given the people favor in the sight of the Egyptians, so that they granted them what they requested. Thus they plundered the Egyptians.*
> —Exodus 12:35-36

Consider for a moment the powerful and devastating word translated *plundered*. In Hebrew the word used is [*natzal*], which means to *snatch away, deliver, rescue, save, strip* and, yes, *plunder*.

Do you remember where you saw this word before? It was in "Passover: An Overview" when we discussed God's promise in Exodus 6:6 to bring Israel out of Egypt.

God not only snatched Israel from the bondage of Egypt, He snatched Egypt's material wealth as well! Israel entered Egypt as a poor family but left as a rich nation. After years of slavery, Israel left Egypt laden with precious metals of gold, silver, brass, and copper as well as luxurious fabrics of purple, scarlet, and white linen. Using their new wealth, Israel built God's tabernacle in the desert.

CELEBRATING UNLEAVENED BREAD IN ISRAEL TODAY

Because of the prohibition against leaven (yeast), this holiday has quite an impact on the daily lives of those living in Israel and in observant religious communities around the world.

Homes are given a thorough cleaning, starting weeks before. Perhaps it's from this holiday that we get the concept of *spring cleaning*. The Jewish mother turns her entire household upside down to make sure that *all* leaven is discovered and removed. Then she brings out special plates to prevent any contamination from dishes used at other times of the year. Among the very observant, the father of the house makes a search to determine if all leaven has been removed. To facilitate the search, a small bit of leaven is left in a conspicuous place. Father and children move through the house with a feather, a flashlight, and a handkerchief. Finding the offending leaven, he whisks it into his handkerchief and takes it outside where he immediately burns it. Then and only then can he proclaim the house "clean" and ready to begin the holiday. The search for leaven is serious business.

When I kept a kosher home, I put all food made with leaven into one kitchen cabinet and taped it shut. Another option used by some is to "sell" everything to a Gentile neighbor and then buy it back. The going rate is usually $1.00!

Consider the task for large food markets. Shelves containing products with leaven are masked with reams of white paper. Seeing such a sight of seeming endless rivers of white is startling to say the least. It's one of the few evidences of God's commandments being followed in an otherwise secular country. Most restaurants in Israel choose to close their doors during this week.

Spiritual

God often identifies Himself as "God who delivered you," reminding Israel (and the world) of who He is and what He has done.[5]

GOD'S FAITHFULNESS

The Feast of Unleavened Bread commemorates God's faithfulness, His covenant-keeping love [*chesed*]. He promised Abraham that his descendants would be enslaved for four hundred years. He promised Moses that He would rescue them with "signs and wonders." And He did:

> *God is not a man, that He should lie, nor a son of man, that He should repent. Has He said, and will He not do? Or has He spoken, and will He not make it*

good? ... Not a word failed of any good thing which the LORD had spoken to the house of Israel. All came to pass.
—Numbers 23:19; Joshua 21:45

God's faithful, covenant-keeping love can never and will never fail:

Through the LORD's mercies we are not consumed, because His compassions fail not. They are new every morning; great is Your faithfulness.
—Lamentations 3:22-23[6]

GOD'S POWER

Lest Israel ever forget His power, God often described Himself in connection with the Exodus from Egypt:

I am the LORD your God, who brought you out of the land of Egypt, out of the house of bondage.
—Exodus 20:2

The demonstration of His power was not only for Israel but also for the surrounding nations. When Joshua and Caleb entered Jericho, God's reputation preceded them. Rahab said to them:

I know that the LORD has given you the land, that the terror of you has fallen on us, and that all the inhabitants of the land are fainthearted because of you. For we have heard how the LORD dried up the water of the Red Sea for you when you came out of Egypt ... And as soon as we heard these things, our hearts melted; neither did there remain any more courage in anyone because of you, for the LORD your God, He is God in heaven above and on earth beneath.
—Joshua 2:9-11

When was the last time you saw a demonstration of God's power? We usually think of His power through His creation: volcanoes, hurricanes, tsunamis. If you've ever experienced one of these catastrophes firsthand, it's an experience you'll never forget. In fact, you'll probably tell your story to anyone who will listen to you. Sadly, many only acknowledge God's power by calling these devastations "acts of God."

On a trip to Thailand soon after the tsunami of 2005, I visited a small fishing village that was almost destroyed by the huge wave. Where homes once stood, there were small lakes created by water trapped inland. Most startling was a large boat that had been driven by the winds and water into what was once the center of town. That's power.

It is important to note that God constantly refers to His power as "His strong right hand and outstretched arm":

> *Behold, the LORD God shall come with a strong hand, and His arm shall rule for Him.* —*Isaiah 40:10a*

> *"As I live," says the LORD God, "surely with a mighty hand, with an outstretched arm, and with fury poured out, I will rule over you."* —*Ezekiel 20:33*

> *Therefore humble yourselves under the mighty hand of God, that He may exalt you in due time.* —*1 Peter 5:6*

His power (omnipotence) is without equal and without end.

GOD'S OMNISCIENCE

Because God understands the end from the beginning, His timing is usually not the same as ours! That God brought Israel out of Egypt exactly when He told Abraham He would in Genesis

15:13 can give us courage that His timing is perfect. I wonder what the waiting was like, especially for the early generations who had no hope of living to see their freedom. We might not, no, we probably will not understand or even like His timing—but it will be perfect.

God taught me about waiting for His perfect timing several years ago when I was forced to move from an apartment I loved. I had expected to remain there either until Jesus returned or called me to Himself. However, the owner wanted to sell and had given me a year's notice. I chose not to think about it until absolutely forced to.

More than wanting to stay, I wanted to do God's will. But God seemed to be silent on the issue. Daily my cry was, "I'll go wherever You want me to, but You must show me." Yet all I heard was silence.

People were knocking on my door, wanting to see the apartment and make a bid on it. Frantic, I ran from city to city, apartment to apartment, to find the "right" place. Friends criticized me for being too fussy. Others encouraged me to hold out for my heart's desire. Round and round I went.

One day, after reading Exodus 14:8-15 and 2 Chronicles 20:17, the Spirit spoke to me in a poem:

The problem grows before my eyes
With demands upon my heart.
My head screams out, "You must move NOW!"
But I don't know where to start.

You tell me Lord to "stand my ground"
To see what You will do.
That takes much faith and trust and love
But there's no one else but You!

I turn to You to show the way
You've chosen just for me;
And know I'll bring You glory
As I walk in victory.

So I will stand or I will move
According to Your voice.
Instant and loving obedience
Is my only choice!

It was an encouraging poem, but it didn't help my emotions when the doorbell rang with another potential buyer.

One morning, in the process of waking up and doing absolutely nothing spiritual, I heard the Lord's voice speak with clarity and urgency, "Go now!" That was it. No map was emblazoned in the sky. No city flashed with neon colors in my mind; just two little words, which didn't tell me much. A friend who happened to be at home in the city that I'd always loved was willing to look through the local paper. By the time I got to his home, he had made some appointments.

You know the rest of the story—the first apartment I entered was *the* place ... and had only become available a few hours before! I was the first to see it—and the last. I signed a contract within days. As hard as it sometimes is to endure the wait, the Lord's timing is always perfect.

What about Israel's waiting? When Israel first came into Egypt, the people were treated well. We don't know when their slavery began or for how long they cried for deliverance from Egypt.

Just a few generations ago, Israel again cried for deliverance. Six million Jews and six million others died in the horror of the Holocaust. Twelve million voices cried to God for help. Was there no answer? Or was there an unexpected answer? Perhaps part of the answer was the re-creation of the state of Israel.

Let these Scriptures bring refreshment to the waiting, weary soul:

> *To everything there is a season, a time for every purpose under heaven.* —Ecclesiastes 3:1

> *But, beloved, do not forget this one thing, that with the Lord one day is as a thousand years, and a thousand years as one day. The Lord is not slack concerning His promise, as some count slackness, but is longsuffering toward us, not willing that any should perish but that all should come to repentance.* —2 Peter 3:8-9

Consider God's longsuffering in His omniscience. For thousands of years, God the Father watched His children in the throes of bondage—yet He waited:

> *We, when we were children, were in bondage under the elements of the world. But when the fullness of the time had come, God sent forth His Son, born of a woman, born under the law, to redeem those who were under the law, that we might receive the adoption as sons.* —Galatians 4:3-5

God's promise to Jeremiah echoes down through the ages for both Israel and the church:

> *"For I know the thoughts that I think toward you," says the* LORD, *"thoughts of peace and not of evil, to give you a future and a hope."* —Jeremiah 29:11

> *And we know that all things work together for good to those who love God, to those who are the called according to His purpose.* —Romans 8:28

God knows what is needed to fulfill His promises in a way that will be right for us and bring Him the most glory. To keep ourselves aligned with Him is what the holidays are all about.

GOD'S HOLINESS

God's holiness is reflected in the name of this holiday—Unleavened Bread.

The definition of *leaven* is *an agency which works in a thing to produce a gradual change or modification.*[7] Leaven is usually associated with the fermentation of either alcohol or bread. It can be used for both good and for bad.

Jesus compared the Kingdom of heaven to leaven, reflecting the positive influence the Kingdom has:

> *The kingdom of heaven is like leaven, which a woman took and hid in three measures of meal till it was all leavened.* —*Matthew 13:33*

However, more often in Scripture leaven is used symbolically for sin:

> *Then Jesus said to them, "Take heed and beware of the leaven of the Pharisees and the Sadducees."* —*Matthew 16:6*

The origin of the Hebrew for *holy/holiness* came from the pagan world and meant *standing in awe of the gods.* Holy or holiness is used as a *description of a state of being, a person, or object, or even the process of sanctification:*

> *Therefore you shall consecrate him, for he offers the bread of your God. He shall be holy to you, for I the LORD, who sanctify you, am holy.* —*Leviticus 21:8*

[*Qadash*], translated *holy*, means *to consecrate, sanctify, prepare, dedicate, be hallowed, be holy, be sanctified, be separate, tabooed; to show oneself sacred or majestic; to be honored, be treated as sacred; to be clean, pure, free from defilement from profane things.*[8]

Perhaps the best and most simple definition of holy when used of God is *other than*. God is without description or comparison.[9] "There is no way the human mind can comprehend His purity and perfection. He is outside His creation and yet the world and mankind are in the process of sanctification (being made holy) in which God (will sanctify) Himself." [10]

"An encounter with God's holiness inevitably demands a response."[11] Isaiah recognized his sinfulness. Daniel, John, and the disciples all fell to the ground in His presence. God warned Moses:

> *Then He said, "Do not draw near this place. Take your sandals off your feet, for the place where you stand is holy ground."*
> —*Exodus 3:5*

The psalmist asked:

> *Who may ascend into the hill of the LORD? Or who may stand in His holy place? He who has clean hands and a pure heart, who has not lifted up his soul to an idol, nor sworn deceitfully.*
> —*Psalm 24:3-4*

God's holiness makes demands. Both the sacrifice and the one offering the sacrifice must be pure.[12] Because God desired to dwell among them, the people and their camp were required to live in holiness:

> *And the LORD spoke to Moses, saying, "Speak to all the congregation of the children of Israel, and say to them: You shall be holy, for I the LORD your God am holy …*

'And you shall be holy to Me, for I the LORD am holy, and have separated you from the peoples, that you should be Mine' ... For the LORD your God walks in the midst of your camp, to deliver you and give your enemies over to you; therefore your camp shall be holy, that He may see no unclean thing among you, and turn away from you."
—Leviticus 19:1-2; 20:26; Deuteronomy 23:14

The worship of heaven focuses on God's holiness:

Holy, holy, holy is the LORD of hosts; the whole earth is full of His glory. *—Isaiah 6:3*

The four living creatures, each having six wings, were full of eyes around and within. And they do not rest day or night, saying, "Holy, holy, holy, LORD God Almighty, Who was and is and is to come!"
—Revelation 4:8

I'm sure by now you've already seen the several ways that Jesus fulfills the Feast of Unleavened Bread.

CHRIST CAME IN THE PROCESS OF TIME

God was prepared to redeem the world even before He created it.[13] He made that promise first to Adam and Eve and repeated the promise to Abraham, to David, and to Isaiah—just to name a few.[14] He even gave Daniel His timetable.[15] Then God waited until the perfect time; the apostle Paul called it "the fullness of time."[16] No one can understand the mind of God or His way of doing things, but we can be certain that His reasons and timing are right:[17]

> *In His forbearance God had passed over the sins that were previously committed, to demonstrate at the present time His righteousness, that He might be just and the justifier of the one who has faith in Jesus.*
> *—Romans 3:25b-26*

CHRIST'S BURIAL

Jesus died on Passover and was buried on Unleavened Bread. On the cross He bore the sins, sickness, and sadness of the world. As He was buried, He took those sins with Him, thus removing them from those who would believe in Him:

> *As far as the east is from the west, so far has He removed our transgressions from us. —Psalm 103:12*

This verse doesn't say that Jesus removes us from our sins, but that He removes our transgressions from us. Those sins are buried, unseen by God and out of our lives. By His blood and burial our sins are gone forever—Hallelujah!

DELIVERANCE FROM BONDAGE

Remember our wonderful word for deliverance used in Exodus 6:6c, "I will rescue you from their bondage"? As discussed earlier, the Hebrew word [*natzal*] has the connotation of being *an act of violence.* We saw the violence as God devastated Egypt through the plagues then ultimately destroyed her army in the Red Sea. Israel's deliverance was through violent signs and wonders.

Now look at the cross. See the violence perpetrated upon God Himself. The movie *The Passion* was such a vivid portrayal that it stunned every audience into silence. The violence upon His body was only one aspect of the cross; there was also violence done to the kingdom of darkness.[18]

JESUS IS GOD'S "RIGHT HAND"

God's "right hand" is consistently used to describe a position of power and authority. Who else but Jesus is God's right hand? Jesus is the source by, through, and in whom God's power and authority flow:[19]

> *...who has gone into heaven and is at the right hand of God, angels and authorities and powers having been made subject to Him.* —1 Peter 3:22

By Jesus, we are delivered:

> *Your right hand, O LORD, has become glorious in power; Your right hand, O LORD, has dashed the enemy in pieces.* —Exodus 15:6

Through Jesus, we are saved:

> *Show Your marvelous lovingkindness by Your right hand, O You who save those who trust in You from those who rise up against them.* —Psalm 17:7[20]

In Jesus, we have victory:

> *For they did not gain possession of the land by their own sword, nor did their own arm save them; but it was Your right hand, Your arm, and the light of Your countenance, because You favored them.* —Psalm 44:3

Jesus, the right hand of God, gives us security, peace, and joy.[21]

JESUS TRIUMPHS

During their last supper as the disciples sang the Great Hallel of Psalms 113–118, I'm sure they were remembering the triumphant entry into Jerusalem just the previous week:

> *The voice of rejoicing and salvation is in the tents of the righteous; the right hand of the LORD does valiantly. The right hand of the LORD is exalted; the right hand of the LORD does valiantly.* —*Psalm 118:15-16*

Perhaps Jesus was thinking of an even greater triumphal procession, when He will lead us into His freedom:

> *Now thanks be to God who always leads us in triumph in Christ.* —*2 Corinthians 2:14a*

The word *triumph* is a translation of the Greek [*thriambeuo*/*three·am·byoo·o*/]. The word comes from the hymn sung by pilgrims during a festival to the Greek god Dionysus (called Baacus by the Romans). Dionysus was the god of wine: "[He] inspired madness. He represents not only the intoxicating power of wine, but also its social and beneficial influences. He was also known as the Liberator, freeing one from one's normal self, by madness, ecstasy, or wine. The 'divine' mission of Dionysus was to mingle the music of the aulos and to bring an end to care and worry." [22]

Can you imagine the revelry of those drunken pilgrims? Despite their attempts to "bring an end to care and misery," their only accomplishment would have been a terrible hangover! Later, [*thriambeuo*] was used as a "public display of a criminal or a defeated enemy to shame."

Remember David's fight with Goliath? David felled the mighty giant with a single stone. Nevertheless, he then took Goliath's own sword and cut off his head. That's what I call making a public spectacle of the defeated enemy.

How much more is the joyous triumphant celebration of Christ Jesus, who has brought us out of our misery and cares. We are the riches of Christ's grace, trophies of His love, and more than conquerors by His power. Read these words about Jesus:

> *Having disarmed principalities and powers, He made a public spectacle of them, triumphing over them in it.*
> —Colossians 2:15

Remember the three R's of the holidays?

- **REMEMBER** God in the past—who He is and what He has done.
- **REJOICE** in God in the present—He is the same today as He was yesterday.
- **REST** in God for the future—He has everything in control!

As we celebrate Unleavened Bread and rejoice in our freedom, we are reminded of our past bondage. No longer bound by sin, we have room to breathe!

FREE TO BREATHE

I've made several life-changing moves. Before moving to Israel, I said good-bye to my parents and headed to the West Coast of North America. It was April 20, 1983. I'd come to a turning point in my life, and I needed to start over. My car was packed with the stuff I thought I couldn't live without and would need on the journey: kayak, skis, tent, camping stove, basic clothes, and even a new set of tires—just in case. I'd left my dog Boffin with friends and stored my furniture; I would send for them later when I was ready to settle. For the moment, as the car pulled out of the driveway, I was free. This was the first day of my new life.

The journey took twenty-one days, but it took much longer than that to really begin my new life.

Each of us is on a journey into freedom, and every journey is different. But every journey, no matter how long, how arduous, or how challenging, begins with one step. Taking the first step out of bondage and into freedom is certainly exciting, although it might also be a bit scary. Yet it need not be so, for Jesus is our "very present help in trouble" (Psalm 46:1). He is our Savior, always available to bring us out of a tight place; He is the way out of all bondage, the exit from all temptation.[24] We can rejoice with the psalmist:

> *Blessed be the LORD, Who has not given us as prey to their teeth. Our soul has escaped as a bird from the snare of the fowlers; the snare is broken, and we have escaped.*
> *—Psalm 124:6-7*

We are set free by His love, His blood, and His power:

> *If the Son makes you free, you shall be free indeed.*
> *—John 8:36*

Our bondage might not be the bondage of sin, but it might be bondage of the soul, keeping us anxious, stressed, uptight, fearful, or confused. Whatever the issue, Jesus can bring us into freedom. There is a little chorus that reminds us of this truth:

"He did not bring us out to bring us back again;

He brought us out to bring us into the Promised Land."[25]

Let each day be another "first step" into the journey of freedom. We need never go back into Egypt.

FREE TO HOPE

Israel's bondage in Egypt wasn't the only time God seemed to have forgotten His promises. Consider the lives of Joseph and David. We can even assume that Moses had a promise from God about being Israel's deliverer. Each of them had to wait. Each of them had to endure horrendous situations. Each of them had reasons to give up.

But God never forgot: He never forgets His promises. He always fulfills His Word, because He places His Word even above His name![26]

Consider the word *hope* [*tiqva*]. The New Testament tells us that *faith* and *hope* are interrelated; without hope there is no faith.[27] In common usage, *hope* is *a wishful thought or desire*. When I tell people that God loves them, their usual response is, "I hope so," without having any assurance or confidence. This is not the hope of the Bible.

When God sent Israel into Babylon, He did so with an incredible promise of hope:

> *For thus says the LORD: After seventy years are completed at Babylon, I will visit you and perform My good word toward you, and cause you to return to this place. For I know the thoughts that I think toward you, says the LORD, thoughts of peace and not of evil, to give you a future and a hope.* —Jeremiah 29:10-11

Daniel was so confident in this promise that when the seventy years were completed, he reminded God of His promise, "God, *now* is the time! [my paraphrase]"[28]

The national anthem of Israel is called *Ha Tiquva*—"The Hope." As we continue to wait for the remainder of God's promises for Israel, we wait with confident assurance.

God has made promises that are personal, specific, and unique to each of us. We can trust Him to fulfill them for His glory and our blessing.

> *In Him, also we have obtained an inheritance, being predestined according to the purpose of Him who works all things according to the counsel of His will, that we who first trusted in Christ should be to the praise of His glory.*
> *— Ephesians 1:11-12*

Our life is a testimony to God's glory. How then can He *not* make good on His promises? Yes, there is a season for everything, but seasons change—He does not:[29]

> *And we know that all things work together for good to those who love God, to those who are the called according to His purpose. For whom He foreknew, He also predestined to be conformed to the image of His Son, that He might be the firstborn among many brethren. Moreover whom He predestined, these He also called; whom He called, these He also justified; and whom He justified, these He also glorified.*
> *—Romans 8:28-30*

We can pray boldly with the psalmist:

> *Remember the word to Your servant, upon which You have caused me to hope. This is my comfort in my affliction, for Your word has given me life.* *—Psalm 119:49-50*

STRENGTH TO PERSEVERE

The level that we trust in God's faithfulness will be the level of our perseverance during the hard times of waiting.

Abraham never possessed the land of his inheritance. There were many in Egypt who didn't see the day of their deliverance. The prophets spoke of God's salvation but never lived to see Him. But they persevered.

King David was a man of action. I doubt his shepherd days were filled with the tranquility and serenity we so often imagine. He had to be vigilant as he protected the sheep. He was adept at killing bears and lions, and, I'm sure, a myriad of other animals. And yet he was able to write: "I waited patiently for the LORD" (Psalm 40:1).

The Hebrew repeats the verb *wait*: "I waited and waited." That's probably a more accurate picture of David's waiting for God's answer. It is an active waiting, full of eager expectation and hope:

> *Wait on the LORD; be of good courage, and He shall strengthen your heart; wait, I say, on the LORD!*
> *—Psalm 27:14*

Perseverance, better translated as "endurance," is rewarded:

> *In returning and rest you shall be saved; in quietness and confidence shall be your strength.*
> *—Isaiah 30:15a*

To enable us to persevere in hope, God sealed us with the Holy Spirit, our guarantee of final and total redemption:

> *You were sealed with the Holy Spirit of promise, who is the guarantee of our inheritance until the redemption*

of the purchased possession, to the praise of His glory.
—Ephesians 1:13b-14

God's glory is magnified as He fulfills His promises to and through us. So let the holiday of Unleavened Bread encourage us that though God's promise tarries, it will be fulfilled!

HOLY UNTO THE LORD

As Israel is required to remove all leaven from her homes, so are followers of Jesus to remove all "leaven" from their lives. See the connection between Passover and the Feast of Unleavened Bread in Paul's exhortation:

> *Do you not know that a little leaven leavens the whole lump? Therefore purge out the old leaven, that you may be a new lump, since you truly are unleavened. For indeed Christ, our Passover was sacrificed for us. Therefore let us keep the feast not with old leaven, nor with the leaven of malice and wickedness, but with the unleavened bread of sincerity and truth.*
> *—1 Corinthians 5:6-8*

The removal of leaven is meant to be the reflection of God's holiness in our lives, as we recognize that we have been delivered for the purpose of being a holy people unto God:

> *And you shall be holy to Me, for I the LORD am holy, and have separated you from the peoples, that you should be Mine.* *—Leviticus 20:26*

Holiness is not an issue of external behavior. Our behavior will flow out of the internal change of new life in Christ Jesus. But it does take determination to walk in the freedom celebrated by Unleavened Bread:

... the truth is in Jesus: that you put off, concerning your former conduct, the old man which grows corrupt according to the deceitful lusts, and be renewed in the spirit of your mind, and that you put on the new man which was created according to God, in true righteousness and holiness ...

Therefore we also, since we are surrounded by so great a cloud of witnesses, let us lay aside every weight, and the sin which so easily ensnares us, and let us run with endurance the race that is set before us, looking unto Jesus, the author and finisher of our faith.
—Ephesians 4:21b-24; Hebrews 12:1-2

Sin is insidious, like leaven; a tiny bit will permeate and defile everything it touches.

I recently watched a soccer field being built. Day by day, the huge machines moved back and forth across the field, leveling the ground. When the heavy work was done, the laborers came with rakes, walking every inch of the field. This was repeated over and over until the field was ready to be fertilized. Finally, the grass cover was put down, creating a lush green carpet.

If that preparatory work had not been done, the field would not be fit for play. Any unevenness would be dangerous to the players, possibly causing falls and serious injury.

The same is true for us. Sin, no matter how small or hidden, defiles and results in separation from God's holy presence.

COME OUT FROM AMONG THEM

God is calling us to be completely free from the power and effects of our Egypt:

> *Depart! Depart! Go out from there, touch no unclean thing; go out from the midst of her, be clean, you who bear the vessels of the LORD.*
> *—Isaiah 52:11*

We each have a different Egypt—that which holds us in bondage. For me, it was chocolate chip cookies.

You might wonder, "How can a little cookie hold you in bondage?" Admittedly, the power of a cookie might be overrated, but I couldn't stop eating them. My bondage became apparent while on a seven-hour drive. The trip had started innocuously enough; but within an hour, the large bag of cookies was empty. My stomach was screaming, "No more!" Chagrined at my lack of control, I whispered, "I'll never eat another chocolate chip cookie again." And I haven't. Not a single one.

There is nothing inherently bad in a little cookie or a bit of chocolate, except together they held me in bondage.

So, what is the "chocolate chip cookie" in your life? What seems innocent or socially acceptable to others may in fact be your Egypt. Allow the Holy Spirit to search and convict you of any hidden fault or presumptuous sin so that you will be holy, as your Father in heaven is holy:

> *Who can understand his errors? Cleanse me from secret faults. Keep back Your servant also from presumptuous sins; let them not have dominion over me. Then I shall be blameless, and I shall be innocent of great transgression.*
> *—Psalm 19:12-13*

FREE TO SERVE

Israel's deliverance was for a purpose. God said to Moses:

> *Then you shall say to Pharaoh, "Thus says the LORD: 'Israel is My son, My firstborn. So I say to you, let My son go that he may serve Me.'"*
> *—Exodus 4:22-23*

> *And you shall say to him, "The LORD God of the Hebrews has sent me to you, saying, 'Let My people go, that they may serve Me in the wilderness.'"*
> *—Exodus 7:16*

The holiday of Unleavened Bread reminds us that God's purpose for our freedom is that we may serve Him:

> *And you shall be to Me a Kingdom of priests and a holy nation.* *—Exodus 19:6*

Paul consistently referred to himself as a "bond slave" or a "servant" of Christ. To some this might seem contradictory. How can freedom be freedom if we are made to serve? Are we just changing masters? YES!

"When the service is offered to God, it is not bondage, but rather a joyous and liberating experience."[30] The reality is that the whole world, apart from Jesus, is under the influence of the evil one.[31] Satan is a worse master, without heart, without grace, without mercy, and without hope. The good news of the gospel of Jesus, which we celebrate on this holiday, is that God gives us the choice to come into His service:

You were slain, and have redeemed us to God by Your blood out of every tribe and tongue and people and nation, and have made us kings and priests to our God; and we shall reign on the earth.
—Revelation 5:9-10

We have taken much time to study the death and burial of our Beloved Savior, so let us proceed to the most thrilling of all celebrations—His Resurrection on the Feast of Firstfruits.

Feast of Unleavened Bread

Endnotes

1. See also: Leviticus 23:6-8; Numbers 28:17-25; 2 Chronicles 30:23-27; Ezra 6:21-22; Matthew 26:17; Luke 22:7.
2. See also Exodus 23:14-17 and Deuteronomy 16:16.
3. Van Gemeren, W. A. (Ed.). *New International Dictionary of Old Testament Theology & Exegesis* (NIDOTTE) [Electronic form]. Zondervan. We look more closely at this Hebrew word as part of our study of the Day of Atonement.
4. HALOT, #4384.
5. Exodus 20:2; 1 Samuel 10:18; Jeremiah 2:6; Daniel 9:15.
6. Mercies: [*chesed*]; compassions: [*rachamim*]; faithfulness: [*'emunah*]. For a complete treatment of these words, see "*Passover: Spiritual*."
7. Barnhart, C. (Ed.). (1956). *The American College Dictionary*. New York: Random House, p. 694.
8. Brown, C. (Ed.). *The New International Dictionary of the New Testament Theology* (Vol. II), pp. 224-238.
9. Isaiah 46:5.
10. Lohmeyer, E. (1965). *The Lord's Prayer*, p. 73.
11. Brown, C. (Ed.). *The New International Dictionary of the New Testament Theology* (Vol. II), p. 224.
12. Leviticus 2:11; 6:14-18.
13. Revelation 13:8.
14. Genesis 3:15; 22:8; Psalm 79:9; Isaiah 53.
15. Daniel 9:24-26.
16. Galatians 4:3.
17. Isaiah 55:9.
18. Colossians 1:13-14.
19. Matthew 28:18; Acts 2:33-34; 5:31; 7:55-56.
20. Lovingkindness: [*chesed*]; save: [*moshi'a*]; trust: [*chasah*]. You have seen these words in the Passover chapters.
21. Psalm 16:8-11.
22. *Wikipedia, The Free Encyclopedia. http://en.wikipedia.org/wiki/Dionysus.* An *aulos* was an ancient Greek wind instrument: *http://en.wikipedia.org/wiki/Aulos.*
23. Colin, B. (Ed.). *The New International Dictionary of New Testament Theology* (Vol. I), p. 649.
24. 1 Corinthians 10:13.
25. Findani, Renzo. (1983). *Zion Song Music.*
26. Psalm 138:2.
27. Hebrews 11:1.
28. Daniel 2:2-19.
29. Ecclesiastes 3:1.

Chapter Ten

Feast of Firstfruits

Harvest of the Spring

The Feast of Firstfruits celebrates God's fulfillment of His promise to bring Israel into the Promised Land.

If we had any question about the orchestration of God's calendar, the redemptive significance of this third holiday of the Passover season would provide the answer. First, let's look at the three spring Passover-related holidays:

- **Passover** commemorates the redemption of Israel through the sacrifice of the lamb.
- **Unleavened Bread** commemorates the actual exodus from Egypt's bondage.
- **Firstfruits** commemorates Israel's coming into the Land of Promise and partaking of its bounty.

These holidays celebrate Israel's deliverance from beginning to end. There is another Passover-related holiday, the Feast of Tabernacles. Tabernacles is celebrated in the fall and commemorates the journey from Egypt to Canaan.

Forty years of wandering. Forty years of manna. Forty years of desert. It was enough. Israel had arrived! The journey was over. Gone was that ever-moving cloud forcing them to pack, move, and unpack! God had fulfilled His promise to plant them in a land of His choosing.

The Feast of Firstfruits is the celebration of the harvest in the land God gave to Israel. It is a unique holiday among the nations of the world. God took Israel out of one nation and brought her into another:

> *You have brought a vine out of Egypt; You have cast out the nations, and planted...You drove out the nations with Your hand, but them You planted.*
>
> *—Psalm 80:8; 44:2a*

You are already familiar with the Feast of Firstfruits but probably refer to it by a different name—Resurrection Day or Easter.[1]

Seasonal

The Feast of Firstfruits is the third and final of the annual holidays of spring.

Spring is always a time of joy. The cold of winter is chased by the warmth of the spring sun. Everywhere the senses are assaulted with the color and smells of new life. Trees and fields once stripped bare are now clothed in radiant blossoms. It is a time of promise and renewal as life bursts from the dead.

Heralding spring in Israel is the early-blooming almond tree. The Hebrew name for *almond* is [*shaqed*], which means *industrious* or *vigilant*. Thus, in ancient Israel, the almond was a symbol of watchfulness and promise.

There are actually three firstfruit holidays: one in the spring, another in the summer, and the last in the fall. All three holidays (Firstfruits, Weeks, and Tabernacles) are pilgrim festivals requiring the Jewish men to come to Jerusalem to present an offering of the firstfruits of the season's harvest.

> *And the LORD spoke to Moses, saying, "Speak to the children of Israel, and say to them: 'When you come into the land which I give to you, and reap its harvest, then you shall bring a sheaf of the firstfruits of your harvest to the priest. He shall wave the sheaf before the LORD, to be accepted on your behalf; on the day after the Sabbath the priest shall wave it.'"* —Leviticus 23:9-11

From this Scripture we see three important aspects of this holiday:

- Celebrating Israel's arrival in the Promised Land
- Reaping the first harvest
- Offering the firstfruits of the harvest

ARRIVAL INTO THE LAND

God gave to Israel as her inheritance a land already inhabited. This is very politically incorrect to many today. Nevertheless, God's ways are not our ways.[2] This is His story and the witness of Israel.

For everyone who reads and believes in the Bible, this feast is especially important in light of the continued battle for the land of Israel. Either God's promises to Israel (and thus to you) are true and trustworthy, or they are not. This is not a political issue; God is a God of real estate.[3] The current situation in Israel must be viewed from the perspective of God's promises to the descendants of Abraham, Isaac, and Jacob:[4]

> *Every place on which the sole of your foot treads shall be yours: from the wilderness and Lebanon, from the river, the River Euphrates, even to the Western Sea, shall be your territory.* —*Deuteronomy 11:24*

REAPING THE HARVEST

What did the spies see? A land flowing with milk and honey! What a wonderful change to a constant menu of manna. In fact, the entire generation entering the land had never eaten anything else:

> *Then the manna ceased on the day after they had eaten the produce of the land; and the children of Israel no longer had manna, but they ate the food of the land of Canaan that year.*
> —*Joshua 5:12*

Once again, God proved His faithfulness to provide and sustain His people. God blessed them abundantly, allowing them to reap where they had not sown and live where they had not built. Rather than presuming on God's goodness and grace, Israel was to always remember the source of her blessing:

> *So it shall be, when the LORD your God brings you into the land of which He swore to your fathers, to Abraham, Isaac, and Jacob, to give you large and beautiful cities which you did not build, houses full of all good things, which you did not fill, hewn-out wells which you did not dig, vineyards and olive trees which you did not plant—when you have eaten and are full—then beware, lest you forget the LORD who brought you out of the land of Egypt, from the house of bondage.* —*Deuteronomy 6:10-12*

OFFERING THE FIRST OF EVERY FRUIT

The Feast of Firstfruits was a time to remember all God had done for them in the past and to respond to God's goodness by giving back to Him the firstfruit of the fields:

> *And it shall be, when you come into the land which the LORD your God is giving you as an inheritance, and you possess it and dwell in it, that you shall take some of the first of all the produce of the ground, which you shall bring from your land that the LORD your God is giving you, and put it in a basket and go to the place where the LORD your God chooses to make His name abide. And you shall go to the one who is priest in those days, and say to him, "I declare today to the LORD your God that I have come to the country which the LORD swore to our fathers to give us."*
>
> *Then the priest shall take the basket out of your hand and set it down before the altar of the LORD your God. And you shall answer and say before the LORD your*

God: "My father was a Syrian, about to perish, and he went down to Egypt and dwelt there, few in number; and there he became a nation, great, mighty, and populous. But the Egyptians mistreated us, afflicted us, and laid hard bondage on us. Then we cried out to the LORD God of our fathers, and the LORD heard our voice and looked on our affliction and our labor and our oppression. So the LORD brought us out of Egypt with a mighty hand and with an outstretched arm, with great terror and with signs and wonders. He has brought us to this place and has given us this land, 'a land flowing with milk and honey'; and now, behold, I have brought the firstfruits of the land which you, O LORD, have given me."

—Deuteronomy 26:1-10a[5]

In remembrance of Israel's redemption and the final plague on Egypt, the firstborn of the womb—both man and beast—was also to be offered unto the Lord:

And it shall be, when the LORD brings you into the land of the Canaanites, as He swore to you and your fathers, and gives it to you, that you shall set apart to the LORD all that open the womb, that is, every firstborn that comes from an animal which you have; the males shall be the LORD's ... So it shall be, when your son asks you in time to come, saying, "What is this?" that you shall say to him, "By strength of hand the LORD brought us out of Egypt, out of the house of bondage. And it came to pass, when Pharaoh was stubborn about letting us go, that the LORD killed all the firstborn in the land of Egypt, both the firstborn of man and the firstborn of beast. Therefore I sacrifice to the LORD all males that open the womb, but all the firstborn of my sons I redeem."

—Exodus 13:11-15

Finally, Israel was to rejoice, knowing that God's provision would continue:

> *Then you shall set it before the LORD your God, and worship before the LORD your God. So you shall rejoice in every good thing which the LORD your God has given to you and your house, you and the Levite and the stranger who is among you.* —*Deuteronomy 26:10b-11*

Spiritual

This holiday highlights God's sovereign choice of Israel:

> *You drove out the nations with Your hand, but them You planted; You afflicted the peoples, and cast them out. For they did not gain possession of the land by their own sword, nor did their own arm save them; but it was Your right hand, Your arm, and the light of Your countenance, because You favored them.* —*Psalm 44:2-3*

Israel was, and remains, a unique nation, chosen by God for His purposes; purposes that are still in effect to this day. Israel was and remains His witness to display His character and His ways.[6]

I sometimes meet people who question me about God's continuing promises for Israel in light of her disobedience. This question is really a challenge to His Word and to His nature. Israel's disobedience resulted in chastening—but not rejection:

> *I will be his Father, and he shall be My son. If he commits iniquity, I will chasten him with the rod of men and with*

the blows of the sons of men. But My mercy shall not depart from him. —2 Samuel 7:14-15

God spoke through Jeremiah:

Thus says the LORD, who gives the sun for a light by day, the ordinances of the moon and the stars for a light by night, who disturbs the sea, and its waves roar (the LORD of hosts is His name):

"If those ordinances depart from before Me," says the LORD, "then the seed of Israel shall also cease from being a nation before Me forever."

Thus says the LORD: "If heaven above can be measured, and the foundations of the earth searched out beneath, I will also cast off all the seed of Israel for all that they have done," says the LORD. —Jeremiah 31:35-37

Paul also addresses the issue of God's continuing choice of Israel in his letter to the Romans:

I say then, has God cast away His people? Certainly not! For I also am an Israelite, of the seed of Abraham, of the tribe of Benjamin. God has not cast away His people whom He foreknew ... Even so then, at this present time there is a remnant according to the election of grace. And if by grace, then it is no longer of works; otherwise grace is no longer grace. But if it is of works, it is no longer grace; otherwise work is no longer work. —Roman 11:1-2a, 5-6

God's favored treatment of Israel does not minimize His love for the world or for His Kingdom community.

GOD'S FAITHFULNESS TO HIS COVENANT

The Feast of Firstfruits showcases God's covenant-keeping love (His faithfulness) to Israel. He promised to bring her out and to bring her into the Promised Land. God doesn't save partially; He saves completely:

> *I have also established My covenant with them, to give them the land of Canaan, the land of their pilgrimage, in which they were strangers … And I will bring you into the land which I swore to give to Abraham, Isaac, and Jacob; and I will give it to you as a heritage: I am the LORD.*
>
> *—Exodus 6:4, 8*

God's character requires that He keep His promises to Israel and to you. Let us never tire of celebrating this truth.

GOD'S GRACIOUS PROVISION

God's provision for His people (houses and harvests for which Israel did not labor) is reflected in Firstfruits. As with the manna during their journey, His provision was an act of His grace and not of Israel's works. Can you already see this holiday's redemptive fulfillment in Jesus as well as its application to our lives?

The greatest gift of God's grace is Himself:

> *He said, "Surely they are My people, children who will not lie." So He became their Savior. In all their affliction He was afflicted, and the Angel of His Presence saved them; in His love and in His pity He redeemed them; and He bore them and carried them all the days of old.*
>
> *—Isaiah 63:8-9*

Redemptive

The resurrection of Jesus is the embodiment and fulfillment of this holiday. Paul makes this connection when he calls Jesus "the firstfruit from the dead." [7]

JESUS IS GOD'S FIRSTFRUIT

How to follow God's instruction to celebrate Firstfruits on a Sabbath became another argument between the Pharisees and the Sadducees; they debated to which Sabbath the Lord was referring:

> *He shall wave the sheaf before the LORD, to be accepted on your behalf; on the day after the Sabbath the priest shall wave it.*
> *—Leviticus 23:11*

The basis of their disagreement was that each of the Lord's feasts was to be a Sabbath—a day holy unto the Lord. Thus the Passover itself was considered a Sabbath. But there is also the weekly Sabbath—from sundown Friday to sundown Saturday.

So which Sabbath was to be used to determine the holiday of Firstfruits? The Pharisees won this argument, insisting that God intended Firstfruits to be observed after the weekly Sabbath (Saturday) following Passover. Therefore, the holiday of Firstfruits is celebrated on the first day of the week—Sunday.

Scholars are still debating the actual day of Christ's crucifixion and burial.[8] I am convinced that He was crucified just before the beginning of the Passover celebration and buried on Unleavened Bread. Regardless, we can be absolutely certain that He rose on Firstfruits! Yes, the most important event in all of history, the resurrection of Jesus the Messiah, occurred on God's holiday of Firstfruits! He is the Firstfruit from the dead:

> *But now Christ is risen from the dead, and has become the firstfruits of those who have fallen asleep.*
> *—1 Corinthians 15:20*

JESUS IS GOD'S PROVISION

Neither Abraham's attempted sacrifice of his son nor any of the sacrifices made in the temple could provide atonement. God promised and provided Himself as the atonement.[9] Probably the clearest prophetic description of God's provision of redemption came through Isaiah:

> *For He shall grow up before Him as a tender plant, and as a root out of dry ground. He has no form or comeliness; and when we see Him, there is no beauty that we should desire Him. He is despised and rejected by men, a Man of sorrows and acquainted with grief. And we hid, as it were, our faces from Him; He was despised, and we did not esteem Him. Surely He has borne our griefs and carried our sorrows; yet we esteemed Him stricken, smitten by God, and afflicted. But He was wounded for our transgressions, He was bruised for our iniquities; the chastisement for our peace was upon Him, and by His stripes we are healed. All we like sheep have gone astray; we have turned, every one, to his own way; and the LORD has laid on Him the iniquity of us all.* *—Isaiah 53:2-6*

As a young woman in university, I studied the Bible and even earned top grades; yet like so many Jewish people, I missed the obvious. But when the "eyes of my understanding were enlightened," I saw Jesus on every page of the Old

Testament. To quote the great hymn by John Newton, I "was blind but now I see."

Who can understand the love of God, who laid aside His glory, took upon Himself the form of man, and came down to deliver, save, and redeem His people?

PROMISE OF FUTURE HARVEST

Just as the Feast of Firstfruits is the first harvest festival, the resurrection of Jesus promises us that there will be another resurrection, which we will discuss in the other harvest festivals.

Kingdom

I was surprised to discover that few Israeli congregations celebrate Firstfruits (Resurrection) as a separate holiday, because they include Resurrection as part of their celebration of Passover. But God created both Passover *and* Firstfruits to reveal and to celebrate Jesus![10]

SAVED BY GOD'S GRACE

How many times have you heard or said, "There's no free lunch"? That may be true today, but not for Israel as she entered the Land. Firstfruits celebrates God's grace—giving the people harvest and homes absolutely free. What a picture of God's gracious gift to us of salvation:

For by grace you have been saved through faith, and that not of yourselves; it is the gift of God, not of works, lest anyone should boast.
—Ephesians 2:8-9

[God], who has saved us and called us with a holy calling, not according to our works, but according to His own purpose and grace which was given to us in Christ Jesus before time began. *—2 Timothy 1:9*

NEW LIFE

Have you ever failed? Maybe in marriage, school, or business? Have you ever wished you could start over?

The resurrection of Jesus provides a new start in life: a brand new, abundant, and eternal life![11] A new life is the inheritance for every child of God:

If anyone is in Christ, he is a new creation; old things have passed away; behold, ALL things have become new.
—2 Corinthians 5:17 [Emphasis added]

All means *all*. From God's perspective, everything about a believer is new even if it does take a bit of time for some of the old things to pass away.

SEATED IN HEAVENLY PLACES

Christ's resurrection on Firstfruits assures His followers that we, too, have been (and will be) raised from the dead. The promised land for the Kingdom community is with Him in heavenly places:

But God, who is rich in mercy, because of His great love with which He loved us, even when we were dead in trespasses, made us alive together with Christ (by grace you have been saved), and raised us up together, and made us sit together in the heavenly places in Christ Jesus.
—Ephesians 2:4-6

What's going on in your life as you read this? Whatever the issue, see it from the perspective of being seated in the heavenlies. Consider:

- You are far above anyone or anything, seen or unseen, that can touch you or separate you from the love, grace, and mercy of God.
- You are seated. You are not preparing for or racing to another meeting. You are not striving or performing to be accepted. You are at rest!
- You are "hidden with Christ in God" (Colossians 3:3).

Take a moment to reflect on what being hidden with the Son in God the Father means in your life.

WALKING IN RESURRECTION POWER

As we've seen, Firstfruits celebrates Israel's arrival in the Promised Land. Life would be different from slavery in Egypt or wandering in the desert. God had given His people everything they needed to live in this new life.

In the same way, God gives us everything we need to walk in His resurrection power:

Grace and peace be multiplied to you in the knowledge of God and of Jesus our Lord, as His divine power has given to us all things that pertain to life and godliness, through the knowledge of Him who called us by glory and virtue. —2 Peter 1:2-3

By faith in His resurrection, you are united with Christ and filled with His life.[12] Therefore, you are no longer bound by sin. You can walk in the newness of life empowered by the Holy Spirit. Once bound by the power of darkness, you are now filled with the same power that raised Jesus from the dead—power to raise you above your situation.

That power dwells in you! You are dynamic! I'm not talking about your personality but about your personhood! The Greek word for *power* is [*doo·nam·is*], which is the base of our word *dynamite*. You have dynamite power to live the life you were designed for.

How many times have you thought or said, "I cannot forgive, love, forget, make a decision"? Or, "I don't have the strength, knowledge, wisdom, finances, ability, talent"? You are right. Whatever the challenge, you are probably incapable of completing the task. The paradox of the Kingdom is that, in our weakness, God shows Himself strong. Christ's power enables you to do what you cannot do.[13]

So which kingdom are you walking in? The kingdom of darkness or the Kingdom of God's resurrected Son? How can you tell? Check the fruit of your life. Walking in the Kingdom of love, being led by the Holy Spirit, will bear His fruit:

... love, joy, peace, longsuffering, kindness, goodness, faithfulness, gentleness, self-control. —Galatians 5:22-23

Walking in the kingdom of darkness will bear the fruit of the flesh:

...adultery, fornication, uncleanness, lewdness, idolatry, sorcery, hatred, contentions, jealousies, outbursts of wrath, selfish ambitions, dissensions, heresies, envy, murders, drunkenness, revelries... —Galatians 5:19-21

And just in case this list isn't exhaustive, Paul adds, "and the like." Because sin and death no longer hold us in bondage, we can walk in the newness of life.[14]

NOT BOUND BY THE PAST

The generation that came into the Promised Land had not lived in the bondage of Egypt. Their only experience was of the wilderness, but they had heard the stories from their elders. It was time to move forward. Thinking of the past would have been a distraction.

Remembering the past is important when it leads to celebrating God for what He has done in our lives. It is also important as a tool in the ministry of deliverance and inner healing. But while it is good to remember the past, we must not be bound in or to it:

One thing I do, forgetting those things which are behind and reaching forward to those things which are ahead, I press toward the goal for the prize of the upward call of God in Christ Jesus. —Philippians 3:13b-14

REAPING AND SOWING

A fundamental principle of the Kingdom is whatever we sow, we shall reap.[15] If we sow into the power of darkness, we will reap bad fruit; if we sow into the Kingdom of God, we will reap good fruit. Yet this holiday seems to contradict this basic principle. Israel reaped where she had not sown.[16]

What better picture is there of the spiritual blessings given to us by God's grace alone because of Messiah Jesus? Consider just a few:

- Life[17]
- A guaranteed imperishable inheritance[18]
- Every spiritual blessing in the heavenlies[19]
- Forgiveness of sin and healing of all our diseases[20]
- A garment of praise for the spirit of heaviness[21]
- Dancing instead of mourning[22]

HOPE

The resurrection is the cornerstone of our faith. Very simply, if Passover were the end of the story, we'd still be bound in our sins, separated from God, and without hope:

> *If Christ is not risen, then our preaching is empty and your faith is also empty… And if Christ is not risen, your faith is futile; you are still in your sins!*
> *—1 Corinthians 15:14, 17*

Union with Jesus

- is the hope of glory;
- removes the fear of death;
- redeems us from the grave;
- is provision for an eternity with God.[23]

You can hope because God has your future in His control.

> *The Lord will perfect that which concerns me.*
> *—Psalm 138:8*

> *He who has begun a good work in you will complete it until the day of Jesus Christ.* *—Philippians 1:6*

We cannot separate hope from rest and peace. Even as God was sending Israel out of the Land and into captivity in Babylon, He gave them hope:

> *For I know the thoughts that I think toward you, says the* L*ORD, thoughts of peace and not of evil, to give you a future and a hope.* *—Jeremiah 29:11*

FAITH, PEACE, AND REST

Entry into your promised land is through faith in Jesus.

Joshua and Caleb were the only ones of the generation that left Egypt to enter the Promised Land. An eleven-day journey took forty years; millions of people died in the desert. Why? Because of unbelief.[24]

Peace is obtained and maintained by communion with God:

> *You will keep him in perfect peace, whose mind is stayed on You, because he trusts in You.*
> *—Isaiah 26:3*

As we saw in the "Passover: Redemptive" chapter, the Hebrew word for *salvation* [*yeshu'ah*] comes from the root [*yasha'*]: *to receive help, to be victorious, to accept help, to save, help, to come to assist as if from a place of trouble, turmoil and constriction.* If you are not experiencing the abundant life of freedom, peace, rest, and fullness of joy—go back to the cross! Take with you whatever burdens you are carrying and leave them there. Breathe deeply the truth that Christ is risen!

THE DEAD DO NOT PRAISE THE LORD

Let's again turn to the Great Hallel sung by Jesus and His disciples at the Last Seder/Supper. The psalmist understood that God delivered Israel so she would praise and worship Him:

> *The dead do not praise the LORD, nor any who go down into silence. But we will bless the LORD from this time forth and forevermore.* —*Psalm 115:17-18*

God has given us new life for the same purpose. The greatest worship comes from the lips of those whose lives have been redeemed by the Passover Lamb:

> *And they sang a new song, saying:*
>
> *"You are worthy to take the scroll,*
> *And to open its seals;*
> *For You were slain,*
> *And have redeemed us to God by Your blood*
> *Out of every tribe and tongue and people and nation,*
> *And have made us kings and priests to our God;*
> *And we shall reign on the earth."* —*Revelation 5: 9-10*

The Party Continues

We've come to the close of the study of the spring holidays: Passover, Unleavened Bread, and Firstfruits. We started in the slave pits of Egypt amid suffering. We ended in the promised land of freedom, love, peace, and joy—all because, and for, the glory of Jesus.

As we have seen, God's ordained feasts are not meant to be merely a Jewish celebration of history, but a time to worship and celebrate the one true God. Each was meant to be an opportunity for God to show His character to His people, to remind them of His provision and miracles, and to foreshadow and point the way to Jesus, our Messiah, our Christ.

In the midst of the everyday busyness of life, God wants His children, including you, to have set-aside times throughout the year to celebrate and worship Him. Therefore, our study doesn't end here; there are still the holidays of the summer, fall, and winter!

The party continues.

Feast of Firstfruits

Endnotes

1. You might have noticed that there is sometimes a gap of one month between Resurrection and Passover, although the dating of Resurrection is tied to Passover/Firstfruits. This is because the Jewish calendar requires an occasional "extra month" in a year. While the date of Passover, and thus Firstfruits, remains the same on the Jewish calendar, it will be "out of sync" with the dating of Resurrection on the Christian calendar. See http://www.jewfaq.org/calendar.htm.
2. Isaiah 55:9b.
3. Deuteronomy 32:8.
4. It is likewise important to remember that God instructed Israel to welcome the "stranger in her midst" (Exodus 22:21). There was to be one law for both native born and stranger (Exodus 12:49). I believe that from God's perspective, Israel's being in the Land is more about stewardship than occupancy. Israel is tasked to prepare the Land for the coming of the King.
5. This portion of Scripture is recited during the modern Passover celebration.
6. Isaiah 43:10ff.
7. 1 Corinthians 15:20.
8. The debate revolves around the calendar (due to the uncertainty of the year) versus the reference to Jesus being in the grave for three days and three nights.
9. Genesis 22:8a; Ezekiel 16:62-63.
10. One year our ministry facilitated a Resurrection service on the beach of Tel Aviv. Needless to say, we drew quite a crowd! Using trumpets, rams' horns, and an assortment of instruments, we gave visual and verbal testimony to the hope, peace, and joy we found in Jesus.
11. John 10:10; 3:16.
12. Romans 6:5, 11; Galatians 2:20.
13. Philippians 4:13.
14. Romans 6:4.
15. Galatians 6:7.
16. Deuteronomy 6:11.
17. Romans 6:23.
18. 1 Corinthians 9:25.
19. Ephesians 1:3.
20. Psalm 103:3.
21. Isaiah 61:3.
22. Psalm 30:11.
23. Colossians 1:27; Hosea 13:14; 1 Corinthians 15:55; Psalm 49:15; John 14:3.
24. Hebrews 3:19.

Chapter Eleven

Feast of Weeks

Harvest of the Summer

And you shall count for yourselves from the day after the Sabbath, from the day that you brought the sheaf of the wave offering: seven Sabbaths shall be completed. Count fifty days to the day after the seventh Sabbath; then you shall offer a new grain offering to the LORD. You shall bring from your dwellings two wave loaves of two-tenths of an ephah. They shall be of fine flour; they shall be baked with leaven. They are the firstfruits to the LORD.
—*Leviticus 23:15-17*

Most of you are already familiar with this holiday, although you know it by its Greek designation, Pentecost. In the Feast of Weeks, "the mystery of God was revealed" in the establishment of a Kingdom community of Jews and Gentiles.[1] God's eternal purpose was to create a community who would know Him, love Him, worship, and celebrate Him. He started with a family from whom He built a nation. Ultimately, He made provision for the entire world to become citizens and members of His Kingdom.[2]

The Bible calls this holiday by several names:

- Feast of Weeks [3]
- Feast of Harvest [4]
- Day of Firstfruits [5]
- Pentecost[6]

Did you notice that this holiday is also called Firstfruits? The Feast of Weeks is the second of the three firstfruit holidays. This has tremendous redemptive implications, so read on!

Seasonal

The Feast of Weeks is celebrated fifty days after the Firstfruits of Passover.[7] It is the festival of the summer harvest, including crops of wheat and barley. It is the second pilgrim festival in which Jewish males would bring the firstfruit of their summer harvest to Jerusalem to offer unto the Lord.

National

Let's consider five points of significance this holiday has to the nation of Israel:

- Possessing their inheritance
- Remembering and rejoicing
- Inclusion of all people

- A unique offering
- Rabbinic tradition

POSSESSING HER INHERITANCE

When Israel came into the Land, God's provision of manna ceased as He provided a harvest for which the people had not labored.[8] They then had to sow and reap their own harvest. This second harvest was another fulfillment of God's covenant promises:

> *On the same day the LORD made a covenant with Abram, saying:*
>
> *"To your descendants I have given this land, from the river of Egypt to the great river, the River Euphrates—the Kenites, the Kenezzites, the Kadmonites, the Hittites, the Perizzites, the Rephaim, the Amorites, the Canaanites, the Girgashites, and the Jebusites."*
>
> *—Genesis 15:18-21*

Before them were two daunting tasks. First, they had to TAKE the land. As harsh as it seems to us today, God's instructions were clear:

> *When you have crossed the Jordan into the land of Canaan, then you shall drive out all the inhabitants of the land from before you, destroy all their engraved stones, destroy all their molded images, and demolish all their high places; you shall dispossess the inhabitants of the land and dwell in it, for I have given you the land to possess.*
>
> *—Numbers 33:51b-53*

The former inhabitants of the land had defiled it to such an extent that God's judgment on them was to come from the hand of Israel. Israel was to take the land, remove those inhabitants, and leave no prisoners!

Second, Israel had to KEEP the land. Taking the land was a long and challenging task, but keeping it was even harder. In fact, Israel was unable to consistently remove the *-ites* who were determined to remain. As God warned, these idol worshippers became a distraction and a snare to Israel, eventually leading her into worship of foreign gods and sins of great disobedience.

Taking and keeping are two different issues. Taking is an activity, whereas keeping is a lifestyle. An activity (program or project) has a beginning and an end. Once the goal is achieved, you can applaud yourself and relax. Or can you?

Possessing your possession—keeping your achievements—requires diligence and perseverance. The difference between an activity and a lifestyle is evident in my clothes closet, where there are sizes ranging from Petite 4 to Regular 14!

REMEMBER AND REJOICE

God wanted the people of Israel to always remember that once they were slaves, but they were delivered and could enjoy the bounty of His covenant promises. The festivals were times to remember and to rejoice:

> *You shall rejoice before the LORD your God, you and your son and your daughter, your male servant and your female servant, the Levite who is within your gates, the stranger and the fatherless and the widow who are among you, at the place where the LORD your God chooses to make His*

name abide. And you shall remember that you were a slave in Egypt, and you shall be careful to observe these statutes.
—Deuteronomy 16:11-12

This festival takes place during the barley season, so the Jewish people read the book of Ruth as part of their celebration of Weeks. The great love scene between Boaz and Ruth takes place at the threshing floor during the harvest, a time of great merriment.

INCLUSION OF ALL

Because Israel had known the bondage of slavery in Egypt, she was always to be gracious to the stranger in her midst. Her doors were to be open to everyone who wanted to come under the protection of God, most especially the widow and the orphan.[9] There was to be only one law for both Israel and the stranger in her midst.[10]

UNIQUE OFFERING

The offering on this firstfruit holiday is different from that of the spring holiday of Firstfruits:

You shall bring from your dwellings two wave loaves of two-tenths of an ephah. They shall be of fine flour; they shall be baked with leaven.
—Leviticus 23:17

This offering was to contain leaven!

Earlier I said that leaven is symbolic of sin. Offerings to the Lord have to be holy, containing neither leaven nor blemish. But for this, the second of the firstfruit holidays, God specifically asks for loaves baked *with* leaven! Furthermore, the loaves were to come from wheat ground at home. Herein lies a clue to the redemptive significance of Weeks.

RABBINIC TRADITION

A wonderful, though non-substantiated, tradition among the religious Jews is that Weeks is the day Moses received the Law from God on Mt. Sinai.

"Can you tell me, please, the foundation of the teaching that Moses received the Torah on Weeks?" I asked a rabbi. He and those around him were a bit shocked and definitely uncomfortable with my question. It was a question that they'd never dare to ask themselves. One finally admitted, "That's an issue still being debated."

"Wouldn't it be incredible if it were true?" I challenged. "Wouldn't it be so like God to fulfill His promise for the Holy Spirit on the very same holiday that He gave the Mosaic Covenant?"

> *And it shall come to pass afterward that I will pour out My Spirit on all flesh; your sons and your daughters shall prophesy, your old men shall dream dreams, your young men shall see visions. And also on My menservants and on My maidservants I will pour out My Spirit in those days.*
> *—Joel 2:28-29*

Needless to say, the rabbi and I had an interesting conversation!

Of this we can be sure, God the Father did give His promised Holy Spirit on the Feast of Weeks!

> *When the Day of Pentecost had fully come, they were all with one accord in one place. And suddenly there came*

a sound from heaven ... And they were all filled with the Holy Spirit ... this is what was spoken by the prophet Joel.
—Acts 2:1-4, 16

According to tradition, Moses was said to have climbed a ladder into heaven to receive the Torah, so on this holiday, challah (sweet bread) is served in the shape of a ladder rather than the braided challah served on Sabbath. Dairy products are also eaten as a reminder of the Promised Land, a land flowing with milk and honey.

Spiritual

Regardless of the veracity of the rabbinic tradition, there are truths about God's character reflected in the Feast of Weeks.

GOD IS A COVENANT MAKER

Four of God's covenant promises come together on this holiday:

- To Abraham:

  In you all the families of the earth shall be blessed.
  —Genesis 12:3

- To Moses:

  He said, "... And this shall be a sign to you that I have sent you: When you have brought the people out of Egypt, you shall serve God on this mountain."
  —Exodus 3:12

ॐ To Jeremiah:

Behold, the days are coming, says the LORD, when I will make a new covenant with the house of Israel and with the house of Judah—not according to the covenant that I made with their fathers in the day that I took them by the hand to lead them out of the land of Egypt… But this is the covenant that I will make with the house of Israel after those days, says the LORD: I will put My law in their minds, and write it on their hearts.
—Jeremiah 31:31-33

ॐ To Joel:

And it shall come to pass afterward that I will pour out My Spirit on all flesh; your sons and your daughters shall prophesy, your old men shall dream dreams, your young men shall see visions. And also on My menservants and on My maidservants I will pour out My Spirit in those days.
—Joel 2:28-29

GOD IS OUR PROVIDER

The second harvest was evidence of God's continual provision. Each of the three pilgrim festivals reminded the people that they could trust Him for their daily bread. Jesus said:

Therefore I say to you, do not worry about your life, what you will eat or what you will drink; nor about your body, what you will put on. Is not life more than food and the body more than clothing? Look at the birds of the air, for they neither sow nor reap nor gather into barns; yet your heavenly

> *Father feeds them. Are you not of more value than they?*
> *—Matthew 6:25-26*

Of course, His ultimate provision was for our salvation. Look at this gem buried in the life of David:

> *God does not take away a life; but He devises means, so that His banished ones are not expelled from Him.*
> *—2 Samuel 14:14*

The means God provided is Jesus, the Provider for both our spiritual and physical needs.

GOD THE HOLY SPIRIT

On this holiday, our focus is drawn to the third person of the triune Godhead, the Holy Spirit.[11] Being part of the Godhead, the Holy Spirit is in every way one in character and essence with God the Son and God the Father. Scripture describes the Spirit by many names including:

- Helper[12]
- Holy Spirit of Promise[13]
- Spirit of Glory[14]
- Spirit of Holiness[15]
- Spirit of Christ[16]
- Spirit of God[17]
- Spirit of His Son, Spirit of Adoption[18]
- Spirit of Truth[19]

Scripture is replete with the functions of the Spirit, including, but not limited to

- baptizing us into the Kingdom of God, guaranteeing our relationship with God by pouring His love into our hearts, giving us access to the Father, sealing us for the Day of Redemption.[20]
- making us alive; producing good fruit; helping us in our weakness; interceding; searching the deep things of God; bringing freedom, unity, peace, and joy; strengthening our inner man.[21]
- convicting of sin, righteousness and judgment, sanctifying, cleansing, purifying, giving wisdom, knowledge, and revelation, empowering for evangelism and ministry.[22]

The sweet communion with God through the indwelling of the Holy Spirit is one of life's greatest joys.

Redemptive

A four-point sermon outline on the prophetic significance of this holiday could be:

- **PROMISE**—The Holy Spirit
- **PEOPLE**—A Kingdom community
- **PURPOSE**—His witness
- **POWER**—Enablement

KINGDOM COMMUNITY

We've established that God's eternal plan was to create a Kingdom community that would fill the earth with the knowledge of His glory. This community would also be a witness to the heavenlies. God first gave Israel the assignment to bring that knowledge to the Gentiles, so the Gentiles could become equal citizens in that Kingdom. Even before the wall of enmity was built between Jews and Gentiles,[23] God had destroyed it.

Jewish and Gentile relationships have not always been easy. I remember the day when God revealed the hardness of my heart regarding the Gentiles through one of the Psalms sung at Passover. Psalm 117 was next on my reading schedule. I was going to skip it, but the Spirit insisted that I read it:

> *Praise the LORD, all you Gentiles! Laud Him, all you peoples! For His merciful kindness is great toward us, and the truth of the LORD endures forever. Praise the LORD!* —*Psalm 117*

I began to meditate, "Yes, may the Gentiles praise You, Lord, for Your merciful kindness to Israel. The Gentiles can trust You because You are faithful and true to Israel."

"No," the Holy Spirit corrected me, "Read it again." I read it as I had done for years: the Gentiles can praise and trust God because He is faithful to Israel.

The Spirit crashed through my meditation, saying, "The Gentiles can praise and trust Me because I am faithful."

Unbeknownst to me, I had not really understood that God's eternal love for the Gentiles is the same love He has for Israel. I was like the disgruntled workers in Matthew 20:1-16.

I now understand that, before my salvation, I was just as far away from God and the promises of the covenant as any Gentile unbeliever. The wonderful mystery of Christ revealed in Ephesians 2:13 is that all of us who "once were far off have been brought near by the blood of Christ." Through Christ, we all become citizens of the Kingdom community:

> *For the promise is to you and to your children, and to all who are afar off, as many as the Lord our God will call.* —*Acts 2:39*

Praise God that in Christ Jesus:

> *...the grace of God that brings salvation has appeared to all men.* —*Titus 2:11*

ONE NEW MAN

The unique offering of Weeks is a picture of the mystery of Jesus Christ hidden deep in the heart of God:

> *...The mystery of Christ...has now been revealed by the Spirit...that the Gentiles should be fellow heirs, of the same body, and partakers of His promise in Christ through the gospel...For through Him we both have access by one Spirit to the Father.* —*Ephesians 3:4-6; 2:18*

I suggest that the two loaves presented on one sheet represent Jews and Gentiles, thus foreshadowing the Scripture:

> *He Himself...has broken down the middle wall of separation...so as to create in Himself one new man from the two, thus making peace, and that He might reconcile them both to God in one body through the cross.* —*Ephesians 2:14-16a*

What a perfect picture of the one new man who would witness and testify to the heavenlies so that:

...the manifold wisdom of God might be made known by the church to the principalities and powers in the heavenly places.
—Ephesians 3:10

The bougainvillea bush growing right outside my window is a wonderful example of the one new man. On one stem there are two blossoms, exact in every way except the color—one is pink and the other is white. Is this not the picture of Jew and Gentile in Christ—different and yet the same?

JEWS AND GENTILES

I believe there is a common, although inaccurate, teaching in some churches that Gentiles become "spiritual Jews" when they are saved, and that the church becomes "spiritual Israel." How can this be? A Gentile does not become a Jew any more than a Jew becomes a Gentile. Salvation means that we both become followers of Christ—a Jewish follower of Christ or a Gentile follower of Christ.[24]

To understand, let's consider men and women. Paul tells us that in Christ men/women and Jews/Gentiles are all the same.[25] And yet Christ does not change men from being men or women from being women. Paul is talking about the spiritual realm. In the natural, men are still men and women are still women. They retain the obvious, God-given differences and functions. It is the same with Jews and Gentiles. In the natural, each group has its own purposes in the community of the Kingdom.

SECOND FIRSTFRUITS

Remember that one of the designations of Weeks is Firstfruits. It is the second of the firstfruit harvests. By His resurrection,

Jesus became the *firstfruits* of the dead. Through faith, believers become the second of the firstfruits; we are the firstfruits of Jesus:

> *Of His own will He brought us forth by the word of truth, that we might be a kind of firstfruits of His creatures.*
> *—James 1:18*

I think it's interesting that James is addressing his letter to the Jewish believers.[26] Paul's statement "for the Jew first and also for the Greek" in Romans 1:16 is exactly what happened on Weeks, circa AD 32. With Weeks being a pilgrim festival, Jerusalem was filled with Jews from "every nation under heaven";[27] thus, the Jews were the first to receive the Holy Spirit.

THE CHURCH IS EMPOWERED

I have often heard it said, "The church was born on the Feast of Weeks." Perhaps a more accurate statement would be that the church was empowered on the Feast of Weeks.

Often in Scripture, wheat is linked with evangelism and harvest with its end result of salvation.[28] On this holiday of wheat harvest, God empowered the Kingdom community (the church) to do the work of evangelism.

While there are many personal blessings bestowed by the Holy Spirit, the Spirit was given corporately to enable the harvest. Consider His immediate effects:

> *Everyone heard them speak in his own language. Then they were all amazed and marveled, saying to one another, "Look, are not all these who speak Galileans? And how is it that we hear, each in our own language*

in which we were born? ... We hear them speaking in our own tongues the wonderful works of God."
—Acts 2:6b-8, 11

The Holy Spirit enabled and empowered these Jews to speak in languages that were unknown to them but understood by the hearers. And what was their message? The wonderful works of God!

The first time I experienced the empowerment of the Holy Spirit was exactly one month after I first prayed to Jesus. I was going through a relationship crisis. While driving to work, amid the tears of a broken heart, I cried out to Jesus, "If this is the pain I cause myself, I give up. You said You wanted control of my life. Well, You have it now!" Immediately my tears stopped.

When I walked into the office, a friend confronted me with a surprising question, "What happened to you?" Apparently my tear-streaked face was glowing. "Jesus!" I practically shouted, "It's all about Jesus." Soon she and everyone else in my office heard and responded to the good news of the gospel! That's the empowerment of the Holy Spirit.

Kingdom

I'd like to suggest seven principles from Weeks that we can apply to our lives:

- We are to be laborers in His harvest.
- We are sealed for adoption.
- We are circumcised by the Spirit.
- We are to possess our possession.

- We are to demonstrate righteousness and justice.
- We are to make good choices.
- The church and redeemed Israel is the one new man.

LABORERS IN HIS HARVEST

As the Feast of Weeks commemorates the harvest for which Israel labored, it reminds us that we are the laborers in His harvest:

> *The harvest truly is great, but the laborers are few; therefore pray the Lord of the harvest to send out laborers into His harvest.* —*Luke 10:2*

You might not be an evangelist, but you are called and empowered to be His witness. If God's purpose is to fill the earth with the knowledge of His glory, you have an important role to fulfill. No one will be able to fill your part in the way God created you to fill it.

God's will is that all might be saved.[29] But how can they, unless they hear the gospel?

> *How then shall they call on Him in whom they have not believed? And how shall they believe in Him of whom they have not heard? And how shall they hear without a preacher?* —*Romans 10:14*

Why are so many Christians silent? Perhaps they hope that their lives will be the only witness necessary. Francis of Assisi is reputed to have said, "Preach Jesus all the time, but use words only when necessary." I suggest that this saying is a complete contradiction of Scripture. Faith does not come through the testimony of believers' lives, but through their lips.[30] Evangelism is everyone's responsibility.

Do you have God's heart for the lost? Consider:

- Jesus wept over the people of Jerusalem.[31]
- Jeremiah's heart was broken over the sins of the people.[32]
- Paul was compelled by love.[33]

"And what about evangelism to the Jews?" you may ask. "Haven't they suffered enough at the hands of Christians? Do we have the right to witness to them about Jesus?"

"YES, a thousand times YES!" I shout. Can there be a more anti-Jewish action than to keep silent? Can love truly be expressed without sharing the gospel? What comfort is there outside of Jesus? Did Jesus die only for the Gentiles?[34] Jesus Himself said that He came for the lost sheep of Israel. Remember that one of God's purposes for His Kingdom community is to provoke the Jews to jealousy.[35]

Scripture promises you great rewards as you labor in God's harvest.[36]

SEALED FOR ADOPTION

The Holy Spirit seals our adoption and is the guarantee of our inheritance. As children of God, we become joint heirs with Christ and are promised an inheritance of unsearchable riches in Him:[37]

> *And because you are sons, God has sent forth the Spirit of His Son into your hearts, crying out, "Abba, Father!" Therefore you are no longer a slave but a son, and if a son, then an heir of God through Christ.*
> *—Galatians 4:6-7*

Are you living as a slave or as a child of a loving Father?

CIRCUMCISED BY THE SPIRIT

God's promise to Israel to circumcise the people's hearts is the same promise He makes to you, and it is fulfilled in Weeks.[38] The Holy Spirit enables us to fulfill God's law of grace and truth.[39] God cried through Jeremiah:

> *Break up your fallow ground, and do not sow among thorns. Circumcise yourselves to the LORD, and take away the foreskins of your hearts, you men of Judah and inhabitants of Jerusalem.*
> *—Jeremiah 4:3-4*

We cannot circumcise our hearts. Without the Holy Spirit, our hearts are as hard as the stone upon which God wrote the Mosaic law. We are unable or unwilling to discern our own sins. If the moral portion of the Mosaic covenant was impossible to keep, how much more the higher expectations of the new covenant?

As we allow the Holy Spirit to convict us of sin, cleanse us, and control our lives, we shall be "innocent of great transgression."[40]

POSSESS OUR POSSESSION

The Feast of Weeks celebrates Israel possessing her inheritance. So I'd like to ask you a personal question. Are you fully possessing and keeping God's promises of an abundant life in Jesus? I'm not referring to wealth, although that is surely an aspect of His abundance. I'm talking about an abundance of love, joy, and peace in the deepest part of you.

I'm confident most people will answer, "No." You might be like me, saying, "The snare is broken, but I haven't escaped!"[41] Yes, the snare might be broken, but pieces often remain. Like

Israel's enemies, they are intruders that need to be removed to avoid needless trouble.

Let me give you an example. There are trees along the sidewalk in front of my home. Although they were just planted a few years ago, their roots are pushing up and breaking the nicely laid bricks. While walking in the dim light of morning, I didn't see the broken bricks and fell hard. Only God's grace kept me from breaking any bones, but I was badly bruised.

In like manner, as we try to put all the pieces of our lives in place, a root of unresolved pain, bitterness, or unforgiveness can break through our nicely ordered lives, causing disruption, destruction, or even devastation to those around us. We suddenly find ourselves confused, discouraged, and defeated (bruised).

These intruding snares prefer to remain hidden in our souls. They attack our minds, distorting God's character and His truth. They cause havoc to our emotions. Then, when our wills get involved, we head straight for danger.

As the enemy attacks our souls, our spirits are affected as well. Consider this:

> *For the enemy has persecuted my soul; he has crushed my life to the ground; he has made me dwell in darkness, like those who have long been dead. Therefore my spirit is overwhelmed within me; my heart within me is distressed.*
> —Psalm 143:3-4

The psalmist has the answer:

> *Cause me to hear Your lovingkindness in the morning, for in You do I trust; cause me to know the way in which I should walk, for I lift up my soul to You.*
> —Psalm 143:8

The psalmist cries to know God's covenant-keeping love. The word used for lovingkindness is [*chesed*].[42] The abundant salvation of Jesus is freedom and wholeness in our bodies, our souls, and our spirits.[43]

How did Israel take the Land? Little by little.[44] Likewise, we, too, are working out our salvation little by little as we possess our possession.

By the power of the Holy Spirit, confront those intruders with God's truth and love [*'emet v^e chesed*]. Then you will be able to

> *... lay aside every weight, and the sin which so easily ensnares us, and let us run with endurance the race that is set before us, looking unto Jesus, the author and finisher of our faith.* —*Hebrews 12:1b-2a*

Recognize your enemies; they are not flesh and blood but powers and principalities. Heed Paul's advice:

> *Finally, my brethren, be strong in the Lord and in the power of His might. Put on the whole armor of God, that you may be able to stand against the wiles of the devil.*
> —*Ephesians 6:10-11*

Glory to the author and finisher of our faith, who has won the victory, disarming those intruders! The battle you are waging will result in the perfection of your faith, as you learn to lean on the arm of Jesus. Often my sweetest time of fellowship with Him is in the midst of a struggle. Sing another of the Passover psalms:

> *I love the LORD, because He has heard My voice and my supplications. Because He has inclined His ear to me, therefore I will call upon Him as long as I live.*
> —*Psalm 116:1-2*

RIGHTEOUSNESS AND JUSTICE

During the Feast of Weeks, we are reminded to leave gleanings from our harvest for the poor. The two great commandments link together righteousness and justice. In God's eyes they cannot be separated.

Righteousness is tied to our relationship with God, and justice is tied to our relationship with others. Our righteousness in Christ will result in our just treatment of others.[45]

Because of Israel's experience in and deliverance from Egypt, she understood the injustice that comes from the hands of the wicked. God commanded and expected Israel to protect the widow, provide for the orphan, and take care of strangers in her midst.

Boaz understood firsthand the righteous justice extended by his father, Salmon, to his mother, Rahab, a stranger in Israel. Later, he extended that same righteous justice to Ruth, a Moabite widow and stranger in Israel. Eventually, he became the grandfather of King David.

Your witness of the righteous justice of Jesus is incomplete until you extend His justice to the poor and needy. I challenge us all to get personally involved with those around us who need to see our faith in action.

CHOICES

When Moses presented God's Law to Israel, the people had to make a choice. He set before them life and death, and they had to choose.

They had already made some bad choices. Choosing to have God speak to Moses while they stood far off, then creating and worshipping a gold calf comes to mind. It seemed that they were ready to make the right choice:

And they said, "All that the LORD has said we will do, and be obedient." —Exodus 24:7

Yet they kept the foreign gods, which their fathers had served in Egypt.[46] So, like Moses, Joshua gave them the same choice. Again Israel promised to serve the Lord; and again, the people rebelled.[47]

Jesus gives the same choice. How will you respond? Will you say, "Yes," but not put away your foreign gods or idols? Will you stand afar off and let someone else meet with God in your place? Or will you accept His gift of salvation, receive the Holy Spirit, and climb the mountain for sweet intimacy with your Savior?

"Freedom gives a person the right to accept God's covenant. But if one rejects, then one is choosing death."[48]

THE CHURCH AND REDEEMED ISRAEL[49]

I will call them My people, who were not My people, and her beloved, who was not beloved. And it shall come to pass in the place where it was said to them,

"You are not My people," there they shall be called sons of the living God. —Romans 9:25-26

As we continue to reflect on the Kingdom community (the one new man), let us consider the relationship between Jews and Gentiles in Christ. Zechariah and John had similar visions:

These are the two anointed ones, who stand beside the Lord of the whole earth. —Zechariah 4:14

These are the two olive trees and the two lamp stands standing before the God of the earth.
—Revelation 11:4

Could the two *anointed ones*, which literally means *sons of fresh oil*, be the church and redeemed Israel?

Let me be clear. I believe that when a Jew is saved and becomes a follower of Jesus, he becomes part of the community of the Kingdom (the church). Yet at the same time, he remains part of Israel. While many of the blessings and promises to the church and Israel are the same, there remains one unique distinction for Israel—the stewardship of the Land in preparation for Christ's return.

Next, we turn our attention to the holy days of the fall.

Endnotes

1. Ephesians 3:5-6.
2. John 1:12.
3. Exodus 34:22; Deuteronomy 16:10.
4. Exodus 23:16.
5. Numbers 28:26.
6. Acts 2:1.
7. Because Passover itself is considered a Sabbath, the Sadducees and Pharisees argued over which Sabbath began the countdown to Weeks! Today it is celebrated on the sixth day of Sivan, seven weeks and one day after the second day of Passover that is also the beginning of the Feast of Unleavened Bread.
8. See "*Firstfruits.*"
9. Ruth 1:16.
10. Exodus 12:49; Numbers 15:16,29.
11. Holy Spirit: [*ruach haqadesh*].
12. John 16:7.
13. Ephesians 1:12-14.
14. 1 Peter 4:14.
15. Romans 1:4.
16. Romans 8:9.
17. Romans 8:14.
18. Galatians 4:6.
19. John 14:17.
20. John 3:5; Romans 5:5; 2 Corinthians 1:22; Ephesians 2:18; 4:30.
21. John 4:14; 7:38; 1 Peter 3:18; Galatians 5:22-23; Romans 8:26; 1 Corinthians 2:10; 2 Corinthians 3:17; Ephesians 4:3; 3:16.
22. John 16:9; 1 Corinthians 6:11; 2 Thessalonians 2:13; 1 Peter 1:22; John 14:26; 16:13; Acts 1:8; 1 Corinthians 12:3-11.
23. Isaiah 43:10; Psalm 117.
24. Many Jewish believers prefer the term "Messianic," but I prefer being called "Christian" as it best describes my faith. I've heard some religious Jews calling themselves "Messianic" because they believe a Messiah will come without knowing for whom they are looking.
25. Galatians 3:28.
26. "To the twelve tribes which are scattered abroad" (James 1:1).
27. Acts 2:5.
28. Matthew 13:24-30; John 4:35-38.
29. 1 Timothy 2:3.

30. Our lives can make them jealous or curious, but it is the Word that has the power unto salvation (Romans 1:16). I will forever be indebted to "John," whose abundant life and personal knowledge of "my" God made me so jealous that I began to listen to the gospel message.
31. Matthew 23:37.
32. Jeremiah 8:18–9:1.
33. 2 Corinthians 5:14.
34. Matthew 15:24.
35. Romans 10:19; 11:11; Deuteronomy 32:21.
36. Proverbs 11:30; Psalm 125:5-6.
37. John 1:12; Romans 8:17.
38. Deuteronomy 30:6.
39. Romans 8:1-17; Galatians 5:16; 2 Corinthians 3:17.
40. Psalm 19:13.
41. Psalm 124:7.
42. This Hebrew word is studied in depth in "*Passover: Spiritual.*"
43. Isaiah 61:1-3; cf. Luke 4:18; Psalm 103.
44. Exodus 23:30.
45. James 2:14-25.
46. Joshua 24:20.
47. Joshua 24:21.
48. Irving Greenburg, source unknown.
49. I am using the more common term "church," but in essence I mean the Kingdom community as I have been using it throughout this book.

Chapter Twelve

Blowing of Trumpets

All about the King

The holidays of the fall begin six months after those in the spring. As in the spring, there are three holidays: Blowing of Trumpets, Day of Atonement, and Feast of Tabernacles.

Through the spring feasts, we saw God's redemptive plan, from the deliverance of Israel out of bondage to their arrival in the Promised Land.

The first two feasts of the fall seem to be a selah … as though God wants us to stop, take a deep breath, and reflect.

Seasonal

In the seventh month, on the first day of the month, you shall have a sabbath rest, a memorial of blowing of trumpets, a holy convocation. You shall do no customary work on it; and you shall offer an offering made by fire to the LORD.
—Leviticus 23:24-25

Blowing of Trumpets is in the seventh month of God's calendar, occurring in late September or early October. Being on the first day of the month, it also coincides with the monthly holiday of New Moon, thus making it a double celebration.

The feast appears on secular calendars by its more common Hebrew name, Rosh Hashanah, which means "head of the year." This designation (contrary to Scripture, which says that Passover is the beginning of the year) is based solely on rabbinic traditions about events that are supposed to have happened on this day.

National

The Bible does not record any significant event in Israel's history that this holiday commemorates.[1] However, there are two significant events the Bible records as having occurred on this holiday:

- Sacrifices were resumed before the foundation for the second temple had been laid.[2]
- Ezra read the Law.[3]

Furthermore, *blowing of trumpets* is not the best translation. The literal Hebrew is translated *you shall have a memorial of blowing*, omitting the word trumpet.

The Hebrew word used is [*t^e^ru'ah*], which means *a shout or a loud blast of alarm or joy.* A more familiar word, [*shofar*], is often used in conjunction with *truah.* The *shofar* is a *curved, musical instrument made of the horn of a ram or kudu.*

We get some clues about this holiday as we look at how the two words, *truah* and *shofar*, are used:

- *Truah:*
    - Alarm for war[4]
    - Signal to march[5]
    - Shout for joy—general[6]
    - Shout for joy—religious[7]
- *Shofar:*
    - God's voice [8]
    - Begins the year of Jubilee [9]
    - Caused confusion in enemy camp[10]
    - Call to war[11]
    - Cessation of war[12]
    - Anointing of a king[13]
    - Feast of New Moon[14]
    - Praise to God[15]
    - Call to repentance[16]
    - Declaration of Israel's sins[17]
    - Regathering of Israel[18]

- Impending judgment[19]

Notable times when *truah* and *shofar* are used together:

- Destruction of the walls of Jericho[20]
- Call to repentance[21]
- Praise to God[22]

When the Bible is silent, the rabbis often develop traditions, which eventually are accepted as explanations.[23] Rabbis claim these events happened on this holiday:[24]

- Creation of the world and Adam
- Adam's fall
- Cain and Abel were born
- Abraham, Isaac, and Jacob were born and died
- Isaac was offered but spared by the substituted ram
- Moses received the second set of the Law

By the time the Mishna[25] was codified (circa AD 200–400), the holiday had a four-fold meaning:

- Beginning of the civil year
- Memorial to the creation
- Day of Remembrance
- Day of Passing for Judgment

The combination of the latter two gave rise to the most notable tradition—that Blowing of Trumpets begins the Days of Awe.

DAYS OF AWE

Tradition explains that the Days of Awe are the ten days between Blowing of Trumpets and Day of Atonement. It is said that after the golden calf incident, Moses went up to Mt. Sinai during Trumpets to receive the second set of tablets while the people spent time in repentance. Moses then returned to camp on the Day of Atonement, when the people had completed their repentance and were ready to receive the second set of tablets.

Based on this tradition, the Days of Awe developed into a time of repentance and preparation to receive from God. The Days begin with the blowing of the shofar on Trumpets. The shofar's harsh sounds are a clarion call, warning the people to prepare for the impending judgment set for the Day of Atonement.[26]

The people are to spend the next ten days remembering and repenting for sins committed during the previous year.

According to the tradition, God has three books before Him:

- The Book of Death
- The Book of Life
- The Book of In-between or Suspension

The Book of Death is for the wicked: those who have done such evil during the previous year that there is no possible redemption.

The Book of Life is for the extremely righteous: those whose deeds are so exemplary there need be no further judgment.

There are very few names written in either of these two books. The vast majority of names are kept in the Book of Suspension.

At the first sound of the trumpet, God reviews the lives of every living soul over the previous year. He then determines their fate for the coming year.

Those judged very wicked are written in the Book of Death. The verdict is issued swiftly.

For the few judged very righteous, their names are written in the Book of Life. They will live. That's why the traditional Jewish greeting for this holiday is, "May your name be inscribed (or endorsed) in the Book of Life for the coming year."

For the rest, the vast majority of the people, God waits ten days until Day of Atonement to make His final judgment.

Thus, based on this tradition, the Days of Awe are a time of preparation. They are to be a time of personal reflection, repentance, and restoration of relationships before God makes His final judgment in the closing moments of Day of Atonement.

As a young woman, these "Days" were very serious to me. I spent many hours trying to remember each and every thing I had done that might not be pleasing to God. It was awful as I realized how many people I'd hurt. There were so many! I had to humble myself and go to each one to apologize. I HATED IT.

But like the rest of my Jewish family and friends, I was preparing myself to stand before God on the Day of Atonement. I was getting myself ready for His judgment.

I desperately hoped that during these ten days, I would do enough good things to make up for all the awful things I had done over the past year, trying to tip the scales in my favor so my name would be written in the Book of Life for another year.

After a while I wondered why I had to go through this every year. Didn't I resolve each year to be good—so good that my name would be immediately written in the Book of Life? And if I were finally good enough, why couldn't it be written there permanently? I wondered but found no answers.

Observant Jews may follow a custom called Tashlich (casting off) in which they walk to flowing water, say a prayer, and symbolically throw their sins into the water.[27] Tashlich is based on God's promise recorded in Micah:

> *Who is a God like You, pardoning iniquity and passing over the transgression of the remnant of His heritage? He does not retain His anger forever, because He delights in mercy. He will again have compassion on us, and will subdue our iniquities. You will cast all our sins into the depths of the sea.* —*Micah 7:18-19*

Although there is no biblical foundation for the Days of Awe, the truth is that one day we will all pass before God for judgment. God's verdict will not be for a year, but for eternity—some for everlasting life and others for everlasting torment.[28]

Praise to God and our Savior Jesus, who has inscribed us in His Book of Life for eternity!

Spiritual

The Blowing of Trumpets reminds us that God is a forgiving judge and king.

GOD IS JUDGE

God's word is final; He is Judge, and His judgments are perfect:[29]

> *He is the Rock, His work is perfect; for all His ways are justice, a God of truth and without injustice; righteous and upright is He.* —*Deuteronomy 32:4*

Testing authority is the result of our sin nature. We challenge God's justice according to our standards and then criticize Him for not being fair.

Parents often say to their stubborn children, "Because I said so!" "Why?" is not only a question of children, but also of many adults. God's answer is the same, "Because I said so!" God is the standard of all justice:

> *I will make justice the measuring line, and righteousness the plummet; the hail will sweep away the refuge of lies.*
> *—Isaiah 28:17*

God's justice is the foundation of His character, just as much as His mercy, grace, and truth.[30] When King David was given a choice, he chose to have God judge him rather than the people. Throughout Scripture, we see many other aspects of God's character as Judge. He is

- jealous[31]
- impartial[32]
- immutable[33]
- just[34]

GOD IS FORGIVING

When God revealed Himself to Moses in Exodus 34:5-6,[35] He included forgiveness as one of His main characteristics. His willingness to forgive is the result of His compassion, mercy, grace, truth, and faithfulness:

> *For You, LORD, are good, and ready to forgive, and abundant in mercy to all those who call upon You.*
> *—Psalm 86:5*

I finally found the answer to my quandary about the Days of Awe. By God's grace, through faith in Jesus, I have absolute assurance that I am forgiven!

If we walk in the light as He is in the light, we have fellowship with one another, and the blood of Jesus Christ His Son cleanses us from all sin . . . If we confess our sins, He is faithful and just to forgive us our sins and to cleanse us from all unrighteousness.
—1 John 1:7, 9

GOD IS KING

The LORD sat enthroned at the Flood, and the LORD sits as King forever. *—Psalm 29:10*

The LORD is King forever and ever; the nations have perished out of His land. *—Psalm 10:16*

As an American, it's hard to appreciate royalty. That changed when I was invited to visit the House of Lords in London, England. Visitors were not allowed to enter the Chamber before the Lords, so along with others I waited in the hallway. The sneer that had been on my lips instantly vanished as the procession of white wigged and robed Lords passed by.

Then I was led upstairs and into the Chamber itself. The sight was breathtaking. More than the magnificence of the highly polished, deep mahogany walls was the throne. Set apart and slightly elevated, the throne dominated the entire room. Even so, it was not the official throne of the Queen, simply a ceremonial one.

All I could think about was the throne of God. If an earthly power can command such awe and respect, how can we comprehend standing before the King of the Universe?

Redemptive

Does Jesus not deserve the utmost attention and adoration of His creation? I submit for your consideration that this day of memorial blowing might revolve around the kingship of Jesus. Could this be the one feast on God's calendar that specifically commemorates His coming, His return, and His coronation?

THE COMING OF THE KING

Jesus,

> *...who, being in the form of God, did not consider it robbery to be equal with God, but made Himself of no reputation, taking the form of a bondservant, and coming in the likeness of men. And being found in appearance as a man, He humbled Himself and became obedient to the point of death, even the death of the cross. Therefore God also has highly exalted Him and given Him the name which is above every name, that at the name of Jesus every knee should bow, of those in heaven, and of those on earth, and of those under the earth, and that every tongue should confess that Jesus Christ is Lord, to the glory of God the Father.*
> —*Philippians 2:6-11*

Even as I write those words, my spirit is soaring. I want to shout, "Hallelujah! Glory to God in the highest! And to all men ... SHALOM!"

But wait. That's been done already, hasn't it?

> *Suddenly there was with the angel a multitude praising God and saying: "Glory to God in the*

highest, and on earth peace, goodwill toward men!"
—Luke 2:13-14

If the appearance of one angel is frightening,[36] can you imagine what this sight was like? The awesomeness of the most spectacular sunset or the northern lights cannot compare with a multitude of heavenly hosts proclaiming, singing, shouting the news that God Himself was born! Glory to God in the highest, indeed!

Can you imagine a better time to blow every trumpet in the Land? Could there be a better accompaniment to the angels' voices? Bethlehem is just a few kilometers from Jerusalem. Imagine the perfection of this orchestration—trumpets blasting in Jerusalem and angels praising overhead.

Could it be that Christ was born on the day of the Blowing of the Trumpets? Perhaps the reason God did not give any further instructions about this feast was because He expected the Jewish people to recognize the time of their visitation. Consider Simeon and Anna, who were both ready and waiting with eager expectation.[37]

Since Jewish culture (as recorded in Scripture) does not celebrate births, we really don't know when Christ was incarnated. Nevertheless, I am confident that it wasn't on December twenty-fifth. Let me give you several reasons why this could not have been the date of the incarnation:

- The shepherds would not have been in the fields at that time of year.[38]
- Travel was virtually impossible at that time of year, so Caesar Augustus would not have called for taxation, which would have required such movement.

- Because Jews do not commemorate birthdays, the date would not have been preserved.
- The date of December twenty-fifth has an unsavory and questionable history.[39]

Unsubstantiated, but believed by some, is that the records of the rotation of the priests survived despite a colorful history! If the course of Zechariah is known and accurate, the birth of John can be determined as well as the birth of Jesus—in the seventh month.

KING OF THE JEWS

Israel rejected God as King twice.[40] Nevertheless, God established Himself as Israel's King, installing Jesus upon the throne of David to reign on His holy hill:

> *Why do the nations rage, and the people plot a vain thing? The kings of the earth set themselves, and the rulers take counsel together, against the LORD and against His Anointed, saying,*
>
> *"Let us break their bonds in pieces and cast away their cords from us."*
>
> *He who sits in the heavens shall laugh; the LORD shall hold them in derision. Then He shall speak to them in His wrath, and distress them in His deep displeasure: "Yet I have set My King on My holy hill of Zion.*
>
> *I will declare the decree: the LORD has said to Me, "You are My Son, today I have begotten You. Ask of Me, and I will give You the nations for Your inheritance, and the ends of the earth for Your possession. You*

shall break them with a rod of iron; You shall dash them to pieces like a potter's vessel."

Now therefore, be wise, O kings; be instructed, you judges of the earth. Serve the LORD with fear, and rejoice with trembling. Kiss the Son, lest He be angry, and you perish in the way, when His wrath is kindled but a little. Blessed are all those who put their trust in Him.
—Psalm 2

Jesus is the fulfillment of the prophecy given to Isaiah:

For unto us a Child is born, unto us a Son is given; and the government will be upon His shoulder. And His name will be called Wonderful, Counselor, Mighty God, Everlasting Father, Prince of Peace. Of the increase of His government and peace there will be no end, upon the throne of David and over His kingdom, to order it and establish it with judgment and justice.
—Isaiah 9:6-7

Mary's child was born and God's Son was given to rule and reign in an everlasting Kingdom:

Then the angel said to her, "Do not be afraid, Mary, for you have found favor with God. And behold, you will conceive in your womb and bring forth a Son, and shall call His name JESUS. He will be great, and will be called the Son of the Highest; and the Lord God will give Him the throne of His father David. And He will reign over the house of Jacob forever, and of His kingdom there will be no end."
—Luke 1:30-33

Even the Gentiles recognized His kingship both at His birth and at His death.[41]

KING OF ALL KINGS

Christ Jesus is King not only of Israel, but of all Kings:

> *...to Him was given dominion and glory and a kingdom, that all peoples, nations, and languages should serve Him. His dominion is an everlasting dominion, which shall not pass away, and His kingdom the one which shall not be destroyed.* —*Daniel 7:14*

He is Lord of all Lords and King of all Kings, Lord of the living and the dead.[42] All things are under His feet; every knee will bow and every tongue will confess that Jesus is Lord.[43]

Any questions?

CHRIST HAS ALL AUTHORITY

Jesus is far above all rule and authority, power and dominion, and every title that can be given. Angels, powers, and authorities are subject to Him.[44]

Just before He ascended, Jesus made this bold proclamation:

> *All authority has been given to Me in heaven and on earth.* —*Matthew 28:18*

To those who say that Jesus never claimed to be God, consider Christ's presumption if this were not true, claiming the same authority as God the Father. So I ask, "Which part of 'all' do you not understand?"

- Jesus has the authority to judge.[45]
- Jesus has the authority to forgive sins.[46]

- Jesus has authority over sickness.[47]
- Jesus has authority over creation.[48]

Above all, Jesus has authority over death: His, mine, and yours![49] As it is written:

> *Death is swallowed up in victory. O Death, where is your sting? O Hades, where is your victory?*
> *—1 Corinthians 15:54-55*

Why, I wonder, do we constantly question or try to usurp God's authority?

Return of the King

There are two, perhaps three, events associated with the coming of the King that we can include in our study of Blowing of Trumpets.

REGATHERING OF ISRAEL

The regathering of the people is a prophetic fulfillment of this feast. Notice:

> *And it shall come to pass in that day that the LORD will thresh, from the channel of the River to the Brook of Egypt; and you will be gathered one by one, O you children of Israel. So it shall be in that day: The great trumpet will be blown; they will come, who are about to perish in the land of Assyria, and they who are outcasts in the land of Egypt, and shall worship the LORD in the holy mount at Jerusalem.*
> *—Isaiah 27:12-13*

Challenging my belief in God, my brother once asked, "Where are the miracles today?" "Israel," I responded. No other country, people, or language was brought back to life after an absence of thousands of years. The great cultures of the past have all disappeared, but as Tevye in *Fiddler on the Roof* sang, "We're still here!" One day we will *all* be here, on the holy mount in Jerusalem!

SALVATION OF ISRAEL

The prophet Zechariah conjoins the return of Jesus with the salvation of Israel. First notice the command to the Jewish people:

> *Rejoice greatly, O daughter of Zion! Shout, O daughter of Jerusalem! Behold, your King is coming to you; He is just and having salvation, lowly and riding on a donkey, a colt, the foal of a donkey.*
> —*Zechariah 9:9*

You might be way ahead of me by now. The Hebrew translation of the New Testament translates *shout* as [*rua'*], the root of [*t*ᵉ*ru'ah*]—the name of this holiday!

Continuing:

> *Then the LORD will be seen over them, and His arrow will go forth like lightning. The Lord GOD will blow the trumpet, and go with whirlwinds from the south. The LORD of hosts will defend them; they shall devour and subdue with slingstones… The LORD their God will save them in that day, as the flock of His people. For they shall be like the jewels of a crown, lifted like a banner over His land.*
> —*Zechariah 9:14-16*[50]

Verse nine was fulfilled when Jesus rode into Jerusalem the week before Passover. The remainder of the text will be fulfilled when Jesus returns and all of Israel will be saved.

Did you notice the description the prophet uses for Israel? They will be "like the jewels of a crown." I believe that the royal diadem that we sing about is Israel and the Jewish people:

All hail the power of Jesus name,
let angels prostrate fall;

Bring forth the royal diadem
and crown Him Lord of all,

Ye chosen seed of Israel's race,
ye ransomed from the Fall;

Hail Him who saves you by His
grace, and crown Him Lord of all.[51]

Israel's salvation, life from the dead, is truly a reason to shout and blow trumpets!

THE RAPTURE OF THE CHURCH

Among Christian evangelicals, there is a common theory called pre-tribulation rapture, contending that the "last great trump" is referring to this feast. Consider these verses:

> *Then the sign of the Son of Man will appear in heaven, and then all the tribes of the earth will mourn, and they will see the Son of Man coming on the clouds of heaven with power and great glory. And He will send His angels with a great sound of a trumpet, and they will gather together His elect from the four winds, from one end of heaven to the other.*
> *—Matthew 24:30-31*

For the Lord Himself will descend from heaven with a shout, with the voice of an archangel, and with the trumpet of God. And the dead in Christ will rise first. Then we who are alive and remain shall be caught up together with them in the clouds to meet the Lord in the air.
—1 Thessalonians 4:16-17

Behold, I tell you a mystery: We shall not all sleep, but we shall all be changed—in a moment, in the twinkling of an eye, at the last trumpet. For the trumpet will sound, and the dead will be raised incorruptible, and we shall be changed.
—1 Corinthians 15:51-52

As much as there would be great symmetry to God's redemptive festival calendar if Jesus returned on Blowing of Trumpets, the timing poses some challenges:[52]

- We do not know the exact time, much less the exact day, of Christ's return.
- The timing of Zechariah 12:10 is not specified.
- The final trumpet blast recorded in Scripture, Revelation 11:15, follows many of God's judgments on earth.

It is possible Christ will return on Blowing of Trumpets, but that is for God alone to know.

The Coronation of the King

While I am not presuming to schedule the Day of the Lord on this Feast, there might be a correlation with the memorial blowing of trumpets.

THE FINAL TRUMP—THE DAY OF THE LORD

There will be seven trumpet sounds in heaven in the end of days:

> *When He opened the seventh seal, there was silence in heaven for about half an hour. And I saw the seven angels who stand before God, and to them were given seven trumpets... Then the angel took the censer, filled it with fire from the altar, and threw it to the earth. And there were noises, thunderings, lightnings, and an earthquake. So the seven angels who had the seven trumpets prepared themselves to sound.*
>
> *—Revelation 8:1-2, 5-6*

By the end of the sixth trumpet, there will be unimaginable destruction:

- One third of the earth and trees will be burned, as well as all the green grass.

- One third of the sea will be turned to blood, killing one third of its life, and one third of all ships will be destroyed.
- One third of waters will be turned bitter, and many will die.
- One third of the sun, moon, and stars will be turned dark, affecting one third of night and day.
- An invasion of locusts will torture all those without God's seal of protection.
- One third of all mankind will die by plagues of fire, smoke, and sulphur.

Then, at the seventh trumpet, worship will erupt in heaven for the long-awaited coronation of the King:

> *Then the seventh angel sounded: And there were loud voices in heaven, saying, "The kingdoms of this world have become the kingdoms of our Lord and of His Christ, and He shall reign forever and ever!"*
> *—Revelation 11:15*

I suggest that the final trump begins what the Bible calls "The Day of the Lord" as the King brings His judgment to the earth.

The joint celebration of the Blowing of Trumpets and New Moon of the seventh month marks another of God's "new beginnings." Perhaps the rabbis are right, that this holiday can be used as a time for reflection and restoration of our relationship with God and with each other. May this holiday be a time of preparation.

PREPARING TO MEET THE JUDGE

Standing before a judge is very stressful, even if you're innocent. My day in court was the result of my failure to renew my driver's license on time. It didn't matter that I was only two blocks from the Transportation Office; the policeman was correct in giving me a ticket. I was guilty, so there was no way to appeal except in person before the judge. Waiting for my turn seemed endless as I watched person after person plead his innocence only to be judged, "Guilty!" No one convinced the judge. No one escaped judgment and a fine. As I waited, I kept thinking of the day when I will stand before another Judge.

Jesus Himself warns us that every idle word will be proclaimed that all might hear:

> *For there is nothing covered that will not be revealed, nor hidden that will not be known. Therefore whatever you have spoken in the dark will be heard in the light, and what you have spoken in the ear in inner rooms will be proclaimed on the housetops.*
> *—Luke 12:2-3*

I don't know your reaction to that warning, but it sure terrifies me. To think we can stand before God clothed in our own righteousness is more than folly; it is a deception that leads to eternal destruction:

> *"But who can endure the day of His coming? And who can stand when He appears? ... And I will come near you for judgment; I will be a swift witness against sorcerers, against adulterers, against perjurers, against those who exploit wage earners and widows and orphans, and against those who turn away an alien—because they do not fear Me," says the LORD of hosts.*
> *—Malachi 3:2-5*

Notice that the last five words of the Lord quoted by Malachi are, "they do not fear Me." Lacking fear of God, the reverential awe, respect, and honor that He deserves, leads us into sin.

I experienced fear as I sat in that court room. The hours droned on and my anxiety increased. The fact that the policeman hadn't seen the previous extension, thinking I was years overdue instead of just a few weeks, really didn't matter. I was guilty. I had no excuse. I had no option. All I could do was bow my head and accept the judgment.

My name was called. With shaking knees, I approached the bench.

The rabbis were correct about one aspect of Days of Awe; God will open His books and we will stand before God for judgment:[53]

> *And I saw the dead, small and great, standing before God, and books were opened. And another book was opened, which is the Book of Life. And the dead were judged according to their works, by the things which were written in the books . . . And they were judged, each one according to his works . . . And anyone not found written in the Book of Life was cast into the lake of fire.*
> —*Revelation 20:12, 13b, 15*

The Scripture above affirms that all people—the living and the dead, the great and the small—will be judged according to God's standards.

Grace and mercy were extended to me by an earthly judge. I was exonerated. The judge looked at my license, looked at me, and declared, "Not guilty." The ticket was expunged and my record was clean, as if my crime had never been committed.

So much more is the grace and mercy that will be extended to me by the heavenly Judge because of the righteousness of Jesus. Remember, nothing is hidden from His judgment except that which is already forgiven. Paul's letter to the Romans gives us hope:

> *But now the righteousness of God . . . through faith in Jesus Christ, to all and on all who believe . . . being justified freely by His grace through the redemption that is in Christ Jesus.* —*Romans 3:21-22, 24*

O the praise and thanksgiving we can give Jesus who has promised:

> *There is therefore now no condemnation to those who are in Christ Jesus.* —*Romans 8:1a; cf. 5:16-19*

Clothed in the righteousness of Jesus, we can enter into God's grace with boldness.[54]

There still remains another throne of judgment where everything we have done for Jesus will be judged:

> *Therefore we make it our aim, whether present or absent, to be well pleasing to Him. For we must all appear before the judgment seat of Christ, that each one may receive the things done in the body, according to what he has done, whether good or bad.*
> —*2 Corinthians 5:9-10*

At that time, fire will reveal the foundations upon which we have built. That which endures will receive rewards, but that which is burnt will suffer loss:

> *No other foundation can anyone lay than that which is laid, which is Jesus Christ. Now if anyone builds on this foundation with gold, silver, precious stones, wood, hay,*

straw, each one's work will become clear; for the Day will declare it, because it will be revealed by fire; and the fire will test each one's work, of what sort it is. If anyone's work which he has built on it endures, he will receive a reward. If anyone's work is burned, he will suffer loss; but he himself will be saved, yet so as through fire.
—1 Corinthians 3:11-15[55]

As the trumpets called a warning to Israel, so let them sound an alarm in our hearts. May this holiday be a "selah" to stop our busyness, catch our breaths, take stock of our lives, and ask ourselves, "Am I ready?"

PREPARING TO MEET THE KING

Consider again the amazing grace and goodness of our God and King, who daily loads us with blessings, promising us every spiritual blessing in the heavenlies, and yet still rewards us for doing what we were created to do![56]

Time and space do not permit me to review the myriad of ways Scripture tells us to prepare to stand before the King. Esther spent a year preparing for one night with her king. We have our entire lives. Whereas Esther was uncertain if she would be accepted, we have absolute assurance that we have been chosen and that we will stand holy, pure, and blameless before Him as a spotless bride.[57]

Now that's reason enough to sound the trumpets in praise and worship!

BLOW THE TRUMPET IN ZION

As you are preparing yourself, do not forget that we must prepare others.

All that we have discussed about evangelism is applicable to this holiday as well. Remember that one of God's primary purposes for these holidays is to fill the earth with the knowledge of His glory. In other words, use each of these holy days to evangelize the lost and bring revival to the believer.

You are God's witness. You are His trumpet. Let Him speak through you constantly. As we each blow the trumpets of our lives, we make a magnificent sound.

Day of Atonement is the next holiday on God's festal calendar.

Endnotes

1. Some evangelical teachers believe there is a prophetic significance to Israel, which I will address later.
2. Ezra 3:6.
3. Nehemiah 8:2.
4. Numbers 23:21; 31:6; 2 Chronicles 13:12; Jeremiah 20:16; 49:2; Ezekiel 21:22; Amos 1:14.
5. Numbers 10:5-6.
6. Job 8:21.
7. 1 Samuel 4:5-6; Ezra 3:11-13; Job 33:26; Psalm 27:6; 33:3; 89:15.
8. Exodus 19:19; 20:18; Revelation 4:1.
9. Leviticus 25:9.
10. Judges 7:16ff.
11. Judges 3:27; 6:34; 1 Samuel 13:3; 2 Samuel 20:1; Nehemiah 4:1, 20; Isaiah 18:3; Jeremiah 4:5, 27; Ezekiel 33:3ff; Joel 2:1; Zechariah 9:14 (partial list).
12. 2 Samuel 2:28; 18:16; 20:22.
13. 2 Samuel 15:10; 1 Kings 1:34, 41; 2 Kings 9:13.
14. Psalm 81:3.
15. Psalm 98:6; 150:3.
16. Joel 2:15.
17. Isaiah 58:2.
18. Isaiah 27:13.
19. Hosea 8:1.
20. Joshua 6:5, 20.
21. 2 Chronicles 15:14.
22. Psalm 47:5; 115:3.
23. Most of these traditional explanations are credited to Moses who, it is said, received not only the written Law but also the oral Law from God on Mt. Sinai.
24. Fruchtenbaum, A. (1986). *Radio Manuscripts*, Ariel Ministries.
25. The Mishna, a collection of sixty-three tractates of the 'oral Law' believed to have been given by God to Moses on Sinai, is the foundation of today's rabbinic Judaism.
26. Tradition teaches there needs to be 100 blasts comprised of three sets plus one final note. The first, "tekia," is a long single blast said to be an expression of joy. The second, "shevarim," is three short blasts representing weeping. The third, "truah," is nine extremely short, staccato notes representing trepidation and sorrow. The final trump is the "tekia gedolah," lasting as long as the blower has breath. This is also called "The Great Trump" and is an expression of the hope of redemption.
27. The practice of Tashlich is not discussed in the Bible, but it is a long-standing custom. See http://judaism.about.com/od/roshhashana/a/shana_tashlich.htm.

28. Daniel 12:1-2; Isaiah 66:24; John 5:28-29; Acts 24:15.
29. Psalm 9:8; 50:6; 94:2.
30. Psalm 89:14; 92:15.
31. Exodus 20:5; Joshua 24:19.
32. Deuteronomy 10:17; Romans 2:11; Colossians 3:25.
33. Numbers 23:19; 1 Samuel 15:29; Malachi 3:6.
34. Psalm 7:11; 18:25-26; 119:137; Nehemiah 9:33; Job 34:10-12.
35. See "*Passover: Spiritual*."
36. Luke 1:30.
37. Luke 19:44; 2:25-38.
38. Because of the rain and cold, sheep were corralled from October to April.
39. From Charlemagne to Constantine, pagan festivals (e.g., Saturnalia, Sol Invictus) and legends ("miraculous" birth of Tammuz) have coincided with the date of December 25th, leading one to wonder which influenced which.
40. 1 Samuel 8:1ff; John 19:15.
41. Matthew 2:2; Luke 2:38.
42. 1 Timothy 6:15; Revelation 17:14; 19:16; Romans 14:9.
43. Philippians 2:10-11; Isaiah 45:23; Romans 14:11; 1 Corinthians 15:27.
44. Ephesians 1:21; 1 Peter 3:22.
45. Acts 17:31.
46. Matthew 9:1-6.
47. Matthew 9:20ff; 15:30; Mark 8:22-26; John 9 (partial list).
48. John 2:1-11; Matthew 15:21-28; 14:22-23; 8:23-27.
49. Matthew 9:18ff; Luke 7:11-16.
50. Trumpet: [*shofar*]; save [*yasha'*].
51. Perronet, Edward. "All Hail the Power of Jesus' Name." (1779).
52. The spring and summer feasts were fulfilled on the actual feast day by the death, burial, and resurrection of Jesus and the giving of the Holy Spirit. For the symmetry to apply to the feasts of the fall, it would require each of the prophetic events in the redemptive plan for the future to occur on the appropriate feast days.
53. Romans 14:12.
54. Hebrews 4:16.
55. See also: Matthew 16:27; Revelation 22:12.
56. Psalm 68:19; Ephesians 1:3; 2:10.
57. Ephesians 1:4; 5:27; Colossians 1:22.

Chapter Thirteen

13

Day of Atonement

Day of National Repentance

And the LORD spoke to Moses, saying: "Also the tenth day of this seventh month shall be the Day of Atonement. It shall be a holy convocation for you; you shall afflict your souls, and offer an offering made by fire to the LORD. And you shall do no work on that same day, for it is the Day of Atonement, to make atonement for you before the LORD your God. For any person who is not afflicted in soul on that same day shall be cut off from his people. And any person who does any work on that same day, that person I will destroy from among his people ... it shall be a statute forever throughout your generations in all your dwellings. It shall be to you a sabbath of solemn rest, and you shall afflict your souls; on the ninth day of the month at evening, from evening to evening, you shall celebrate your sabbath."

—Leviticus 23:26-32

In my first year as a follower of Christ, the Day of Atonement (Yom Kippur) was approaching. I asked my pastor, "The holidays are coming; what do we do?" [1]

He replied, "*We* don't do anything. You don't understand. Christ has done it all."

"But Pastor, it's you who doesn't understand. Every year on the Day of Atonement I sat in the synagogue praying, begging God to forgive me of my sins, but at the end of the day, I never knew if I'd been forgiven. I even asked the rabbi one day, 'How do we know that our sins are forgiven?' He could only tell me, 'We don't know, but because God is merciful, we just act as though we're forgiven.' Pastor, now that I *know* I'm forgiven, I want to CELEBRATE!"

My family was considered liberal, or Reform Jews, yet this holiday was important to us. You could say this was the defining time of the year in our identity as Jews. We might not have attended the synagogue any other time of the year, but we were always there on the Day of Atonement. In fact, we usually spent most of the day there. Eagerly I waited for the time I was considered old enough to fast for the duration of the holiday.

This day remains the holiest of all the biblical feast days for Jewish people around the world.[2] For many, it is the one time of the year when they consider the reality of sin.

The Hebrew verb *atone* is [*kafar*]. In our study of Unleavened Bread, we learned that it means *to appease, make amends, to make atonement.*[3] The noun *atonement* is the resulting *satisfaction or reparation of wrong doings.*[4] In its theological sense, it is the reconciliation of God and man by means of the atoning propitiation.

Let's explore this most solemn day on God's calendar.

Seasonal

Day of Atonement comes five days after Blowing of Trumpets and is the second of the fall holidays in the seventh month.

After seven sabbatical agricultural years, the year of Jubilee (the fiftieth year) is proclaimed by the blowing of the trumpet on the Day of Atonement:

> *And you shall count seven sabbaths of years for yourself, seven times seven years; and the time of the seven sabbaths of years shall be to you forty-nine years. Then you shall cause the trumpet of the Jubilee to sound on the tenth day of the seventh month; on the Day of Atonement you shall make the trumpet to sound throughout all your land. And you shall consecrate the fiftieth year, and proclaim liberty throughout all the land to all its inhabitants.*
> *—Leviticus 25:8-10a*

National

God dwelled in the midst of Israel, and the entire nation was expected to live according to God's holy standards.[5] As the people could not, atonement was necessary for the entire nation.[6] Furthermore, they were required to afflict their souls: their minds, their hearts, and their wills.[7]

The verb *to afflict* means *to oppress, humble, be bowed down, to be put down, become low, to be depressed, be downcast.*[8] Another word for affliction of the soul is repentance. Affliction of the soul is a necessary step on the way toward atonement.

You might ask, "How can one afflict his own soul?" The answer is by recognizing our sins in the face of God's holiness. As we see the horror of our sins and the holiness of our Savior, we afflict, or humble, our souls. I believe this affliction results in accepting the honor of serving our wonderful Lord.

Interestingly, the Hebrew form for Day of Atonement is plural (atonements), thus reflecting the purpose of the holiday. On this day, the priest would make atonement for the corporate sins of the nation. Jewish people today have changed the purpose of this holiday by focusing on their personal sins. But God expects individuals to confess and repent for their sins on a daily basis.

Let's consider the other unique elements of this holiday.

NO WORK PERMITTED

God commands a complete cessation of work on Sabbath and on Atonement. On the other holidays, He simply commands a cessation of customary work. On Atonement, His command goes further, declaring that anyone who works will be destroyed, eliminated, killed!

> *For any person who is not afflicted in soul on that same day shall be cut off from his people. And any person who does any work on that same day, that person I will destroy from among his people.*
> *—Leviticus 23:29-30*

ELABORATE DETAILS

While we hear echoes and references to Passover throughout Scripture, Atonement exceeds Passover in its minutiae of details. Leviticus 16 is devoted to its observance, and the holiday is the basis for the entire letter written to the Hebrews.

EMPHASIS

This holiday emphasizes the High Priest and the atoning sacrifices.

- The High Priest

  Day of Atonement was the only time that the High Priest was permitted to enter the Holy of Holies. I don't think we can fathom the intensity and solemnity of that responsibility. Any mistake could be fatal, as recorded in Leviticus 10, when Nadab and Abihu offered profane fire.

  Before entering, the High Priest had to perform an elaborate ritual of cleansing—bathing his entire body twice. Furthermore, he exchanged his golden robes for plain white linen, which was discarded at the end of the day.

  The Most Holy place was dark, lit only by the censer of burning coals, which the priest carried within. Besides the censer, the priest also carried sweet incense, possibly frankincense.

  Before making atonement for Israel, the priest had to make atonement for himself, for the priesthood, and for the sanctuary.

- Dual sin offerings

  Another unique feature of this holiday was the dual offerings for sin. Two goats were to be used, as similar in appearance as possible, so it would appear that both goats were one sacrifice:

Then Aaron shall cast lots for the two goats: one lot for the LORD and the other lot for the scapegoat. And Aaron shall bring the goat on which the LORD's lot fell, and offer it as a sin offering. But the goat on which the lot fell to be the scapegoat shall be presented alive before the LORD, to make atonement upon it, and to let it go as the scapegoat into the wilderness.
—Leviticus 16:8-10

The order of the offerings was important. First, the priest would sacrifice the goat for YHWH. Then he turned the scapegoat toward the people:

Aaron shall lay both his hands on the head of the live goat, confess over it all the iniquities of the children of Israel, and all their transgressions, concerning all their sins, putting them on the head of the goat, and shall send it away into the wilderness by the hand of a suitable man. The goat shall bear on itself all their iniquities to an uninhabited land; and he shall release the goat in the wilderness.
—Leviticus 16:21-22

Sins had to be atoned for through the shedding of blood before they could be removed!

Though not recorded in Scripture, the holy day is traditionally concluded with a feast, a most fitting response to forgiveness of sins:

Blessed is he whose transgression is forgiven, whose sin is covered. Blessed is the man to whom the LORD does not impute iniquity. *—Psalm 32:1-2a*

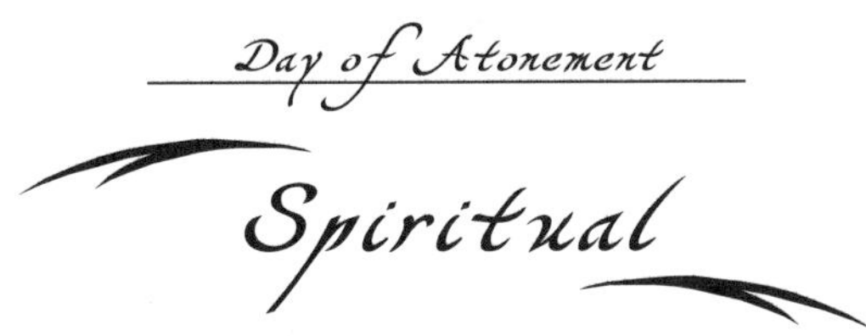

God's holiness and His grace are highlighted on this holiday. God's holiness is intolerant of sin and results in His just punishment for the sinner. His grace provides the means (atonement) by which that same sinner can be forgiven.

HOLINESS

And the LORD spoke to Moses, saying, "Speak to all the congregation of the children of Israel, and say to them: 'You shall be holy, for I the LORD your God am holy.'"
—Leviticus 19:1-2

We often overlook God's holiness, preferring His grace. Yet without recognizing the extent of His holiness, we will not fully appreciate His grace, which enables us to stand before Him:

If You, LORD, should mark iniquities, O LORD, who could stand? *—Psalm 130:3*

Who may ascend into the hill of the LORD? Or who may stand in His holy place? *—Psalm 24:3*

Consider how swiftly God responded to those who would not honor Him with obedience: Nadab, Abihu, Uzzah, Ananias, and Sapphira.[9]

God's holiness is also the focus of worship in heaven:

And they do not rest day or night, saying: "Holy, holy, holy, Lord God Almighty, Who was and is and is to come!"
—Revelation 4:8b

GRACE

Juxtaposed with God's holiness is His grace. The psalmist well understood the tension between God's holiness and His grace. He understood that only by God's grace could there be salvation, deliverance, and atonement:

> *Help us, O God of our salvation, for the glory of Your name; and deliver us, and provide atonement for our sins, for Your name's sake!* —*Psalm 79:9*

We've studied the Hebrew for grace, mercy, and loving kindness. Now let's look at *grace* in Greek: [*charis*]. Interestingly, of the 190 times *charis* is used in the Septuagint, 61 of the 75 times where there is a direct equivalent, *charis* is used for the Hebrew [*chen*], which we discussed in "Passover: Spiritual":[10]

> The use of the Hebrew [*chen*] clarifies the meaning of 'grace' in history. It denotes the stronger coming to the help of the weaker, who stands in need of help by reason of his circumstances or natural weakness. He (the stronger) acts by a voluntary decision, though he is moved by the dependence or the request of the weaker party.[11]

Christ's incarnation and crucifixion were the ultimate fulfillments of God's grace, His coming "down to deliver them":[12]

> *Being justified freely by His grace through the redemption that is in Christ Jesus, whom God set forth as propitiation by His blood.* —*Romans 3:24-25a*

I often meet people who say, "Any God who would willingly sacrifice His Son, allowing Him to be tortured and suffer, is not a God I want." And yet, despite the horror of the cross, Isaiah tells us that extending His grace by providing atonement gave (and continues to give) God pleasure:

> *Yet it pleased the* LORD *to bruise Him; He has put Him to grief.*
> —*Isaiah 53:10a*

The word *pleased* [*chafetz*] means the same in Hebrew as it does in English, *to take delight in, to feel great favor toward something.*[13]

Obviously, God's idea of pleasure surpasses and transcends ours. Pleased? God was pleased to bruise His "only begotten Son in whom He was well pleased."[14] How could God the Father be pleased to bruise His Son? Is the Father a sadist, or was Jesus a masochist? No! God could be pleased because of His grace—His grace and love for you!

God the Father was pleased to be gracious. He was pleased to provide our atonement. Jesus, God the Son, was pleased—joyful—to be that atonement.[15]

O the depth and breadth and height of God's grace!

Redemptive

Jesus fulfilled every aspect of the Day of Atonement as both the High Priest and the propitiation for sin. Furthermore, He was a better mediator of a better covenant.

We do not know the tenure or the scope of responsibilities of the High Priest. What we do know is that he was the only one permitted into the Holy of Holies, and then only on the Day of Atonement. His ministry on that day was so critical that, by the second temple period, he was annually instructed in the details of the ritual.

Remember the announcement of John when he saw Jesus, "Behold, the Lamb of God who takes away the sin of the world," as recorded in John 1:29? In this one sentence, two Levitical holidays were combined: Passover and Atonement. On Passover, a lamb was killed, but it was never meant to be a sin offering. On Atonement, it was a goat that bore and carried away sins. Jesus is both the Passover Lamb and the sacrifice of Atonement.

JESUS IS A BETTER HIGH PRIEST

According to historians, within a few years after Israel returned from Babylon, the priesthood was corrupted. The office (which God ordained to be hereditary) had denigrated into cabal, crime, or bribery.[16] The priests were undisciplined men, easily given to temptation.

Every year the High Priest had to make atonement for himself before he could make atonement for the people. Jesus, who was without sin, had no need to make atonement for Himself.

The final word of Jesus on the cross, "It is finished!" is the Greek word [*tetelestai*] from the root [*teleo*], which means *to bring to a conclusion, accomplish, finish*.[17] Jesus' death was completely efficacious, thus ending the need for additional atoning sacrifices. His resurrection ended the need for the Levitical priesthood:

> *He, because He continues forever, has an unchangeable priesthood. Therefore He is also able to save to the uttermost those who come to God through Him, since He always lives to make intercession for them. For such a High Priest was fitting for us, who is holy, harmless, undefiled, separate from sinners, and has become higher than the heavens; who does not need daily, as those high priests, to offer up sacrifices, first for His own sins and then for the people's,*

for this He did once for all when He offered up Himself.
—Hebrews 7:24-27

As a man, Jesus knew all the temptations we face: "In all their affliction, He was afflicted."[18] Able to understand by experience all of our weaknesses, He is able to extend grace, aid, and strength for any of our temptations and needs:

> *For we do not have a High Priest who cannot sympathize with our weaknesses, but was in all points tempted as we are, yet without sin. Let us therefore come boldly to the throne of grace, that we may obtain mercy and find grace to help in time of need.*
> *—Hebrews 4:15-16*

Who among us hasn't experienced temptation? I wear a ring especially designed to remind me that, because He understands, Jesus will always provide an escape from any temptation I might face.[19]

JESUS IS A BETTER MEDIATOR OF A BETTER COVENANT

The High Priest was responsible to make intercession for the people before God. Jesus, as the ultimate High Priest, is the better mediator. By His death, He made intercession for us all; and by His life, He continues to do so.[20]

A common misconception among the Jewish people is that it is unnecessary to have a mediator between man and God. I had often insisted, "I don't need a middle man to pray to God." And yet, the entire system of the temple was based on the need to have a mediator, especially on the Day of Atonement. Normally, it was the sinner himself who laid his hands upon his offering, transferring his sins to the animal. But on Atonement, the priest had to place the sins of all Israel onto the scapegoat:

> *For on that day the priest shall make atonement for you, to cleanse you that you may be clean from all your sins before the LORD.*
> *—Leviticus 16:30*

Even before the temple, Moses, then Phinehas, had mediated (interceded) between Israel and God.

As a better priesthood was needed, a new covenant was necessary. The new covenant was cut (all covenants are cut) by the sacrifice of Jesus. Jesus said over the cup of redemption, "This cup is the new covenant in My blood."[21] He exchanged His death for our life; He gave His life that we might have new life, abundant and eternal.

From the moment I entered into the new covenant through faith in Jesus, I really did feel born again. There was newness about everything. I was a new creation. But that was only the beginning of the transformation that is still taking place in my life.

A transformed life is only one of the blessings of the new covenant. Consider just a few improvements over the Mosaic covenant:

- Adoption, becoming a child of God
- Better promises
- Circumcision of the heart, changing it from stone to flesh
- Eliminating, not just covering, sins
- Indwelling of the Holy Spirit
- Assurance of everlasting life

JESUS IS A BETTER SACRIFICE

Day of Atonement is about Christ and the cross. During the movie *The Passion*, many people closed their eyes rather than watch the brutality inflicted upon Jesus. But we must not turn away from the cross. We must not avert our eyes from Christ's suffering and shame. Nor can we see the cross as anything other than His absolute surrender to the love of His Father. The cross stands as a beacon in the midst of darkness, a lighthouse in the storm:

- It is seen by sinners and shunned by the wicked.
- It is gory, yet glorious.
- It wasn't fair, yet defines love.
- It doesn't make sense, and yet is perfectly logical.
- It is as efficacious today as it was yesterday, and will be tomorrow.

Through the cross, Jesus' sacrifice fulfilled the dual offerings required:

- He was the offering for sin, bearing on His broken body the punishment that brings us peace.
- He was the scapegoat that carried our sins into the uninhabited land of the grave.

Eschatological

While Jesus has already fulfilled many aspects of the Day of Atonement, there remains the issue of Israel's corporate repentance. To the praise and glory of God, there will be a day when Israel recognizes Jesus as her Messiah and repents:

And I will pour on the house of David and on the inhabitants of Jerusalem the Spirit of grace and supplication; then they will look on Me whom they pierced. Yes, they will mourn for Him as one mourns for his only son, and grieve for Him as one grieves for a firstborn. In that day there shall be a great mourning in Jerusalem.
—Zechariah 12:10-11

Repentance was my response the moment I recognized Jesus as my Savior.

I was watching a sculptor shape the bust of Jesus out of clay, accompanied by the words of Isaiah 53. Suddenly the artist began to beat the clay; what appeared to be blood spurted out of the then misshapen head. This was a much different picture of Jesus than I had seen before. This Jesus understood rejection. This Jesus understood betrayal. This Jesus knew abandonment. This Jesus suffered, and He suffered for me!

I wanted this Jesus.

I didn't understand much more than that. I didn't understand the "Why?" of the cross. I needed Jesus, and that was enough for me. In a moment of revelation, I had my answer about the Day of Atonement. The rabbi had forgotten the words of Moses:

For the life of the flesh is in the blood, and I have given it to you upon the altar to make atonement for your souls; for it is the blood that makes atonement for the soul.
—Leviticus 17:11

I understood the gospel message in that moment. I had my answer. The why of the cross led me to repentance. And repentance resulted in my being forgiven:

If we confess our sins, He is faithful and just to forgive us our sins and to cleanse us from all unrighteousness.
—1 John 1:9

The same will be true for the nation of Israel. One day, Jesus will return to Jerusalem, where He will be seen and recognized by the Jewish people. Refined and purified, Israel will cry out:

"Barukh haba' b^{e}shem 'adonay!"
Blessed is He who comes in the name of the Lord![24]

And in that day, the Day of Atonement will be fulfilled:

For I do not desire, brethren, that you should be ignorant of this mystery, lest you should be wise in your own opinion, that blindness in part has happened to Israel until the fullness of the Gentiles has come in. And so all Israel will be saved, as it is written: "The Deliverer will come out of Zion, and He will turn away ungodliness from Jacob; for this is My covenant with them, when I take away their sins."
—Romans 11:25-27

Kingdom

Neither my pastor nor I knew the extent of the personal application of this holy day. For my Gentile pastor, it had no real significance. For me, a Jewish follower of Jesus, it was a time to rejoice. Many years later, I know that there are crucial and relevant applications of this holiday to all of our lives: to the lost—both Jews and Gentiles, and to Christians—both Jewish and Gentile. Let's consider just a few.

REPENTANCE

Before knowing Christ, my thoughts and feelings were in turmoil as the Day of Atonement ended. Tired and hungry, I wanted to eat, but I knew that food would not satisfy my real hunger. Even after many hours of prayers, I questioned, "Had I really done penance?" I was remorseful, but had I repented?

Jewish followers of Jesus are often ostracized by unbelieving Jews who criticize us for converting to another religion. Actually, that accusation is half true. We have converted, but not to another religion. What do the words *convert* and *repent* mean, and how are they applicable to this holiday?

The most common use of *convert* is to change from one religion to another, or to adopt a new religion. But technically, *convert* means to change into something of different form or properties, to transform, to change in character.[25] Transformation of character is the fruit of repentance; therefore, we can consider conversion to be the effect of repentance.

The Hebrew word for *repent* is [*shub*] and means *to return, or to turn back*. Theologically it has two elements: turning away from evil and turning back to God. Repentance is a responsibility of a covenant relationship with God:

> To be sure there is no systematic spelling out of the doctrine of repentance in the Old Testament, it is illustrated (Psalm 1) more than anything else. Yet the fact that the people are called [to repent] implies that sin is not an ineradicable stain; but by turning, a God-given power, a sinner can redirect his destiny.[26]

Repentance affects God's response to man. We see in Jonah 3:9-10 that a change in man's conduct resulted in a stay of God's judgment. The New Testament expands the meaning of repentance to include the mind, the emotions, and the will:

> When men are called to conversion, it means a fundamentally new turning of the human will to God ... Conversion and surrender of the life to God is done by faith in Jesus Christ. Such conversion leads to a fundamental change of the whole of life. It receives a new outlook and objectives ... The effect of conversion is the forgiveness of all sins.[27]

Repentance is often missing from our gospel presentations, but it is the foundation and fundamental ingredient in receiving God's forgiveness, subsequently making Christ's atonement efficacious for the sinner. True repentance must include action and will result in a transformation of behavior.

For the Kingdom community, repentance is not an option; it is a way of life.

BRINGING GOD PLEASURE

Earlier we considered what God does that pleases Him. On this holiday of Atonement, consider what pleases God in our lives:

- Faith[28]
- To walk humbly, justly, and with mercy[29]
- Truth in the innermost parts[30]
- A broken and contrite heart[31]

Have you considered how much pleasure you give to God when you accept His offer of salvation? Listen to the words of Isaiah:

> *When You make His soul an offering for sin, He shall see His seed, He shall prolong His days, and the pleasure of the LORD shall prosper in His hand.*
> *—Isaiah 53:10b*

Pleased is the same word that we saw earlier from the same verse. When a sinner makes Jesus an offering for his sin, God's pleasure is satisfied. Not only is His pleasure satisfied, so is His demand for holiness and His offer of grace. Furthermore, we become the fruit of Jesus' labor:

> *Of His own will He brought us forth by the word of truth, that we might be a kind of firstfruits of His creatures.*
> *—James 1:18*

You are His seed, His eternal and everlasting posterity!

WE MUST NOT "NEGLECT SO GREAT A SALVATION"

This warning to the Hebrews (2:3) is just as important today as it was then. The warning is first to those who refuse to accept God's offer of salvation. To them, He continuously extends His love. But there will come a day when He will no longer strive or wait for the wicked to turn to Him.[32]

This warning can also apply to those who confess Jesus as their Atonement (Savior) without making Him their Lord. We neglect His salvation every time we turn away from Him in doubt or disobedience.

In the heart of Jerusalem, there is a garden that many people believe is the actual burial place of Jesus. Right beyond its fence is a rock formation that looks like a skull, lending credibility to its claim of being Golgotha. I often go there to meditate and reflect on the wonder of God's love.

One day, a young woman sat nearby; often people weep in the garden, but her tears seemed different. She was greatly distressed. Apologetically, Dana poured out her complaint: "I just cannot believe God loves me. I keep asking Him to prove His love to me, but He is so silent."

How well I understand that sense of frustration, knowing God hears and understands but being unable to hear His voice, see His salvation, or feel His love.

I have found the best way to remember God's love is to journey to Golgotha, starting at the top of the Mount of Olives. From that hill, God's plan from eternity past until eternity future coalesced in twenty-four hours.

Take a few moments to look at Jerusalem. Look through the eyes of Jesus as He takes one final look at His beloved city. Let your heart break, as His breaks, with love for the people as well as for the city. Look with Him at the city where He has chosen to put His name. Look at the temple with all its ritual sacrifices. See the smoke rising up from the burnt offerings and the altar of incense, filling the city with a sweet but pungent fragrance. Remember the sacrifice Abraham was willing to make. Then consider what may be in the heart of Jesus in knowing that He, the spotless Lamb, is about to be sacrificed by the very people He came to save.

Then allow tears of passion and compassion, tears of love, to flow down your cheeks.

Continue down toward Gethsemane.

Stop at the place where Jesus is scourged. Count the strokes—thirty-nine in all. See His flesh ripped apart. Feel the crown of thorns piercing His scalp.

Walk along the Via Dolorosa. Hear the crowds of people, feel the crush as they press in to get a better look. Listen to their jeers and taunts of mocking. But also hear that some are crying.

Finish your pilgrimage at Golgotha.

Please don't rush to the empty tomb. Pause. Look at Golgotha:

> See from His head, His hands, His feet,
> Sorrow and love flow mingled down!
> Did ere such love and sorrow meet,
> Or thorns compose so rich a crown?[33]

Sorrow. Not shame, but sorrow. Not anger or fear, but sorrow. Sorrow for those who refuse and reject His love. Sorrow for them and for us today. Sorrow for anyone who refuses or neglects so great a salvation.

COME BOLDLY INTO HIS PRESENCE

God's presence began to envelop Dana as I prayed for her. Surprised by a surge of joy, she began to giggle. Embarrassed, she tried to hide her smile. She, like so many, believed that God was unapproachable. However, the words of Scripture assure us that God desires, and has provided for, an intimate and joyful relationship with His children. Because of His grace and mercy, we *can* laugh in God's presence, we *can* enjoy Him, and we *can* approach Him boldly with our needs and concerns. Let us come boldly, but not brashly, into His presence.

Notice that the High Priest had to remove his "golden" robes and put on pure white linen garments: tunic, trousers, sash, and turban. There was nothing in his appearance to identify him as anything other than a repentant seeker of atonement. In like manner, Jesus set aside His glory to humble Himself by wearing the garment of flesh.

We should approach the throne of grace with humility as well as with confidence. How better to embrace and honor God's gift of salvation?

INTERCESSION

I'd like to suggest that intercession is a biblical, practical, and effective Kingdom application for this holiday. I suggest that as Jesus, our High Priest, is making intercession for us, we can use this holiday to make intercession for the Jewish people, the church, our leaders, our countries, and Israel.

Corporate identity is missing from our intercession. According to E.M. Bounds, intercession is "the hallmark of all true prayer as the soul of a man is stirred to plead with God for men."[34] At the heart of intercession is a dichotomy: our fear of God's holiness and our love for those for whom we are interceding. The tension is to keep both emotions in balance. Without a love for the people, we become critical and judgmental, overlooking God's grace and mercy. Yet without a fear of God's holiness, we may overlook the sins of the people.

Thus, the intercessor must identify with both God and the people. In that position, the identification becomes so complete that the people become our people; their corporate sins become our own. We no longer stand apart, separating ourselves from those for whom we are praying.

Besides Jesus, there are other examples of the righteous identifying with the sins of the people. Ezra confessed:

> *O my God, I am too ashamed and humiliated to lift up my face to You, my God; for our iniquities have risen higher than our heads, and our guilt has grown up to the heavens. Since the days of our fathers to this day we have been very guilty, and for our iniquities we, our kings, and our priests have been delivered into the hand of the kings of the lands, to the sword, to captivity, to plunder, and to humiliation, as it is this day.*
> —*Ezra 9:6-7*

Daniel was a righteous man, yet he cried:

> *We have sinned and committed iniquity, we have done wickedly and rebelled, even by departing from Your precepts and Your judgments.* —*Daniel 9:5*

We who are saved and considered righteous (the Kingdom community) can stand before God carrying the burden for the lost. Let your heart break with the litany of their sin. Go beyond your natural affinity for the people, see their sins as God does, and cry out for His mercy. If we will not, who will?

EVANGELISM

In that great and glorious reappearing of Jesus, when Israel will see those nail-scarred hands and all mouths will be shut, faith will come by seeing the Word of God. But until that day, faith will come by hearing it!

We are all called to be watchmen on the wall, to not only warn the lost of God's impending judgment, but also to extend

His offer of salvation. Whether compelled by love or by fear, we cannot keep silent.

Today, the gospel is the best-kept secret. The Jewish people especially believe that Christianity is a religion of Gentiles with no relevance to them. They have no idea:

- The new covenant was first offered to Israel and the Jewish people.
- God's covenant with Israel is eternal.
- Following Jesus is the most Jewish expression of love and faith in the God of Abraham.

Put your prayers for Israel, the world, and your nation into action:

> *O Zion, you who bring good tidings, get up into the high mountain, O Jerusalem, you who bring good tidings, lift up your voice with strength, lift it up, be not afraid; say to the cities of Judah, "Behold your God!"*
> *—Isaiah 40:9*

After the somber holiday of Atonement, the next Levitical holiday has the most joy and celebrates the final chapter in God's redemptive plan.

Endnotes

1. To many Jewish people, Trumpets (Rosh Hashanah) and Atonement (Yom Kippur) are considered "the holidays."
2. The rabbis have imposed more restrictions regarding "work" on this day than on any other, calling Atonement "The Day."
3. HALOT, #4384.
4. Barnhart, C. (Ed.). (1956). *The American College Dictionary.* New York: Random House, p. 79.
5. Exodus 29:45-46; Leviticus 26:12; Numbers 5:3; Deuteronomy 23:14.
6. Today, the importance of a day to repent for their nation's sins is being recognized. In 2008, 214 countries participated in the Global Day of Prayer on May 11. Perhaps one day, this auspicious event could be moved to coincide with God's calendar.
7. Today, many Jewish people afflict their bodies by fasting. While a worthwhile practice, a fast afflicts the body; therefore, one can fast without afflicting one's soul.
8. Strong, J. (1996). *The Exhaustive Concordance of the Bible* [Electronic Form]. Ontario: Woodside Bible Fellowship.
9. Leviticus 10:1-3; 2 Samuel 6:3-6; Acts 5:1-10.
10. In the New Testament, "grace" is primarily a Pauline concept. It is no wonder that this Pharisee scholar who was trained by the doctrine of "justification by works" would be overwhelmed by the miraculous freedom of salvation by an act of God's grace. "For Paul, *charis* is the essence of God's decisive saving act in Jesus Christ, which took place in His sacrificial death, and also of all its consequences in the present and future." Esser, H., in Brown, C. (Ed.). (1969). *The New International Dictionary of New Testament Theology.* Grand Rapids, MI: Zondervan, p. 119.
11. *Ibid*, p. 116.
12. Exodus 3:8.
13. TWOT, #712.
14. John 3:16; Matthew 3:17.
15. Hebrews 12:2.
16. Edersheim, A. (1976). *The Temple: It's Ministry and Services.* Grand Rapids, MI: Eerdman's, p. 92.
17. John 19:30.
18. Isaiah 63:9.
19. 1 Corinthians 10:13.
20. Isaiah 53:12; Romans 8:34.
21. 1 Corinthians 11:25.
22. Isaiah 53:5c.
23. Psalm 103:12.
24. [*barukh haba' beshem 'adonay*], Luke 13:35.

25. Webster, C. (Ed.). (1956). *The American College Dictionary*. New York: Random House.

26. TWOT, #2340.

27. Brown, C. (Ed.). (1971). *The New International Dictionary of New Testament Theology, Vol. 1*. Grand Rapids, MI: Zondervan, p. 355.

28. Hebrews 11:6.

29. Hosea 6:6.

30. Psalm 51:16,19.

31. Psalm 51:17.

32. Psalm 103:9.

33. Isaac Watts.

34. Bounds, E.M. *The Weapon of Prayer: Prayerless Christian*. New Kensington, PA: Whitaker House.

Chapter Fourteen

Feast of Tabernacles

Final Ingathering

Then the LORD spoke to Moses, saying, "Speak to the children of Israel, saying: 'The fifteenth day of this seventh month shall be the Feast of Tabernacles for seven days to the LORD ...

'Also on the fifteenth day of the seventh month, when you have gathered in the fruit of the land, you shall keep the feast of the LORD for seven days; on the first day there shall be a sabbath-rest, and on the eighth day a sabbath-rest. And you shall take for yourselves on the first day the fruit of beautiful trees ... and you shall rejoice before the LORD your God for seven days ... You shall dwell in booths for seven days. All who are native Israelites shall dwell in booths, that your generations may know that I

made the children of Israel dwell in booths when I brought them out of the land of Egypt: I am the LORD your God.'"
—Leviticus 23:33-34, 39-40, 42-43

Now the Jews' Feast of Tabernacles was at hand.
—John 7:2[1]

The next holiday on God's calendar is about a journey. The Feast of Tabernacles is about Israel's journey between Egypt and the Promised Land. Because of its connection with the exodus from Egypt, I think of Tabernacles as being part of the Passover event. Let's review all the Passover-related holidays:

- Passover commemorates the salvation of Israel from the plague of death.
- Unleavened Bread commemorates Israel's exodus from Egypt.
- Firstfruits commemorates Israel's arrival in the Promised Land.
- Feast of Tabernacles commemorates Israel's forty-year journey through the wilderness.

This holiday doesn't only look to the past. It has tremendous eschatological significance, as it will be celebrated in the Millennial Kingdom. In that day, when Jesus rules and reigns from Jerusalem, all nations will join in the celebration. Thus, Tabernacles spans the entirety of Israel's history.

I remember my first big journey, driving alone across the United States. I was just as excited about the trip itself as I was about my impending move. During the trip, I would be without any responsibility or commitment. I planned the journey carefully, considering weather and sights along the way.

The three-week journey gave me lots of time to think. I thought about the past, the people, and places I was leaving behind. Other times, I wondered about the future. But mostly, I just enjoyed each day. Wherever I was, was the perfect place to be. Each day brought new adventures, which I'd remember for the rest of my life.

It wasn't where I'd been or where I was going that mattered but the journey itself. Aren't we all on a life-changing journey?

Seasonal

The Feast of Tabernacles begins on the fifteenth day of the seventh month, exactly six months after the Feast of Unleavened Bread. It occurs in the fall, usually in October, and is five days after the Day of Atonement.

Tabernacles is the festival of the third harvest: grapes, figs, dates, olives, and wheat. It is the final ingathering of the year and begins what Scripture calls the time of the latter rains. The rainfall during the next few months will determine the bounty of the spring harvest.

Scripture identifies this holiday by several names:

- Feast of Tabernacles [2]
- Feast of the Lord [3]
- Feast of Ingathering [4]
- The Feast[5]

National

From various Scripture references, there are eleven important elements of the Feast of Tabernacles:[6]

- It is celebrated on the fifteenth day of the seventh month.
- It lasts for seven days plus one.
- It is a harvest festival.
- The first and eighth days are declared a Sabbath rest.
- It is a time of rejoicing with the firstfruit of "beautiful trees."
- The people are to live in booths to remember the journey from Egypt.
- There was an abundance of sacrifices.
- The Law was to be read.
- Solomon dedicated the temple during Tabernacles.
- It is a holiday of great rejoicing.
- It will be celebrated in the Millennial Kingdom.

Let's consider some of these elements in greater detail.

THE DATE

The alignment of Tabernacles and Passover forms the foundation of the entire history of Israel. Passover begins Israel's history as a nation; Tabernacles is part of her future, as it will be celebrated in the Millennial Kingdom.

BOOTHS FOR REMEMBERANCE

The booth, or sukkah, is a visual and experiential reminder of Israel's wilderness journey and consequently is the focus of the celebration of Tabernacles. Handcrafted booths of all sizes and shapes can be seen on apartment patios, in backyards, on synagogue lawns, and wherever Jewish people meet and congregate. Most families try to eat at least one meal in their booth each day, and children love to sleep in them under the stars.[7] The booths are often decorated with children's drawings, strings of lights, and fresh or dried fruit.

Arnold Fruchtenbaum points out that the flimsy construction of the booth was also a reminder of the hope of future restoration:[8]

> *On that day I will raise up the tabernacle of David, which has fallen down, and repair its damages; I will raise up its ruins, and rebuild it as in the days of old.*
> —*Amos 9:11*

THIRD PILGRIM FESTIVAL

The Feast of Tabernacles was the preferred of the three pilgrim festivals because of Israel's pleasant weather in the fall. The hot summer months were past, and the latter rains usually held off until just after the eight holy days. Thus, the roads were dry, hard, and easy to navigate. Jerusalem swelled as pilgrims came from everywhere.[9] For miles one could see and hear the singing and laughing of great companies of pilgrims. The memory of those days haunted the people in isolation or exile:

> *My soul thirsts for God, for the living God. When shall I come and appear before God? My tears have been my*

food day and night, while they continually say to me, "Where is your God?" When I remember these things, I pour out my soul within me. For I used to go with the multitude; I went with them to the house of God, with the voice of joy and praise, with a multitude that kept a pilgrim feast.

—Psalm 42:2-4

HOLIDAY OF GREAT JOY

Rejoicing is the natural outcome of remembering God's goodness. In fact, more than for any other holiday, God commands the people to rejoice during Tabernacles:

And you shall rejoice in your feast, you and your son and your daughter, your male servant and your female servant and the Levite, the stranger and the fatherless and the widow, who are within your gates. Seven days you shall keep a sacred feast to the LORD your God in the place which the LORD chooses, because the LORD your God will bless you in all your produce and in all the work of your hands, so that you surely rejoice.

—Deuteronomy 16:14-15

Coming so soon after the affliction of the Day of Atonement, the joy of Tabernacles reflects God's gracious forgiveness of sin.[10]

ABUNDANCE OF SACRIFICES

Responsibility naturally flows from remembering and rejoicing. Rejoicing without responsibility is vain and foolish, but responsibility without rejoicing is death.

An abundance of sacrifices was required during the Feast of Tabernacles. In addition to the regular daily offerings, at the end of the seven days the following had been given to the Lord:

- Burnt offerings
  - fourteen rams
  - ninety-eight he-lambs
  - seventy bulls[11]

  (Let it not escape notice that the number of sacrifices is divisible by seven!)
- Meal and drink offerings
- Sin offerings: one he-goat per day

The eighth day required additional sacrifices: a bull, a ram, and seven he-lambs for the burnt offering; a meal offering, a drink offering, and the sin offering.[12]

DEDICATION OF THE TEMPLE

Both the first and the second temples were dedicated on the Feast of Tabernacles. In our study of Hanukkah, this fact becomes very important.

Spiritual

Through Israel's journey, God revealed Himself as her Patient Father, Good Shepherd, and King.

As He did for Israel, God designs a unique journey for each of us.

My journey across America was designed to bring me to God. I hadn't thought much about Him for many years. But in the quiet and aloneness of my car, I thought about Him a lot. I wondered if He really existed; I wondered if He saw me. I wondered if He really cared about me, and if He'd take care of me. Finally, I wondered if He had a plan for my life, or was the future entirely up to me?

A journal entry revealed my answer to those questions. "Yes!" There was a God, He did care about me, and He did have a plan for my life. I wrote, "Today I am a clean slate for God to write upon. Wherever He wants me to go, whatever He wants me to do, I am His."

I realize now that I didn't understand the depth of my questions or the impact of my answer. God had only begun to open my eyes to see Him. And see Him I did!

The rolling green hills of Virginia and Tennessee declared His existence. The blooming cherry trees of Oklahoma declared His creativity. The expanse of Texas declared His sovereignty. The Grand Canyon declared His power, and the colors of Arizona declared His glory.

Day by day and night by night, I recognized God's protective hand around me and the car.

In the Painted Desert, I could no longer resist. After making sure no one would see, I got out of my car, knelt down, and worshipped.

Israel had those kinds of moments in her journey when she turned to God and worshipped. But her journey is better described as cyclic, going from one trial to another, from severe testing to momentary triumph.

PATIENT AND PERFECTING FATHER

When God delivered Israel from Egypt, He revealed Himself as Father; Israel was His firstborn son.[13] A stubborn and rebellious child, Israel often rebelled against His authority, tested His patience, and limited His blessings.[14]

Mercifully, God is patient and longsuffering:

> *He, being full of compassion, forgave their iniquity, and did not destroy them. Yes, many a time He turned His anger away, and did not stir up all His wrath ... God carried [them], as a man carries his son, in all the way ...*
> *—Psalm 78:38; Deuteronomy 1:31*

In His love, God used the journey to perfect as well as to punish His people. For those who refused to believe the good report of the Land, He brought punishment; yet He used those forty years to perfect the next generation, preparing them to enter the Promised Land.

> *And you shall remember that the LORD your God led you all the way these forty years in the wilderness, to humble you and test you, to know what was in your heart, whether you would keep His commandments or not. So He humbled you, allowed you to hunger ... that He might humble you and that He might test you, to do you good in the end— ... You should know in your heart that as a man chastens his son, so the LORD your God chastens you.*
> *—Deuteronomy 8:2-3a, 16a, 5*

GOOD SHEPHERD

As God looked at Israel, He saw a nation of sheep in desperate need of a Shepherd. With a heart of mercy, God became their Shepherd to guard, protect, provide, and bring them into perfect rest:

> *"You are My flock, the flock of My pasture; you are men, and I am your God," says the Lord* GOD.
> *—Ezekiel 34:31*

Note the ways He cared and provided for Israel:

- His Presence

  God's presence never left them. His glorious presence separated Israel from all other nations of the world:

  > *And the* LORD *went before them by day in a pillar of cloud to lead the way, and by night in a pillar of fire to give them light, so as to go by day and night. He did not take away the pillar of cloud by day or the pillar of fire by night from before the people.*
  > *—Exodus 13:21-22*

- His Protection

  Israel's enemies could not withstand the power and protection of God:

  > *When they went from one nation to another, from one kingdom to another people, He permitted no one to do them wrong; yes, He rebuked kings for their sakes, saying, "Do not touch My anointed ones, and do My prophets no harm."*
  > *—Psalm 105:13-15*

- His Provision

  Even in the most challenging times, there is no lack under the Shepherd's care:

  For the LORD your God has blessed you in all the work of your hand. He knows your trudging through this great wilderness. These forty years the LORD your God has been with you; you have lacked nothing.
  —Deuteronomy 2:7

- His Rest and Restoration

  The Shepherd leads us into rest and restoration:

  The LORD is my shepherd; I shall not want. He makes me to lie down in green pastures; He leads me beside the still waters. He restores my soul.
  —Psalm 23:1-3

  The Hebrew word translated as *still* is [*m^{e}nuchot*] from the root [*nu'ach*], which we saw in our study of Sabbath.[15]

MESSIANIC IMPLICATIONS

Over the years, Israel's bright future had dimmed because of continued rebellion:

- The kingdom was split.
- The north was dispersed.
- The south was under severe discipline.

The people longed for rest and restoration. By the time of Israel's prophets, this holiday was filled with messianic hope. Through His prophets, God brought messages of challenge, correction, and comfort. All eyes and hearts were eagerly anticipating the arrival of the Messiah and the establishment of His Kingdom. The celebration of Tabernacles shone a spotlight on their hopes. The prophets Ezekiel and Zechariah made reference to this holiday within the context of the Millennial Kingdom.[16]

LIGHT AND WATER

Light and water are two symbols often linked with God's presence:

> *You give them drink from the river of Your pleasures. For with You is the fountain of life; in Your light we see light.* —*Psalm 36:8b-9*

The context of the following prophecy from Zechariah takes these two symbols of God's presence throughout Israel's wilderness journey and conjoins them with the Millennial Kingdom:

> *It shall come to pass in that day that there will be no light; the lights will diminish. It shall be one day which is known to the LORD—neither day nor night. But at evening time it shall happen that it will be light. And in that day it shall be that living waters shall flow from Jerusalem, half of them toward the eastern sea and half of them toward the western sea; in both summer and winter it shall occur.* —*Zechariah 14:6-8*

Light and water are also descriptive of the New Jerusalem, thus linking Israel's wilderness journey with her ultimate goal:

> *The city had no need of the sun or of the moon to shine in it, for the glory of God illuminated it. The Lamb is its light . . . And he showed me a pure river of water of life, clear as crystal, proceeding from the throne of God and*

of the Lamb . . . There shall be no night there: They need no lamp nor light of the sun, for the Lord God gives them light.
—Revelation 21:23; 22:1, 5

SHEPHERD KING

In that day, the Shepherd of Israel will also be the King of Kings:

And the LORD shall be King over all the earth. In that day it shall be—"The LORD is one," and His name one.
—Zechariah 14:9

CELEBRATION IN JERUSALEM, CIRCA 32 BC

By the time of Christ's incarnation, the themes of light and water had developed into two important ceremonies in the observance of the Feast of Tabernacles—the Pouring of Water and the Temple Illumination.[17]

POURING OF WATER

Each day during the Feast, the priests made a procession from the Temple to the Pool of Siloam, where they drew from its water using golden pitchers.

The procession returned to the Temple Mount, accompanied by blasts from silver trumpets. There they met other priests who were carrying golden pitchers of wine. The priests then poured their libations through two silver funnels into the base of the altar, accompanied by the shouts of the worshippers, encouraging them to lift their hands so that all could see the pouring. This ceremony was based on the prophesy of Isaiah:

Therefore with joy you will draw water from the wells of salvation. —*Isaiah 12:3*[18]

It was said that one has never seen joy until he has seen the Water-Pouring.

This ceremony was followed by the chanting of the Great Hallel, Psalms 113–118, which is sung during Passover, further linking the two holidays. The public services concluded with a procession round the altar by the priests chanting:

Save now, I pray, O Lord; O Lord, I pray, send now prosperity. —*Psalm 118:25*[19]

On the eighth and last day of the feast, the procession circled the altar seven times. The circuits had a three-fold meaning:

- Anticipating the outpouring of the Holy Spirit[20]
- Remembering the march around Jericho [21]
- Ingathering of the nations

TEMPLE ILLUMINATION

At the close of the first day, the worshippers descended to the Court of the Women. Four golden candelabras were there, each with four golden bowls, and against them rested four ladders. Four youths of priestly descent, each carrying a pitcher of oil, filled each bowl. The old, worn breeches and girdles of the priests served as wicks for these lamps. There was not a court in Jerusalem that was not lit up by the light of "the House of Water-Pouring."[22]

The remainder of the night was filled with rejoicing and blasts of the trumpets. The men danced and sang while the priests and worshippers chanted the Hallel.

Redemptive

Whether the preceding holidays of the fall are the fulfillment of Jesus' first coming or anticipatory of His second coming, there is no doubt that Tabernacles points to His return.

I wonder what thoughts Jesus had as He celebrated these holidays. By using Israel's culture, customs, and ceremonies, He communicated the full prophetic meaning (past, present, and future) of the holiday. But only those with hearts and ears to hear understood. Let's consider how Jesus used the great themes of Tabernacles to declare His identity as He celebrated for the last time before His crucifixion.

WATER

Try to imagine the joyous frenzy during the Water Pouring on that last great day of the Feast. In accordance with the command to cut branches of goodly trees, the people carried with them a lulav: a twist of branches from the palm, myrtle, and willow. During the Water-Pouring, the people shook the lulavs while singing the final verses of Psalm 118:25-29.

Suddenly a loud voice was heard:

> *If anyone thirsts, let him come to Me and drink. He who believes in Me, as the Scripture has said, out of his heart will flow rivers of living water.*
> *—John 7:37b-38*

The connection with Isaiah 12:3 was unmistakable. Jesus was claiming that He was the fountain, the well, the source of salvation.

LIGHT

Now imagine all of Jerusalem bathed in light, giving a golden cast to Jerusalem's stone. The sky was lit by the light of the full moon. The psalms being chanted stirred memories of Israel's journey through the wilderness, being led by a cloud and a pillar of fire. Once again, the voice of the Carpenter broke through the noise:

> *I am the light of the world. He who follows Me shall not walk in darkness, but have the light of life.*
> *—John 8:12*[23]

THE GOOD SHEPHERD

Amid the rising messianic fervor and furor swirling around Him, Jesus made another bold declaration before leaving Jerusalem. He claimed to be the Good Shepherd of Israel:

> *I am the good shepherd. The good shepherd gives His life for the sheep . . . I am the good shepherd; and I know My sheep, and am known by My own . . . I lay down My life for the sheep. And other sheep I have which are not of this fold; them also I must bring, and they will hear My voice; and there will be one flock and one shepherd.*
> *—John 10:11, 14-16*

By declaring Himself to be the Good Shepherd, Jesus was blatantly taking for Himself a title ascribed to God the Father. Then He went a step further. Not only was Israel part of His flock, but He confirmed the Father's original intention of bringing in other sheep, that is, the Gentiles.[24]

Jesus, by implication rather than by declaration, assumed the fulfillment of the eschatological implications of the Feast, namely that He was the King of all Kings.

Eschatological

Despite differences in theologies and doctrines regarding the timing and context of the Millennial Kingdom, the Feast of Tabernacles has the most eschatological significance of all the holidays.

THE MILLENNIAL KINGDOM

There will come a day that Christ will rule and reign from a rebuilt temple in a restored Jerusalem. I personally believe that rule will consist of a thousand years. Furthermore, I believe that His reign will take place after these important events have taken place:

- A major, but localized, war against Israel
- The physical return of Jesus
- The binding of Satan
- The destruction of two-thirds of the Jewish people

Scripture connects the Feast of Tabernacles with the beginning of that Millennial Kingdom:

> *And it shall come to pass that everyone who is left of all the nations which came against Jerusalem shall go up from year to year to worship the King, the* L*ORD* *of hosts, and to keep the Feast of Tabernacles.*
> *—Zechariah 14:16*

At that time, the Gentile nations will join the Jewish pilgrims flowing to His throne to celebrate Jesus and the Feast of Tabernacles. In fact, celebrating Tabernacles will be so important that any nation that does not observe this Feast will suffer judgment:

> *And it shall be that whichever of the families of the earth do not come up to Jerusalem to worship the King, the* Lord *of hosts, on them there will be no rain; they shall receive the plague with which the* Lord *strikes the nations who do not come up to keep the Feast of Tabernacles.*
> *—Zechariah 14:17-18*

According to the prophet Ezekiel, the Prince Himself will offer the sacrifices during Passover and Tabernacles.[25] While scholars debate the identity of the Prince, I believe this is none other than Jesus. Who else can enter the temple by the Eastern Gate? Who other than a priest can offer sacrifices? Only the Messiah!

Can you imagine the joy as all His subjects join the King in Jerusalem in celebrating the Feast of Tabernacles? Beyond simply remembering God's faithfulness in their past journeys, they will be able to rejoice in His actual Presence.

It will be a day spoken of by most of the Hebrew prophets, promised by Jesus, anticipated by the disciples, and longed for by religious Jews.

Let us consider three aspects of the Millennial Kingdom and, consequently, the eschatological aspects of Tabernacles:

- Regathering of the remnant of Israel
- Restoration of Israel
- Worldwide worship

Regathering of Israel's Remnant

Prior to 1948, many people did not take literally God's promises to return Israel to her Land but spiritualized them to make them applicable to the church. Eyes could not see or minds imagine that the Jews would one day reoccupy their Promised Land. No other people, land, or language had ever lain dormant for thousands of years and then been restored. Yes, Israel might be a fluke in the history of nations, but she is evidence that we serve a God of resurrection and second chances:

> *It shall come to pass in that day that the LORD shall set His hand again the second time to recover the remnant of His people who are left, from Assyria and Egypt . . . and the islands of the sea. He will set up a banner for the nations, and will assemble the outcasts of Israel, and gather together the dispersed of Judah from the four corners of the earth.*
> *—Isaiah 11:11-12*

There are many who understand that day to be now, that the regathering of Israel began in earnest in the nineteenth century. But note that the Lord says the ingathering is the second time He brings back Israel from the four corners of the earth. Since every previous return has been more localized (from one place), perhaps the current ingathering from all nations is the first time. I believe the ultimate timing of this promise is revealed by the context of the verses previous to the ones above from Isaiah:

> *The wolf also shall dwell with the lamb, the leopard shall lie down with the young goat, the calf and the young lion and the fatling together; and a little child shall lead them. The cow and the bear shall graze;*

their young ones shall lie down together; and the lion shall eat straw like the ox. The nursing child shall play by the cobra's hole, and the weaned child shall put his hand in the viper's den. They shall not hurt nor destroy in all My holy mountain, for the earth shall be full of the knowledge of the LORD as the waters cover the sea.
—Isaiah 11:6-9

Restoration of Israel

In that day, Israel's long journey from Egypt's bondage will be over. She will finally be out of the wilderness and firmly established in the Promised Land.

Listen carefully to this prophecy of Isaiah, which links Israel's journey through the wilderness with that great and glorious day:

And it shall come to pass that he who is left in Zion and remains in Jerusalem will be called holy—everyone who is recorded among the living in Jerusalem. When the Lord has washed away the filth of the daughters of Zion, and purged the blood of Jerusalem from her midst, by the spirit of judgment and by the spirit of burning, then the LORD will create above every dwelling place of Mount Zion, and above her assemblies, a cloud and smoke by day and the shining of a flaming fire by night. *—Isaiah 4:3-5*

In that day, God's promise to dwell among them will be totally fulfilled:

I will dwell among the children of Israel and will be their God. And they shall know that I am the LORD their God, who brought them up out of the land of Egypt, that I may dwell among them. I am the LORD their God.
—Exodus 29:45-46

The final harvest is another conjunction of Tabernacles and the Millennial Kingdom. As Tabernacles is the final harvest of the agricultural year, the Messianic Kingdom will be the final ingathering of souls—both Jews and Gentiles:[26]

> *He who scattered Israel will gather him, and keep him as a shepherd does his flock . . . Therefore they shall come and sing in the height of Zion, streaming to the goodness of the LORD.*
> *—Jeremiah 31:10, 12*

> *He will set up a banner for the nations, and will assemble the outcasts of Israel, and gather together the dispersed of Judah from the four corners of the earth.*
> *—Isaiah 11:12*

During this time, Israel will fulfill her destiny to be God's most fruitful witness:

> *Thus says the LORD of hosts: "In those days ten men from every language of the nations shall grasp the sleeve of a Jewish man, saying, 'Let us go with you, for we have heard that God is with you.'"*
> *—Zechariah 8:23*

Worldwide Worship

In that day, a purged and holy remnant of Israel will lead the nations in worship of the Messiah:

> *Many people shall come and say, "Come, and let us go up to the mountain of the LORD, to the house of the God of Jacob" . . . for out of Zion shall go forth the law, and the word of the LORD from Jerusalem . . .*

> *"Also the sons of the foreigner who join themselves to the LORD, to serve Him, and to love the name of the*

Lord, to be His servants—everyone who keeps from defiling the Sabbath, and holds fast My covenant—even them I will bring to My holy mountain, and make them joyful in My house of prayer ... for My house shall be called a house of prayer for all nations." The Lord God, who gathers the outcasts of Israel, says, "Yet I will gather to him others besides those who are gathered to him." —*Isaiah 2:3; 56:6-8*[27]

THIRD FIRSTFRUITS

We have seen the previous two Firstfruits holidays being fulfilled by the resurrection of Christ and the salvation of Jews and Gentiles.[28] The third and final Firstfruits will be the resurrection of the dead:

I am the resurrection and the life. He who believes in Me, though he may die, he shall live. And whoever lives and believes in Me shall never die. —*John 11:25b-26a*

This Firstfruits holiday has eschatological applications:

- The Resurrection of the Living and the Dead

  For this we say to you by the word of the Lord, that we who are alive and remain until the coming of the Lord will by no means precede those who are asleep. For the Lord Himself will descend from heaven with a shout, with the voice of an archangel, and with the trumpet of God. And the dead in Christ will rise first. Then we who are alive and remain shall be caught up together with them in the clouds to meet the Lord in the air. —*1 Thessalonians 4:15-17a*

- Fulfillment of the Holy Spirit and Redemption of Creation

  For I consider that the sufferings of this present time are not worthy to be compared with the glory which shall be revealed in us. For the earnest expectation of the creation eagerly waits for the revealing of the sons of God. For the creation was subjected to futility, not willingly, but because of Him who subjected it in hope; because the creation itself also will be delivered from the bondage of corruption into the glorious liberty of the children of God. For we know that the whole creation groans and labors with birth pangs together until now. Not only that, but we also who have the firstfruits of the Spirit, even we ourselves groan within ourselves, eagerly waiting for the adoption, the redemption of our body. —*Romans 8:18-23*

Kingdom

The Feast of Tabernacles is a pilgrim festival and reminds us that we, too, are pilgrims on a journey. We can glean Kingdom principles applicable to our lives from Israel's journey.

It's always wonderful to imagine the end of a journey; but reaching the goal can be met with both excitement and fear.

I remember how my heart skipped a beat the first time I saw my destination on a road sign: "California—176 miles." Suddenly my goal seemed attainable; I was close.

Fear, excitement, dread, and confusion assaulted me. Somewhere deep inside was a hope that this was all a dream.

Secretly I had hoped that someone would stop me and tell me that I was crazy and acting foolishly. I would not have been offended if someone had challenged me that I was having a mid-life crisis. At last I was near, confronting my goal with less than enthusiastic confidence.

In God's Kingdom, life is just as much about the journey as it is about the goal.

That was true for me. My journey west was over, but another journey was about to begin. Exactly three years from my first journal entry about being "a clean slate for God to write upon," I began my journey of faith in Jesus. I had a new goal. The goal was not a place but a Person.

Not unlike Israel's journey, my new journey is preparing me for my permanent and eternal home. While we are seated with Christ in heavenly places, we must work out our salvation with fear and trembling. Positionally, we are with Christ; but practically, we are striving toward the goal—to be more like Him. This is the process of sanctification.

God intends for our journey to be a process and not a program. Our journey is meant to transform us in this life, preparing us for our eternal life as we go from liberation to destination.

When God is our destination, there is a promised blessing throughout the journey:

> *Blessed is the man whose strength is in You, whose heart is set on pilgrimage. As they pass through the Valley of Baca, they make it a spring; the rain also covers it with pools. They go from strength to strength; each one appears before God in Zion.*
> *—Psalm 84:5-7*

With God, every valley of weeping becomes a place of blessing and a place of strengthening.[29]

KNOWING GOD

The most important purpose of our journey is knowing God, His character, and His ways. Every step of life's journey is an opportunity to

- draw into His presence;
- abide with Him;
- be filled and refilled with His love;
- recognize His transforming power in our lives;
- see His mighty hand working on our behalf and in the lives of others.

Every step forward gives us a new perspective of where we've been. Remembering God's goodness in the past will strengthen us to push forward. When the hard times come, and they will, we can hold on to His promises:

> *My lovingkindness I will not utterly take from him, nor allow My faithfulness to fail.* —Psalm 89:33

> *Surely goodness and mercy shall follow me all the days of my life.* —Psalm 23:6a

Our journeys will prove to us that He is good, loving, protective, and providing for all our needs.

THE JOURNEY

The journey of faith must begin with a commitment to make that journey—regardless of cost, comfort, or circumstances.

Here are other Kingdom principles gleaned from Israel's journey:

- Life Is Temporary

  The Feast of Tabernacles reminds us that our life on earth is temporary. Whether our lives are short or long, we will eventually die to this life and be raised to the next. According to the prophet Daniel, some will be raised to "everlasting life and some to shame and everlasting contempt" (Daniel 12:2a). Paul compares our bodies to the flimsy booths of Tabernacles, assuring us that one day we will have glorified and incorruptible bodies.[30]

- A Time of Perfecting

  To the unbelieving mind, God's perfecting us through trials seems cruel. Yet, who hasn't experienced an extra measure of intimacy with God during hard times? A gospel that does not present God's grace in the bumps of our journey is an incomplete gospel message. Consider the lives of Abraham, Joseph, Moses, and David. These men walked a journey of trials and tests, yet they emerged leaning on the arm of their Shepherd. Broken and restored, they became vessels of grace. Above all, let us remember Christ's journey to the cross:

  ...in the days of His flesh, when He had offered up prayers and supplications, with vehement cries and tears to Him who was able to save Him from death, and was heard because of His godly fear, though He was a Son, yet He learned obedience by the things which

He suffered. And having been perfected, He became the author of eternal salvation to all who obey Him.
—Hebrews 5:7-9

The Greek word translated as *perfected* is [*tel·i·o·o*]. It means "*to add what is missing to reach the intended goal, to complete, to accomplish.*"[31] In other words, our trials are designed to bring us to maturity. As we journey, we have a choice whether to focus on the trials or on the goal. Scripture suggests the latter:

My brethren, count it all joy when you fall into various trials, knowing that the testing of your faith produces patience. But let patience have its perfect work, that you may be perfect and complete, lacking nothing.
—James 1:2-4

God turns our hearts to Him so that we will walk in all His ways, fully committed to Him. He knows what's best for us, even if it seems illogical to us.[32] Let us all hold fast to God's promises as we face the bumps in our journey:

For who is God, except the LORD? And who is a rock, except our God? It is God who arms me with strength, and makes my way perfect. He makes my feet like the feet of deer, and sets me on my high places... You have also given me the shield of Your salvation; Your right hand has held me up, Your gentleness has made me great. You enlarged my path under me, so my feet did not slip.
—Psalm 18:31-36

Victorious Striving

Paul encourages us to strive toward victory. Throughout our journey, God trains our hands for war while equipping us with a full set of armor so that we will experience the victory that Christ has already won for us.[33]

Perseverance

Every journey begins and ends with one little step. God did not give Israel a map for her journey, nor does He give one to us! He tells us just what we need to know at the moment—and always just in time. To run and to finish the journey takes determination and perseverance:

> *Not that I have already attained, or am already perfected; but I press on, that I may lay hold of that for which Christ Jesus has also laid hold of me. Brethren, I do not count myself to have apprehended; but one thing I do, forgetting those things which are behind and reaching forward to those things which are ahead, I press toward the goal for the prize of the upward call of God in Christ Jesus.*
> *—Philippians 3:12-14*

The journey may be arduous, but He sustains, protects, and provides for our every step. His glory surrounds us and His banner over us is love! So, let us run the race to win![34]

Dependence

Every journey, in fact every step, requires total dependence on God's grace. Whether we recognize or admit it, our lives are completely in His hands. The lesson of Israel's journey reflects our amazing and gracious partnership with God. He provided manna daily, but it had to be collected. First He allows us to have a need. Then He satisfies that need. Yet, because

He requires us to be actively involved in meeting that need, He gives us the grace to accomplish the task! Someone once said, "We cannot do what God will do, but He will not do what we are supposed to do!" Remember, the Bride makes herself ready! And His grace is sufficient.

ல Oasis

Jesus is not only our future goal; He is our present reality. Despite the bumps and twists of our journey, He is our oasis in the wilderness, an ever-present place of rest and refreshment.

REMEMBER AND REJOICE NOW

It is important that we continually rejoice in our journeys.

There's something contagious about rejoicing, singing God's praises, joining with others and remembering the goodness and the salvation of God. The Bible says that the joy of the Lord is our strength, giving us strength to go on, strength to persevere in the valleys of the journey, and strength to climb the mountains.

Rejoicing is not always a matter of how we feel; anyone can rejoice when our journeys take us into meadows filled with flowers, blue skies, and mountaintops. But we'll never see a rainbow unless it rains, and we'll never notice the rainbow if we're focused on the puddles.

In the midst of terrible challenge and devastation, Habakkuk determined to rejoice in God:

> *Though the fig tree may not blossom, nor fruit be on the vines; though the labor of the olive may fail, and the fields yield no food; though the flock may be cut off from*

the fold, and there be no herd in the stalls—yet I will rejoice in the L*ORD, I will joy in the God of my salvation.*
—Habakkuk 3:17-18

Look up and remember who God is and what He's done. Rejoice in His promises for today and tomorrow.

THE REAL JOURNEY'S END

God has graciously given us the motivation to keep going—the promise of what awaits us at the end of our journey. There will come a day when we will enter into the peace, rest, and joy of the Lord:

Eye has not seen, nor ear heard, nor have entered into the heart of man the things which God has prepared for those who love Him. *—1 Corinthians 2:9*

At the end of the journey will be a hero's welcome with imperishable rewards:

The Son of Man will come in the glory of His Father with His angels, and then He will reward each according to his works. *—Matthew 16:27*

There is nothing that we are experiencing here that goes unnoticed by His watchful eye. Everything done in and for Him will be rewarded. Every time we turn the other cheek, stand for righteousness, or help the poor and needy. Every time we give a cup of cold water to the thirsty and a blanket to the cold. Every little thought and word of encouragement will be weighed and rewarded!

AN AFTERTHOUGHT

Why wait until the return of Jesus to celebrate this Feast? Fulfill prophecy by coming up to Jerusalem to celebrate the Feast of Tabernacles.

We now leave the feasts of the fall and move into the winter holidays of Hanukkah and Purim.

Endnotes

1. For the complete context, see John 7:2–10:21.
2. Leviticus 23:34.
3. Leviticus 23:39.
4. Exodus 23:16.
5. 1 Kings 8:2.
6. Exodus 23:14-17; Leviticus 23:33-43; Numbers 29:12-18; Deuteronomy 16:13-16; 31:9-13; 1 Kings 8:1-66; Nehemiah 8:13-18.
7. Though not a scriptural regulation, the rabbis teach that the booths must not be roofed and branches must be laid loosely over the top to provide shade and slight protection without blocking out the sky.
8. Fruchtenbaum, A. (1987). *The Feast of Tabernacles,* Manuscript #120. Tustin, CA: Ariel Ministries.
9. Jesus' visit to the Bethany home of Mary and Martha was probably at the beginning of the Feast. This would explain the absence of Lazarus, who would have been at the Feast in Jerusalem. Jesus and Mary would have been sitting in the outdoor booth, causing Martha to run back and forth to the house, "distracted with much serving" (Luke 10:38-42).
10. Nehemiah 8:1-8.
11. Rabbinic tradition teaches that the number of bulls represents the seventy Gentile nations (Deuteronomy 32:8; 10:22).
12. This eighth day, now called "Shmini Atzeret," has developed with rabbinic traditions apart from the Feast of Tabernacles.
13. Exodus 4:22-23.
14. Psalm 78:41.

15. [*nu'ach*] "signifies not only an absence of movement, but being settled in a particular place (whether concrete or abstract) of victory, salvation, a sense of security." TWOT #1323. See also "Sabbath."

16. Ezekiel 45:25; Zechariah 14:16.

17. For a more thorough description, see Edershiem, A. *The Temple: Its Ministries and Services*, at http://philologos.org/__eb-ttms/temple14.htm.

18. We've seen this word for salvation, [*y^eshu'ah*] from [*yesha'*], the same root as the name of Jesus.

19. "Save" [*hoshi'ah*] is the imperative form of [*yesha'*]. "Save now!" is [*hoshi'ah-na*] from which our word *hosanna* is derived.

20. Isaiah 12:3; Joel 2:28-29.

21. Joshua 6.

22. Edersheim, A. (1958). *The Temple: Its Ministry and Services*. Grand Rapids, MI: Wm. B. Eerdmans, p. 283.

23. cf. John 9:5; Isaiah 60:19.

24. John 10:16.

25. Ezekiel 45:25.

26. Ezekiel 34:10ff.

27. See also Jeremiah 3:14-17.

28. See *"Firstfruits"* and *"Feast of Weeks."*

29. Romans 8:28ff.

30. 1 Corinthians 15:42-44; 2 Corinthians 4:16–5:9.

31. http://cf.blueletterbible.org/lang/lexicon/lexicon.cfm?Strongs=G5048&t=kjv.

32. Romans 8:28ff; Isaiah 55:10-11.

33. Ephesians 6:10-18.

34. Song of Solomon 2:4; 1 Corinthians 9:24-27.

Chapter Fifteen

Hanukkah

Holiday of Dedication

Now it was the Feast of Dedication in Jerusalem, and it was winter. And Jesus walked in the temple, in Solomon's porch.
—John 10:22-23

"I hate this time of year!"

"Me, too," her friend replied as they walked into the synagogue. "I hate having Christmas shoved down my throat."

I knew exactly how the two women felt. I'd felt the same way. Every December, the entire world seemed to separate between Christians and Jews. As for me and my house, we felt isolated and rejected, as though we hadn't been invited to a wonderful party.

It didn't matter to me that we didn't believe in Jesus, who was at the center of all the fun. I wanted what Christmas seemed to be: family, fun, and PRESENTS!

My family succumbed to my pleadings and we "did" Christmas. My brother and I made our wish lists and saved our pennies to find the perfect presents for others. Daddy took us shopping to find the largest tree, which we quickly festooned with both hand-made and store-bought decorations. Of course, the tree was crowned with a Jewish star to identify it as a Hanukkah bush.

Eventually, however, we stopped the charade. Hanukkah was our holiday. I just didn't know too much about it.

Many people don't know what Hanukkah is all about. I thought Hanukkah was about Judas Maccabee, the temple, and some oil. But now I know it's much more than that. Hanukkah is about God's blessing upon a faithful remnant that would not compromise its faith.

For all the wrong reasons, my family compromised their beliefs to be just like the world. The message of Hanukkah challenges us to stand firm in and for the name of the Lord Jesus despite personal costs and consequences. This is an important message for all of us today.

Seasonal

Hanukkah takes place on the twenty-fifth day of the Hebrew month of Kislev, sometime between the middle and the end of December. It is celebrated for eight days, starting at sundown.

National

Hanukkah commemorates the dedication of the temple after it had been defiled by the Seleucid emperor Antiochus IV.

Hanukkah is not an Old Testament-ordained holiday. Our understanding comes from Daniel (chapters 8–12), the books of the Maccabees, and from Josephus. It was first celebrated in the year 163 BC and remained a minor holiday until recently. A legend surfaced about a miraculous supply of oil, "a most difficult and beclouded point in the history of Hanukkah."[1] None of the histories above mentioned any such occurrence. So let's set the record straight.

HANUKKAH—THE SETTING 198–165 BC

The historical context actually began with Alexander the Great (356–323 BC), who controlled his empire by Greek acculturation of the peoples he conquered.

Before his death, Alexander divided his kingdom among his faithful generals. For the next hundred years, the Ptolemys of Egypt and the Seleucids of Greece fought for control of Israel.

The Ptolemys gave greater religious and political freedom, and Israel was able to govern itself. The High Priest became both the religious leader and the political representative.

The Seleucids, however, were Hellenizers. Allegiance and participation in the Greek culture proved loyalty to the crown and brought economic, political, and social benefits. In the year 198 BC, Israel came under the domination of the Seleucids. Within twenty years, the traditional disciplines of Jewish life were almost completely destroyed.

As Jerusalem became a commercial center, many of the more liberal Jews saw the benefits of embracing the Hellenistic lifestyle. They didn't want the restrictions of a religious life, preferring the freedom and sensual pleasures of their secular neighbors. They pursued social acceptance, regardless of the cost. Assimilation for the men meant attending the gymnasium and performing in the nude; thus, many of the men subjected themselves to painful surgery to remove the sign of their circumcision, exalting the Hellenistic culture over their own. Just like Esau before them, they despised their birthright and the sign of their covenant with God.[2]

In opposition to these apostates were the Orthodox, religious Jews who held to the Word of God. The temple, not the gym, was the center of their lives.

Besides the breakdown of traditional values, there were other distinct changes in the local Jewish society:

- Establishment of the synagogue. The Jews were to worship at the temple in Jerusalem. According to Malachi 2:7, the priests were the messengers of the Lord responsible for deciding matters of ritual and morals. During the exile, however, while separated from the temple, the synagogue was established as a local place of fellowship, study, and lively debate. Even today, observant Jewish life revolves around the neighborhood synagogue.
- The scribes were a new class of "intelligentsia," separated from, and not dependent on, the priests. The scribes came to power when Israel was in exile and unable to fulfill God's commandments concerning temple worship. Since the scribes were well versed in the Law of Moses, they devised a religion adapted to their circumstances. When Israel returned to Jerusalem from exile in Babylon, the scribes and priests contended for power. Influenced by a Hellenistic love of debate, the scribes challenged the wisdom of God and the principles of His Word and argued for the wisdom of man's religion and philosophies.
- Corruption of the priests. The priests eventually buckled under the social and political pressure. Some sought to accommodate traditional Judaism to the times.[3] "Their intention was to preserve those characteristics of the

Jewish religion that suited Greek taste, but to remove everything that smacked of the cultural separation of the conservatives."[4]

The compromising of the priests soon led to their corruption and involvement in political alliances.[5]

Cry for religious tolerance. In those days, every nation had its own god. These gods and religions were territorial and exclusive. No foreigner or outsider was able to sacrifice to the gods.

But Jerusalem was different. With the fragmentation of society and the constant flow of foreigners around the city, the cry for religious tolerance was heard. Even though Israel's God was God of the world, the Jews encouraged everyone to worship his own deity in order to maintain an accommodating status quo. They had come so far as to believe that everyone in Israel had the right to worship his own god in his own way.

Tolerance enabled some strange political and religious alliances. The characteristics of Israel in 165 BC bear a striking resemblance to our world today:

- Society was fragmented.
- Everyone wanted the right to "do his own thing."
- God's Word was reinterpreted to accommodate the times.
- Argument challenged authority.
- Materialism and humanism were the order of the day.
- Local taxes were collected by local notables, giving them a stake in their political situation.

- Religion and traditions replaced a simple faith-/grace-based relationship with God.
- The clergy was compromised by those more concerned with money and politics than with worship and care for the people.

HANUKKAH—THE STORY

In 165 BC, Antiochus IV came to power. He has been described as restless, energetic, opinionated, and emotionally unbalanced. He could not stand to be contradicted and was totally undisciplined. His aides had to detangle him constantly from one error after another.

Antiochus considered himself to be a god and gave himself the nickname Epiphanes, which means "god in the flesh," or "god manifest." The Jews nicknamed him Epimanes, which means "madman." Antiochus was determined to eliminate anyone who rebelled or challenged him. Inspired by a demonic hatred, he turned against the righteous remnant of the Jews. He issued terrible decrees against them and against their worship. He forbade the practice of Judaism, including:

- Sacrifices of burnt offerings in the sanctuary
- Keeping the Sabbaths and feasts
- Keeping the dietary laws
- Circumcision

  In fact, if a male child was found circumcised, the child was killed and the dead body was hung around the mother's neck until she too died.

- Reading of the Scriptures

  Anyone found in possession of a Torah was condemned to death; and the Torah was taken, torn into pieces, and burned.

Antiochus built altars and shrines for idols; defiled the temple by erecting a statue of Zeus, which looked very much like himself; and demanded the sacrifice and eating of swine (considered unclean animals).

Each person had to decide if he would obey God or Antiochus, some preferring death to apostasy. The final showdown took place in a small town outside of Jerusalem called Modi'in.

The accounts of this event set the scene: Appelles, a messenger from the king, strode into town carrying a squealing piglet. The townspeople gathered around a priest named Mattathias and his five sons.

Face to face with Mattathias, Appelles said:

> *You are a leader, honored and great in this town ... Now be the first to come and do what the king commands ... Then you and your sons ... will be honored with silver, gold and with many gifts.* —*1 Maccabees 2:17-18* (NRSV)

A hush settled upon the people as the two men faced each other. Echoing the words of Joshua, Mattathias answered:

> *Even if all the nations that live under the rule of the king obey him, and have chosen to do his commandments ... I and my sons and my brothers will continue to live by the covenant of our ancestors ... We will not obey the king's words by turning aside from our religion to the right hand or to the left.*
>
> —*1 Maccabees 2:19-22; cf. Joshua 24:14-17* (NRSV)

Tension mounted. Another hush blanketed the people. Suddenly, a man rushed forward from the crowd and, in sight of all the people, sacrificed the pig upon the altar. In a righteous rage, Mattathias slew the villager, Appelles, and a few of his soldiers. Turning to the stunned villagers, he issued this challenge: "If any one be zealous for the laws of this country, and for worship of God, let him follow me."[6] With that, Mattathias and his sons left everything and ran into the desert.

Their decision began three years of warfare. This was a defining war in Israel's history. It set Jew against Jew, separating those who were determined to follow God from those who were willing to compromise.

Mattathias and his sons were soon joined by other righteous men and women, zealous for God and His city. Their ranks were thin and poorly armed. Most of them were farmers using their tools as weapons. Their commander was Judas, soon nicknamed Judas the Hammer (Maccabee in Hebrew) because of his style of guerilla warfare.

Night after night this ragtag army would come down from the hills and hammer away at the Greek army. Completely outnumbered and ill-equipped against the Antiochus' forces, the Jews were continually inspired by Judas' battle cry. For three years the battle raged until God gave Judas and his army a miraculous victory.

Without hesitation, their victory march went straight to the temple. The city was in ruins, filled with pagan idolatry and immoral living.

The condition of the temple was worse. Before them was the defiled altar. It had once been dedicated to God but could never be used again. Legend tells that they took apart the altar stone by stone, saying that "one day Messiah will come, and He will tell us what to do with the defiled stones." Then they built a new altar—a memorial of God's victory and faithfulness.

THE LEGEND OF THE OIL

Legend claims that when Judah went to light the temple menorahs, he found only a small cruse of oil. Although only enough for one day, that oil burned for eight days until new oil could be consecrated. Hence, Hanukkah today is celebrated for eight days and is often referred to as the Festival of Lights.

But the history books never mention this miraculous provision. God could, of course, stretch the oil; but the greater miracle is the victory of a small group of ill-suited men, women, and children who fought for God and defeated a mighty, powerful army. The miraculous provision was the victory of the faithful righteous!

HANUKKAH—THE CELEBRATION

"So," you ask, "if the legend of the oil is subject to debate, then why is Hanukkah celebrated for eight days? And why do we light candles?"[7]

Glad you asked. Our historians give us a clue by calling the holiday "Sukkot of Kislev."[8] Remember that Solomon and Ezra dedicated the temple on the Feast of Tabernacles [*Sukkot*]. I imagine that the Maccabees worked furiously to finish cleansing the temple in time to rededicate it on the same festival, but time ran out.

Consequently, they simply patterned their dedication celebration after the Feast of Tabernacles. Their choice of date was exactly three years to the day since Antiochus had first defiled the temple; thus Hanukkah became an eight-day celebration including the illumination of Jerusalem!

Spiritual

Hanukkah reveals one of my favorite aspects of God's character—He loves to show off!

> *For the eyes of the LORD run to and fro throughout the whole earth, to show Himself strong on behalf of those whose heart is loyal to Him.*
> *—2 Chronicles 16:9a*

He loves to come to the aid of His people, especially when they are in (humanly) impossible situations. But don't miss the condition of receiving God's strength—having a heart that is loyal to Him.

THE LORD IS STRONG IN BATTLE

There is no enemy in the natural or the supernatural realm that can stand before God. Sadly, some have considered that God of the Old Testament is violent, while God of the New Testament is peaceful. God cannot change. Yes, God does not take pleasure in battle but will always fight for righteousness and justice:

> *The LORD is a man of war; the LORD is His name. Pharaoh's chariots and his army He has cast into the sea; his chosen captains also are drowned in the Red Sea … Your right hand, O LORD, has become glorious in power; Your right hand, O LORD, has dashed the enemy in pieces. And in the greatness of Your excellence You have overthrown those who rose against You.*
> *—Exodus 15:3-7*

YHWH NISSI—THE LORD IS MY BANNER

The battle might be the Lord's, but sometimes He expects us to march into the battle with Him. When we do so under His banner, He assures us of the victory:

Then David said to the Philistine, "You come to me with a sword, with a spear, and with a javelin. But I come to you in the name of the LORD of hosts, the God of the armies of Israel, whom you have defied. This day the LORD will deliver you into my hand, and I will strike you and take your head from you. And this day I will give the carcasses of the camp of the Philistines to the birds of the air and the wild beasts of the earth, that all the earth may know that there is a God in Israel. Then all this assembly shall know that the LORD does not save with sword and spear; for the battle is the LORD's, and He will give you into our hands."
—1 Samuel 17:45-47

ISRAEL'S PROTECTOR

Hanukkah reminds us that God's plans will always prevail. Throughout Israel's history, many have tried to bring her to destruction. These attempts have always, and will always, come to nothing. Israel belongs to God, and He will never fail her:[9]

Run, speak to this young man, saying: "Jerusalem shall be inhabited as towns without walls, because of the multitude of men and livestock in it. 'For I,' says the LORD, 'will be a wall of fire all around her, and I will be the glory in her midst.'" *—Zechariah 2:4-5*

Take counsel together, but it will come to nothing; speak the word, but it will not stand, for God is with us.
—Isaiah 8:10; cf. Psalm 2:1-4

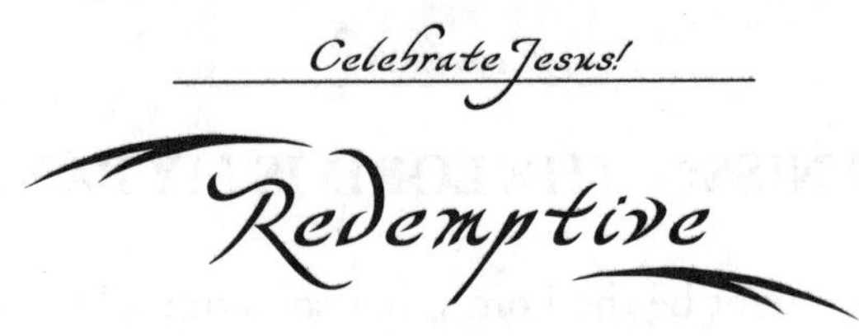

As Jesus used the ceremonies and traditions of Tabernacles to declare His identity, so He did again on Hanukkah.

To appreciate how Jesus fulfills the redemptive aspect of Hanukkah, let's advance time from 163 BC to approximately AD 32. The Jews are under the domination of Rome and longing for a Messiah who would bring political and religious freedom.[10] I'm sure that, since the appearance of Jesus at the Feast of Tabernacles just a few months prior, many of the Jews had pondered His declarations about Himself. Now Jesus is in Jerusalem for the last time before His return for Passover ... and His crucifixion. The religious leaders and the people are anxiously waiting for Him to appear publicly. When he finally does, you can hear the anxiety in their challenge:

> *Then the Jews surrounded Him and said to Him, "How long do You keep us in doubt? If You are the Christ, tell us plainly."* —*John 10:24*

Moses had not been their Messiah. Judah Maccabee had ultimately failed them as a messiah. The people were obviously looking for the Messiah, but just as obviously not willing to recognize Him. This is still true of many today, particularly among the religious Jews in Jerusalem.

Saturday nights, at the close of the Sabbath, many Orthodox celebrate at the pedestrian mall in downtown Jerusalem, dancing with abandon and singing: "Messiah, Messiah!"

"Why are you dancing?" I asked once. "We're rejoicing because the Messiah is coming soon," was the response.

"But how will you know Him?" I asked.

"We just will," was the answer and the answer of many people today.

Will they? Listen to Jesus' answer:

> *Jesus answered them, "I told you, and you do not believe. The works that I do in My Father's name, they bear witness of Me. But you do not believe, because you are not of My sheep, as I said to you. My sheep hear My voice, and I know them, and they follow Me."*
> *—John 10:25-27*

Jesus *had* told them, with His words and His works. So the problem wasn't His communication or their ears. The problem was their hearts. Hanukkah would be His last public declaration of His deity—that He was their long-awaited Messiah. He, not Antiochus, was God made flesh.

The people wanted a warrior Messiah. Jesus was declaring that He was the Good Shepherd of Israel. The declarations Jesus made during Hanukkah clearly refute the argument that He never claimed to be God.

JESUS IS THE TRUE SHEPHERD

Just prior to Hanukkah, Jesus claimed to be the Good Shepherd, thus taking on Himself a messianic title.[11] Now He then went further, claiming to give eternal life. Who else but God can promise eternal life?

> *And I give them eternal life, and they shall never perish; neither shall anyone snatch them out of My hand.*
> *—John 10:28*

JESUS AND THE FATHER ARE ONE

Jesus' next statement was such a clear declaration of His equality with God the Father that the Jews took up stones to stone Him:

> *My Father, who has given them to Me, is greater than all; and no one is able to snatch them out of My Father's hand. I and My Father are one.*
> —John 10:29-30

JESUS IS THE SENT ONE

Jesus gave one more opportunity for their hard hearts and blind eyes to see Him for who He really was and is:

> *Jesus answered them, "Is it not written in your law, 'I said, "You are gods"'? "If He called them gods, to whom the word of God came (and the Scripture cannot be broken), do you say of Him whom the Father sanctified and sent into the world, 'You are blaspheming,' because I said, 'I am the Son of God'? If I do not do the works of My Father, do not believe Me; but if I do, though you do not believe Me, believe the works, that you may know and believe that the Father is in Me, and I in Him."*
> —John 10:34-38

The people finally understood His words, but their hard hearts rejected them, and "they sought again to seize Him" (John 10:39).

Eschatological

The history of Hanukkah is actually foretold by the prophet Daniel. Immediately after Daniel prophesies the seventy weeks of Israel's future history (9:24-26), the prophet then seemingly details the upcoming wars of Antiochus against Israel. Daniel's account is so precise that many Bible critics dispute his authorship, saying that these chapters were written years after the facts.[12]

The prophetic details missing from Antiochus' reign seem to indicate a future fulfillment. When answering the disciples' questions about the end of times, Jesus refers to Daniel's prophecy:

> *Therefore when you see the "abomination of desolation," spoken of by Daniel the prophet, standing in the holy place . . . then let those who are in Judea flee to the mountains.*
> *—Matthew 24:15-16*

Jesus, Paul, and John expanded Daniel's description of the one foreshadowed by Antiochus.[13] The antichrist will do all the things that Antiochus did, but on a greater scale and with greater intensity. The hatred of the Jewish people will be unprecedented, dimming even the horrors of the Holocaust. He will deceive by flatteries and intrigues, and many will willingly, or unwittingly, follow him.

Knowing the challenges that are ahead for Israel, I receive comfort and hope from the real miracle of Hanukkah—the victory of the faithful righteous.

The story of Hanukkah is the story of a righteous remnant that refused to be part of the world, insisting and fighting for the right to worship and obey God.

While we might say that many people are fighting for the same right today, in reality many have perverted the commandments of God, insisting on the right to do what they want to do in the name of religious freedom. Today is just like the days of Israel's judges:

> ... *everyone did what was right in his own eyes.*
> *—Judges 21:25*

Let me suggest that we all ask ourselves some soul-searching questions. If we are honest, our answers will prepare us to stand firm in the shakings that are coming:

- Who is my Shepherd?
- Who is my Commander-in-Chief?
- How completely will I obey the commands of God?
- What price am I willing to pay?

Let's consider each of these in greater detail.

WHO IS MY SHEPHERD?

It's easy to be led astray, especially when confronted by flattering words. Sin loves company and will seek those who can be lured by temptation. We might suddenly find ourselves in a place we had no intention of being.

My dog Boffin showed me how easily I could follow the wrong shepherd. Although I always kept Boffin on a leash, I often didn't hold it; it simply dragged behind him, giving him an element of freedom. One day I noticed that he was gone. The neighbor's dog had left his yard, picked up Boffin's leash, and was leading him in the other direction. The look on Boffin's face showed confusion and fear. He knew he was being led astray but wasn't quite sure how it happened!

How often do we do the same thing? We allow a bad shepherd to lead us in the wrong direction!

Jesus said that His sheep hear and follow His voice. Any other voice is that of the enemy of our souls:

> *But he who enters by the door is the shepherd of the sheep. To him the doorkeeper opens, and the sheep hear his voice; and he calls his own sheep by name and leads them out. And when he brings out his own sheep, he goes before them; and the sheep follow him, for they know his voice.*
>
> *—John 10:2-4*

Look at the description of the sheep:

- They know the Shepherd with knowledge from an intimacy born of abiding in Him.
- They hear His voice with an understanding that leads to obedience.
- They trust Him because He calls them by name.
- They follow Him.

Please note that knowledge comes before obedience. God is much more concerned about our relationship with Him than our service for Him.

WHO IS MY COMMANDER-IN-CHIEF?

The first person or thing that we turn to in a crisis is actually our commander, revealing to whom (or to what) we automatically turn to fight our battles. Sadly, I often run to the refrigerator, seeking comfort and strength to fight my battles. Or I run to the telephone to call whomever I know is available, hoping someone else will fight the battle. Eventually, I pray; but turning to God is not my immediate reaction (other than a quick "O God!").

Neither food nor people can take the place of God as my Commander:

> *The eternal God is your refuge, and underneath are the everlasting arms; He will thrust out the enemy from before you, and will say, "Destroy!"*
>
> *—Deuteronomy 33:27*

HOW COMPLETELY WILL I OBEY THE COMMANDS OF GOD?

What is my level of obedience? When I do finally seek God's direction, how quickly and how fully do I respond?

From the beginning of recorded time, mankind used religion to mimic an intimate relationship with God.

The word *religion* is very interesting. The prefix "re" usually indicates a repetition (repeat, return, renew). "Legion" comes from the same root as "ligament," which is a connecting tie. In other words, "religion" is man's attempt to reconnect with God. Although this is an admirable effort, it's impossible. Man simply cannot make the connection, much less the reconnection. That is what the gospel is all about—God doing what man cannot. God takes the initiative and offers to restore the relationship. Hopefully, we respond.

Hanukkah reminds us that by trying to adapt God's commands, attempting to make them more relevant to our lives, or substituting traditions of men, religion will often (sometimes insidiously) lead us away from God.

WHAT PRICE AM I WILLING TO PAY?

Every decision impacts destiny. Our decision to follow Jesus will determine our eternal destiny, which is heaven. Decisions, however small, will also impact our lives on earth. Decisions impact relationships, lifestyle, and ministry—just to name a few key areas. Life choices will also affect our eternal rewards. Every choice, every decision, has consequences.

The reality of our lives today is that each of us is being confronted with three paths:

- Comfort
- Compromise
- Commitment

Success can only be measured by our unflinching, unfailing obedience to the revealed will of God—regardless of the consequences.

At the time of this writing, most of the world is being shaken. There are economic and natural disasters. Similar pressures attack us from the spiritual realm. To stand firm in the face of challenge, catastrophe, and crisis takes the grace of God. We've spoken before about God's purposes in the midst of trial. According to the prophetic word from Daniel, our situation will get worse before getting better. But we can be encouraged by God's promises:

> *The people who know their God shall be strong, and carry out great exploits. And those of the people who*

> *understand shall instruct many; yet for many days they shall fall by sword and flame, by captivity and plundering. Now when they fall, they shall be aided with a little help; but many shall join with them by intrigue. And some of those of understanding shall fall, to refine them, purify them, and make them white, until the time of the end; because it is still for the appointed time.*
> —*Daniel 11:32-35*

Let us all write these words upon our souls, our minds, our emotions, and our wills. Only as we believe will we be established and kept in perfect peace. God promises that we will do great exploits while being refined and purified. That's a goal worth striving for!

REDEDICATE YOUR TEMPLE

As you celebrate Hanukkah, remember that you are the temple of the Holy Spirit. Your body is His dwelling place. Perhaps you have been defiled by sin and trampled upon by the enemy. Hanukkah gives us a unique opportunity to "present our bodies a living sacrifice" (Romans 12:1) and "to lay aside every weight and sin" (Hebrews 12:1). On each day, present a specific part of your body/temple unto the Lord for His cleansing and service:

- Mouth[14]
- Lips[15]
- Tongue[16]
- Heart[17]
- Mind[18]
- Feet[19]
- Ears[20]
- Eyes[21]

LET YOUR LIGHT SHINE

The traditional celebration of Hanukkah includes lighting a candle, or candles, on each of the eight nights of the holiday. A special nine-branch candelabra (called a Hanukkiah) is used. The ninth candle is called the *Shamos* or Servant. This candle is lit first and then it lights all the others designated for that night.

In like manner, when you are lit by the flame of God's love, the light of Jesus ignites the other eight fruits of the Holy Spirit:

- Love releases joy.
- Joy releases peace.
- Peace releases longsuffering.
- Longsuffering releases kindness.
- Kindness releases goodness.
- Goodness releases faithfulness.
- Faithfulness releases gentleness.
- Gentleness releases self-control.

You then become the fully-lit candelabra of God, shedding His light and love into the dark world.

We have one more holiday to go, the last holiday of the year, the holiday of Purim.

Endnotes

1. Schauss, H. (1938). *The Jewish Festivals: History and Observance.* Union of American Hebrew Congregations, p. 223.
2. "In those days there came forth out of Israel transgressors of the law, and persuaded many saying, 'Let us go and make a covenant with the Gentiles that are around us; for since we parted from them many evils have befallen us.' And the saying was good in their eyes. And certain of the people were forward herein, and went to the king and he gave them license to do after the ordinances of the Gentiles. And they built a place of exercise in Jerusalem according to the law of the Gentiles; and they made themselves uncircumcised, and forsook the holy covenant, and joined themselves to the Gentiles and sold themselves to do evil" (1 Maccabee 1:11-15).
3. This is why the Judaism of today looks so different from the Judaism of the Bible.
4. Bickerman, Elias, source unknown.
5. This fascinating, yet depressing, history is recorded by Flavius Josephus, *Antiquities of the Jews, Book XII.*
6. Maccabees 2:27.
7. Among Jewish homes today, the holiday is observed by lighting a special nine-branch candlebra. Songs are sung and presents are exchanged, which is why some consider Hanukkah to be the "Jewish Christmas." Foods fried in oil (e.g., potato pancakes, jelly donuts) are eaten.
8. Kislev is the Jewish month that corresponds approximately to December. [*Sukkot*] is the Hebrew name for the Feast of Tabernacles.
9. Psalm 121.
10. Within 100 years, the Maccabees (the Hasamonean dynasty) became corrupt and eventually made alliances with Rome. In 63 BC, Pompey attacked and conquered Jerusalem, once again bringing Jews under the yoke of the Gentiles.
11. John 10:1; Psalm 23:1; Isaiah 40:11.
12. Daniel's prophecy is so accurate that one of my students exclaimed, "This proves to me that the Bible is true. I'm getting my life straightened out NOW."
13. Matthew 25:15-22; 2 Thessalonians 2:3-4; Revelation 12:1-5; 13:15-17.
14. Romans 10:10; Isaiah 49:2.
15. Psalm 34:13.
16. Proverbs 27:2; Psalm 145:21.
17. Deuteronomy 6:5.
18. Isaiah 26:3.
19. Romans 10:15.
20. Proverbs 23:12; Psalm 40:6.
21. Ephesians 1:18; Psalm 119:37.

Chapter Sixteen

Purim

For This Purpose

So they called these days Purim, after the name Pur. Therefore, because of all the words of this letter, what they had seen concerning this matter, and what had happened to them, the Jews established and imposed it upon themselves and their descendants and all who would join them, that without fail they should celebrate these two days every year, according to the written instructions and according to the prescribed time, that these days should be remembered and kept throughout every generation, every family, every province, and every city, that these days of Purim should not fail to be observed among the Jews, and that the memory of them should not perish among their descendants.
—Esther 9:26-28

It was 1995, and I was coming to Israel for the first time. As the Land came into view, I was shocked by its appearance and by my reaction. The land of milk and honey was anything but that. All I saw was a tiny strip of brown. Yet I began to cry, whispering, "Daddy, I'm home."

During the next few weeks, God confirmed that Israel was to indeed become my home, although the process would take three years. The wait seemed interminable. Finally, after a week of fasting, praying, and devouring books on Israel's prophetic future, I heard the Lord's voice. He gave me a date: December ninth. Then He gave me a purpose: *Declare the good news of My salvation, first to the Jews and then to the nations.*

Purpose is one of the main themes of Purim—for Israel, for the church, and for each of us.

Seasonal

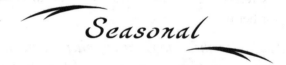

Purim is celebrated during the final days of winter, exactly one month before Passover.[1] There are two components to the celebration of Purim: fasting on the first day and feasting on the second day.

National

Purim is not a Levitical holiday but is mandated in the book of Esther. The holiday commemorates Israel's deliverance from annihilation in the Persian Empire.

The dramatic story begins with a beauty pageant and ends with a banquet. It is as much a love story as it is an adventure story. Full of twists and turns, it ends with a reversal of fate, as the intended victims become the victors. At the end of the story, the villain, Haman, is hung on the same gallows he built to hang the hero, Mordecai:

> *Behold, the wicked brings forth iniquity; yes, he conceives trouble and brings forth falsehood. He made a pit and dug it out, and has fallen into the ditch which he made. His trouble shall return upon his own head, and his violent dealing shall come down on his own crown.*
> —*Psalm 7:14-16*

Esther, our story's heroine, experiences a different reversal of fate. Esther, who began her life as an orphan, became the Queen of Persia. The turning point of the entire drama hinges on Esther's response to Mordecai's challenge to consider the purpose for her life:

> *And Mordecai told them to answer Esther: "Do not think in your heart that you will escape in the king's palace any more than all the other Jews. For if you remain completely silent at this time, relief and deliverance will arise for the Jews from another place, but you and your father's house will perish. Yet who knows whether you have come to the kingdom for such a time as this?"*
> —*Esther 4:13-14*

Esther's response resulted in the salvation of her people:

> *Then Esther told them to reply to Mordecai: "Go, gather all the Jews who are present in Shushan, and fast for me; neither eat nor drink for three days, night or day. My maids and I will fast likewise. And so I will go to the king, which is against the law; and if I perish, I perish!"*
> —*Esther 4:15-16*

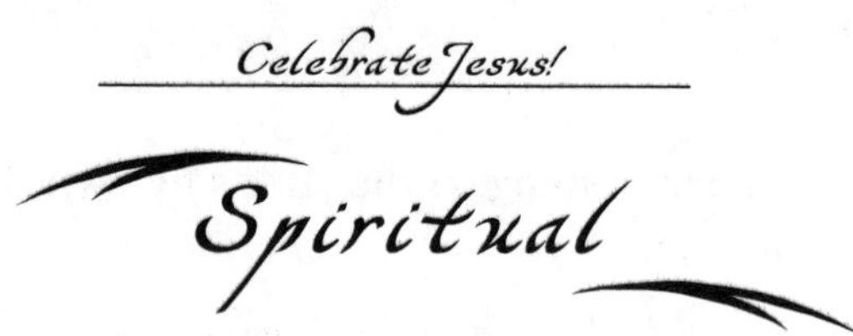

Let's consider four aspects of God's character that we can celebrate at Purim.

OMNIPRESENCE

Although God's name is never mentioned, His presence throughout the story is undeniable. God is everywhere, whether we see Him, ignore Him, or deny Him. The psalmist asks:

> *Where can I go from Your Spirit? Or where can I flee from Your presence?* —*Psalm 139:7*

The answer is, "Nowhere!"

OMNISCIENCE

In our earlier discussion of God's character, we learned that "He is God Who Sees" [*'el ro'i*]. He sees us with understanding and compassion, knowing exactly what we are experiencing and feeling.

OMNIPOTENCE

Then God, who is always present and always seeing, acts on our behalf. Consider these sovereign acts without which the story would have had a very different ending:

- Removal of Vashti
- Placement of Esther within the palace and Mordechai at its gates
- Esther crowned queen
- Sleepless night of the king

GOD'S COVENANT WITH ISRAEL

Purim is another example of the blessings of God's covenant relationship with Israel. He is her defense against Satan's determination to thwart God's redemptive plans. The core of Satan's demonic strategy is the annihilation of Israel and the Jewish people. If the Jews could be destroyed and Israel "washed into the sea," so could all of God's promises and purposes for Israel, and God would become impotent and a liar.

Two aspects of God's covenant with Israel are reflected in the story of Purim.

- His protection:

  "For I," says the LORD, "will be a wall of fire all around her, and I will be the glory in her midst."
  —Zechariah 2:5

- His vengeance against her enemies:

  He sent Me after glory, to the nations which plunder you; for he who touches you touches the apple of His eye.
  —Zechariah 2:8

  For the indignation of the LORD is against all nations, and His fury against all their armies; He has utterly destroyed them, He has given them over to the slaughter ... For it is the day of the LORD's vengeance, the year of recompense for the cause of Zion.
  —Isaiah 34:2, 8

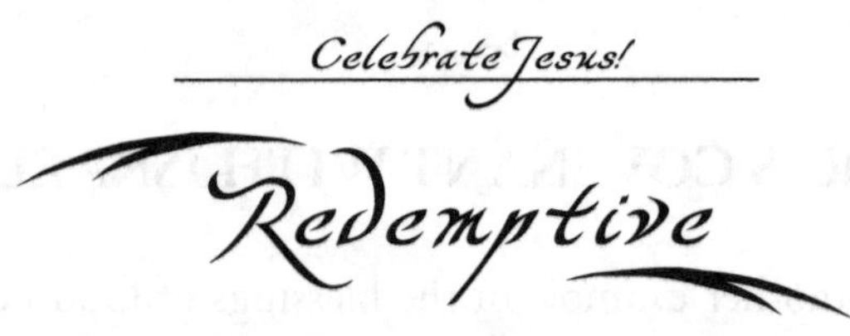

The redemptive aspect of Purim revolves around purpose. Here, we will consider "purpose" as it relates to the nation of Israel and to Jesus.

GOD'S PURPOSES FOR ISRAEL

God chose Israel as His witness to be a light to the Gentiles; through her, He would reveal to the Gentiles His character and His ways.

> *The LORD has made known His salvation; His righteousness He has revealed in the sight of the nations. He has remembered His mercy and His faithfulness to the house of Israel; all the ends of the earth have seen the salvation of our God.* —*Psalm 98:2-3*[2]

To that end, Israel was tasked:

- Preserve His word[3]
- Fulfill God's purposes of election[4]
- Birth the Messiah in human form[5]
- Initiate His return[6]
- Be a watershed for judging the nations[7]

JESUS CAME FOR AND WITH A PURPOSE

Queen Esther was determined to fulfill her destiny, regardless of the cost. Esther was able to save her people without giving her life. Jesus was not. In fact, He came knowing that the cost of salvation for Israel and the world would be His life:

Christ Jesus, who, being in the form of God, did not consider it robbery to be equal with God, but made Himself of no reputation, taking the form of a bondservant, and coming in the likeness of men. And being found in appearance as a man, He humbled Himself and became obedient to the point of death, even the death of the cross.
—Philippians 2:5b-8

Volumes have been written about God's purposes through Jesus. Below I've listed just a few:

- Destroy the works of the devil[8]
- Enable adoption by the Father[9]
- Offer salvation[10]
- Forgive, cleanse, justify, and make righteous[11]
- Offer abundant and eternal life[12]
- Call the sinners to repentance[13]
- Establish God's eternal reign on earth (a restoration of all things)[14]

JESUS, THE ULTIMATE ISRAEL

Jesus envelops Israel's destiny and fulfills all the Father's prophesies about, and promises to, her.

- A light to the Gentiles:

  For my eyes have seen Your salvation which You have prepared before the face of all peoples, a light to bring revelation to the Gentiles, and the glory of Your people Israel. *—Luke 2:30-32: cf. Isaiah 49:6*

- Israel's protector:

  Jerusalem, Jerusalem, the one who kills the prophets and stones those who are sent to her! How often I wanted to gather your children together, as a hen gathers her chicks under her wings. —*Matthew 23:37*

- Israel's avenger:

  Then the Lord will go forth and fight against those nations, as He fights in the day of battle. And in that day His feet will stand on the Mount of Olives. —*Zechariah 14:3-4a*

Kingdom

Before we apply the Kingdom principle of purpose, I'd like to look at the aspect of grace. As we discussed in our study of Hanukkah, a relationship with God is more important than service to God. The grace (favor) Esther received from her husband, the king, is a mere reflection of what we can expect from our Husband/King.

THE FAVOR OF GOD

As part of our studies on Passover and Atonement, we discussed the Hebrew and Greek words for *grace*. We pointed out that, of the 190 times the Greek [*charis*] is used in the Septuagint, 61 of the 75 times where there is a direct equivalent to the Greek, the Hebrew word for *grace* is [*chanan*]. This word is usually used with God as the subject, with Him bestowing grace upon the needy. In Purim, we find the derivative [*chen*] being used "primarily in a secular context where the focus is on the recipient not the giver. In a number of cases, [*chen*] means '*charm*' or *an attractive personality that creates a favorable impression*."[15] [*Chen*] describes how the king felt about Esther:

> *The king loved Esther more than all the other women, and she obtained grace and favor in his sight more than all the virgins; so he set the royal crown upon her head and made her queen instead of Vashti.*
> *—Esther 2:17*

The dramatic turn of events in our story hinged on Esther receiving grace/favor:

> *Now it happened on the third day that Esther put on her royal robes and stood in the inner court of the king's palace, across from the king's house, while the king sat on his royal throne in the royal house, facing the entrance of the house. So it was, when the king saw Queen Esther standing in the court that she found favor in his sight, and the king held out to Esther the golden scepter that was in his hand. Then Esther went near and touched the top of the scepter.*
> *—Esther 5:1-2*

Try to put yourself in this real-life example:

> It's your wedding day. Groom, you are standing at the altar, waiting for the woman who has agreed to be your bride to walk with you for the rest of your lives. In a few moments, you will stand together, making vows to love, honor, and cherish until death parts you.
>
> All eyes dart between you and the closed door through which she will come. The door remains shut.
>
> Butterflies are multiplying in your stomach. You begin to doubt. You begin to wonder. You start asking, "Where is she?" "Will she come?" "Has she changed her mind?"

> You're sure something is wrong because the aisle remains empty. Family has now been seated. The music drones on—but not the bridal song.
>
> You panic. You sweat. The back door is still frustratingly closed.
>
> The pianist lifts her fingers off the keys . . . waiting. A hush falls. The door opens.
>
> There! Billows of white peek from behind the attendants. You strain to get a better look at her.
>
> You cannot breathe. You cannot move. Your entire past has dissolved in this one moment. Your future is beyond comprehension. Just this one moment exists for all eternity.
>
> There is no one else in the room. Just your bride. Your bride.
>
> She's agreed to forsake all others, committing only to you. Although you belong to each other, all you can think of is, "She's mine!"

As we saw above in Esther 2:7, *chen* described how the king felt about Esther. Remember that it means *grace* and *favor*? It also has the meaning of *a charming, attractive personality that creates a (very) favorable impression*. And it describes how the King feels about you.

The moment you said "Yes" to Jesus, the angels did flips in heaven. The Father might have turned to the entire heavenly host saying, "She's mine!" or "He's mine!" Jesus the Son is beyond joy. He's too much in love with you to do anything but murmur, "I am My beloved's and My beloved is Mine."

One glance from you ravishes the heart of God. One cry from you, and He is ready and able to comfort and rescue you. You belong to each other in covenant relationship for eternity.

Now, glowing with God's love, we are ready to talk about His purposes for the Kingdom community and for each of us.[16]

THE KINGDOM COMMUNITY

God has distinct purposes ordained for the Kingdom community as a whole:

- To advance the Kingdom of God

  God's purpose for the church is similar to His call upon Israel. Perhaps this is the cause of so much confusion and, worse, the rise of replacement theology.

  - Same mandate: Fill the earth with the knowledge of God's glory.
  - Same mission: Be a witness to the world.
  - Same message: "Salvation by grace through faith."

  And Jesus came and spoke to them, saying, "All authority has been given to Me in heaven and on earth. Go therefore and make disciples of all the nations, baptizing them in the name of the Father and of the Son and of the Holy Spirit, teaching them to observe all things that I have commanded you."
  —Matthew 28:18-20

- To pray for the peace of Jerusalem

  The church is commanded to pray specifically for the peace of Jerusalem. Someone once said to me, "God is not interested in real estate." That statement is fundamentally false. God apportions land to the nations, and He has chosen Israel as His home and Jerusalem as His capital. From there, He will rule His Kingdom. For those who have become citizens of this Kingdom, Israel becomes our adopted home. How can we NOT pray for her?

I have set watchmen on your walls, O Jerusalem; they shall never hold their peace day or night. You who make mention of the LORD, do not keep silent, and give Him no rest till He establishes and till He makes Jerusalem a praise in the earth.
—Isaiah 62:6-7

Pray for the peace of Jerusalem: "May they prosper who love you. Peace be within your walls, prosperity within your palaces." For the sake of my brethren and companions, I will now say, "Peace be within you." Because of the house of the LORD our God I will seek your good. *—Psalm 122:6-9*

GENTILE BELIEVERS

There are purposes given specifically to the Gentile believer:

- To make the Jews jealous

  Most Jewish believers were introduced to Jesus through the witness of Gentiles. God specifically purposes the Gentiles to make the Jews jealous:

  But through [Israel's] fall, to provoke them to jealousy, salvation has come to the Gentiles.
  —Romans 11:11b

  That is what happened to me. I was angry, resentful, and jealous that John knew my God better than I did. It only took a few months of watching his life and his relationship with God before I had to know God the way he did!

❧ To help rebuild Jerusalem

God called the Gentile King Cyrus to fund the rebuilding of the temple and the walls of Jerusalem.[17] God is still calling on the Gentiles to help rebuild Israel today:

Then you shall see and become radiant, and your heart shall swell with joy; because the abundance of the sea shall be turned to you, the wealth of the Gentiles shall come to you ... The sons of foreigners shall build up your walls, and their kings shall minister to you.
—Isaiah 60:5, 10a

❧ To rejoice over the destruction of Israel's enemies

Alignment with God's purposes will result in rejoicing over the destruction of His enemies. Israel's enemies are His enemies. Notice:

Rejoice, O Gentiles, with His people; for He will avenge the blood of His servants, and render vengeance to His adversaries; He will provide atonement for His land and His people.
—Deuteronomy 32:43

❧ To receive God's blessings

Standing with God's purposes will always result in receiving His blessings. We must ask ourselves, however, "What is my motivation?" We cannot do something in order to receive God's promised blessings but to receive them in response to obedience. God's promise was to Abraham and his seed:

I will bless those who bless you, and I will curse him who curses you. *—Genesis 12:3a*

JEWISH BELIEVERS

I hope I have made a strong case that when a Jewish person becomes a follower of Jesus, his identity as a Jew neither ends nor does it change… nor does the call of God upon his life as a part of Israel change. Therefore, I suggest that there is a unique and distinct purpose placed upon the Jewish believer—to prepare the Land for the coming of the King.[18] Israel has been given the responsibility and authority to steward this Land for God's future purposes.

GOD'S PURPOSES FOR YOU!

One of the three universal questions of life is, "What is my purpose?"[19] We can find the answer to this question through faith in Jesus. This one verse gives you all the answers:

> *For by grace you have been saved through faith, and that not of yourselves; it is the gift of God, not of works, lest anyone should boast. For we are His workmanship, created in Christ Jesus for good works, which God prepared beforehand that we should walk in them.*
> *—Ephesians 2:8-10*

Your identity is the workmanship of Christ. You belong in relationship with Him because you have been saved through faith. Your purpose and destiny is to walk in the good works that already have been prepared for you.

Purim confronts and challenges us to fulfill those good works (purposes) in at least four ways:

Be obedient

The son who said, "No" at first later obeyed and did the will of his father.[20]

I believe that God doesn't look askance if we struggle with a life assignment. Jesus Himself earnestly prayed for a different cup:[21]

And He said, "Abba, Father, all things are possible for You. Take this cup away from Me; nevertheless, not what I will, but what You will."
—Mark 14:36

The outcome, not the struggle, is what matters. The issue is, "Will we be obedient?" One single act of disobedience can result in catastrophe. Haman was an Agagite, a descendent of Amalek whom God ordered King Saul to destroy. Saul disobeyed and spared the Amalekite king. The descendants of that king have continued to harass Israel to this very day.

No matter what the assignment, what purposes God has for you, His grace will be sufficient for you to obey.

Be intentional

Esther was intentional. She knew her purpose and developed a strategy for success. Where God puts you is irrelevant. Fulfilling God's purpose in and through you is the issue. Through prayer, allow God to give you His strategy. Then obey!

- Trust in God for the results

Can you imagine the fear Esther might have felt when approaching the King without a summons? I believe that it was her trust in God that enabled her to go forward. We studied the Hebrew words for *trust* [*chasah*] and [*batach*] in our study of "Passover: Kingdom."[22] Trust is both *a feeling* and *an action*. Trust is the first step toward faith:

> *Those who trust in the LORD are like Mount Zion, which cannot be moved, but abides forever. As the mountains surround Jerusalem, so the LORD surrounds His people from this time forth and forever.*
> *—Psalm 125:1-2*

Confidence leads to action:

> *The name of the LORD is a strong tower; the righteous run to it and are safe.* *—Proverbs 18:10*

- Obey unto death

All around the world today there are men, women, and children who are being tortured and killed for the name of Christ Jesus. Without doubt or hesitation, I tell you that in the coming days we will all have the opportunity and privilege to stand for Jesus, even unto death.

I was a new believer at seminary. The professor asked the class, "For what would you die?" There was an uneasy silence as the students (mostly pastors) carefully pondered their answers. Not me. My bravado was quick and confident, "I would die for the gospel!" While I might not answer so quickly today, I hope my answer would be the same.

Let us press onward, resting in the victory and grace God gives to those who will stand faithfully for Him.

"Causes may come and go, but we are born for a purpose."[23]

Endnotes

1. The thirteenth and fourteenth days of the twelfth month, according to the Jewish calendar, fall in February–March.
2. "Salvation" [*ye shu'ah*] [*yesha'*]; "mercy and faithfulness" [*'emet v^e chesed*].
3. Romans 9:4; 15:4.
4. Romans 9:11.
5. Genesis 3:15; Galatians 4:4-5.
6. Matthew 23:37-39.
7. Joel 3:1-3; Zechariah 1:18-21; 12:1-4; Matthew 25:31-46.
8. Hebrews 2:14.
9. John 1:12-13.
10. Acts 4:12.
11. Ephesians 5:26; 1 John 1:9; Matthew 1:21; Romans 3:24-25.
12. John 10:10; 3:16.
13. Matthew 9:13.
14. Psalm 51:12; Isaiah 57:18; Jeremiah 3:22.
15. TWOT, #694a.
16. While the church consists of Jewish and Gentile believers of Christ with equal standing before God, in this and in the coming age, God seems to make a distinction in their purposes, especially for the Gentiles in their relationship to Israel.
17. Ezra 5:13.
18. This does not negate or contradict retaining and maintaining Jewish culture as an expression of faith in Jesus.
19. The other two are "Who am I?" and "Where do I belong?"
20. Matthew 21:28-31.
21. Matthew 26:42.
22. See "*Passover: Kingdom.*"
23. Dr. O. Virginia Phillips.

Chapter Seventeen

End of the Journey

Cherished reader, we've come to the end of our journey together—or have we?

If I have succeeded in stirring your interest or stimulating your enthusiasm to celebrate Jesus through the feasts of the Lord, we will surely meet at His feet!

To encourage you to embrace, adopt, and adapt His feasts into your lives, ministry, and culture was my motivation, so that together we will fill the earth with the knowledge of His glory.

Beloved, imagine God's pleasure as His Kingdom community worships Him according to His established calendar. Around the world and around the clock, each week, each month, and nine times during the year, praise would ascend from every tribe and language in unison.

Imagine also the impact on the lost—among Jews, Arabs, and Gentiles—to see us worshipping as a community, despite differences in style.

Thank you for allowing me to share my vision, passion, and life through these pages. If in any way my story has blessed you, challenged you, or convicted you, may God be praised.

Let us all draw closer to Him and to each other as we *Celebrate Jesus!*

Lovingly,

joanie

If I can be of any assistance, please don't hesitate to contact me.

Share your holiday stories and pictures on our blog:

http://celebratejesus-thebook.blogspot.com/

Appendix

Practicalities

Some "How To's"

Holidays are a time of community—the gathering together with family, friends, and the stranger in your midst. Regardless of your choice of activities, make each holiday a special time of abiding with God.

The premise of *Celebrate Jesus!* is that the Kingdom community consists of people of every tribe, nation, and language. Like the Word of God itself, the Kingdom transcends any one culture. We are enriched as we share our various styles of worship and celebration. It is my hope that you will each take the information gleaned herein to embrace, adopt, and adapt the feasts of the Lord to your unique culture.

I offer only a sampling of ideas to get you started. Most of the references that follow are from a Jewish perspective, thus the teaching in those pages will differ (sometimes vastly) with what I've shared. Please explore and experiment. Develop your own family and church traditions, then share them with the rest of us. Just maintain your focus as you *Celebrate Jesus!*

SABBATH

Sabbath evening is a time for family and friends to gather for a special meal. The cares and work of the week are set aside, and God is a welcomed guest. Make your table and meal something special to set this night apart from the rest of the week. Take communion as a family and bless each person at your table.

NEW MOON

Gather as a community to praise and worship God, thanking Him for the beginning of a new month. Enjoy a community meal. Take time to reflect on the past month as you prepare for the next.

PASSOVER

The Passover Seder can be simple or elaborate. *Celebrate Passover Haggadah* is an excellent resource for both first timers and the more experienced. Containing practicalities as well as the liturgy, it's the one book for all your needs. It can be used for a small or a large church family. The book is available through the Web site www.celebratejesusthebook.com.

UNLEAVENED BREAD

This is a great time for some good cleaning of your homes as well as your lives. The biblical mandate is to remove all leaven from your homes. While this might be a bit extreme, you can remove leavened products from your diet for the week. Matzo is rather hard to digest, but pita is a good substitute.

This month also begins God's calendar. Take time as a family to share God's goals for your lives for the coming year. Write them down, and then pray with and for each other. Next year, praise God for what He has done.

FIRSTFRUITS

Celebrate the Resurrection!

WEEKS

God described the Promised Land as "flowing with milk and honey." Therefore, forget cholesterol and delight your palates with lots of dairy and honey recipes like cheesecake, cheese blintzes (Jewish crepes), or honey cookies and cakes. Don't forget plenty of fresh fruits and vegetables! There are recipes available at the Web site www.celebratejesusthebook.com as well as links to additional resources.

BLOWING OF TRUMPETS

Because this holiday is considered the civil Jewish New Year, foods traditionally related to provision (apples), fertility (fish), and sweetness (honey) are served. Round challah (bread) is used to symbolize the continuous cycle of the seasons of life. Again, visit the Web site for some great recipes to try!

- **Craft:** Make shofars from papier maché or clay.

DAY OF ATONEMENT

Jesus expected fasting to be a regular part of the life of prayer, and the Day of Atonement is a perfect time to engage in fasting. A fast demonstrates a willingness to submit physical needs for undistracted time with God. A family fast provides unique opportunities for spiritual growth and bonding. In place of the business of preparing meals, use the time for talking and praying. Keep the time focused on God. If health is not jeopardized, people of any age can fast. Fast according to your own convictions. Drink lots of water.

- **Intercession:** On this special day, intercede on behalf of your nation and Israel.
- **Craft:** On a waterproof card (a piece of plastic), write the sins of which God is convicting you. Write them in red water-soluble ink. Then place the cards into a bowl of water and watch the water turn blood red as those sins are washed away.

FEAST OF TABERNACLES

Construct a booth large enough for a small table where you can have a meal or maybe take communion. Booths can be simply made with garden lattice tied together. Cover the booth with branches, then decorate with dried or fresh fruit, lights, and pictures. The whole family can get involved.

HANUKKAH

- **Craft:** Hanukkiah—a nine-branch candelabra. Any material makes a good Hanukkiah—wood, egg cartons, clay, papier maché. The ninth candle is, in some manner, separated from the others.
- **Foods:** Fried foods are a reminder of the Legend of the Oil. Potato latkes (pancakes) and jelly donuts are plentiful at this time.

PURIM

Scripture gives us the plan of celebrating this holiday: fasting on the first day and then feasting and merriment on the second. Giving of gifts to the poor is a very important part of this celebration. Since "purpose" is our theme for Purim, take this time to refocus on God's call on your life, on your church, and on your community. A focus on missions or an evangelistic outreach is always appropriate on Purim.

ADDITIONAL RESOURCES

You, dear readers, are the best resource for ideas and suggestions. Please feel free to send in your thoughts, ideas, recipes, and stories of how you have learned to celebrate Jesus through the feasts: http://celebratejesus-thebook.blogspot.com/.

Celebrate Passover Haggadah by Joan Lipis. For over sixteen years, this book has been used in various ministries to share the joy of Passover with individuals, families, and church groups.

Links to various online and hardcopy resources are available at www.celebratejesusthebook.com, including traditional Jewish Web sites, children's curriculum for teaching the feasts, instructions for building your own Tabernacles booth, and holiday recipes (both traditional and modern).

Hanukkah in the Book of Daniel

Daniel's precise description of the events of Antiochus' reign has led some Bible critics to reject the prophet's authorship. The books of the Maccabees corroborate Daniel's historical accuracy while pointing to a future fulfillment as well.

The following material is based exclusively upon the radio transcripts of Arnold Fruchtenbaum.[1]

Daniel 8:9-12 describes the events of Antiochus' reign:

- Rise to power
- War against the Jews after his defeat in Egypt
- Magnified himself by claiming to be deity, demanding worship (the Abomination of Desolation)
- Forbid daily sacrifices
- Desecrated the Temple
- Received support of some Jews
- Perverted the Jewish people

Chapter 8:13-14 gives the length of Antiochus' persecutions.

Chapter 11:21-35 lists the strategic actions of Antiochus:

> In these verses we find a supernatural alignment between the activities of Antiochus and the anti-Christ. What follows is the fulfillment of the former:

- Verse 21: Antiochus "contemptibly" or illegitimately usurped the throne. He came at a time of security and obtained the kingdom by intrigue (flatteries).
- Verse 22: Antiochus consolidated his power and overthrew the High Priest (prince of the covenant).
- Verse 23: Antiochus made a political alliance with Egypt by having his sister marry into the royal family yet constantly plotted against them.
- Verse 24: After plundering Israel, Antiochus squandered her resources on himself.

Chapter 11:25-28 describes the failure of Antiochus' Egyptian campaign:

- His failed war against Egypt
- Retribution against the Jews
- Return to his own land

Chapter 11:29-30a describes the failure of the third Egyptian campaign and Antiochus being forced to retreat by ships from Rome.

Chapter 11:30b-35 describes the persecutions of the Jews.

Messiah in the Passover

Details from the Old Testament	Fulfillment in the Messiah	New Testament Scriptures
Must be celebrated by all generations to come (Exodus 12:14)	Messiah celebrated with His disciples (The Last Supper)	Matthew 26:20-35 Luke 22:14-36 John 13–17
Victim must be a lamb (Exodus 12:13)	Messiah was the Lamb of God	Isaiah 53:6-8, 10 John 1:29, 36 Revelation 5:6, 12
Lamb must be male in the prime of life (Exodus 12:5)	Messiah was approximately 33 years old	Luke 3:23
Lamb must be carefully selected for death and kept separated before being slain (Exodus 12:5-6)	Messiah's sacrifice was "foreknown" before the world's foundation	1 Peter 1:19-20
Lamb must be taken from the flock (Exodus 12:5-6)	Messiah was from the tribe of Judah	Hebrews 2:17

Details from the Old Testament	Fulfillment in the Messiah	New Testament Scriptures
Lamb must be perfect without blemish (Exodus 12:5)	Sinless life and voluntary sacrifice	2 Corinthians 5:21 Hebrews 7:26 1 Peter 1:19 1 John 3:5
Lamb must be proven from the 10th–14th (Exodus 12:6)	Messiah taught the people and was tested by the rulers	Matthew 21:1–26:14 Mark 11–13 Luke 19:28-44; 20:1–22:6 John 12:12-50
Lamb must be sufficient for all who wished to eat it (Exodus 12:3)	Messiah's provision is sufficient for the sins of the world	John 3:16 1 John 2:22 Hebrews 7:27
Lamb was killed between the first and second evening (Exodus 12:6)	Death on the cross at 3:00 p.m.	Matthew 27:46 Mark 15:34
The bones were not to be broken (Exodus 12:46; Psalm 34:20)	Messiah's bones were not broken	John 19:33, 36
Lamb's blood must be shed and sprinkled that the firstborn might live (Exodus 11:4-7; 12:13)	Messiah's blood was shed that all might live	John 3:16 Romans 5:8 1 Corinthians 15:3 Hebrews 9:22 1 John 1:7

THE LAST WEEK IN THE LIFE OF JESUS[2]

SUNDAY

Triumphal entry into Jerusalem

MONDAY

Jesus curses the fig tree and cleanses the temple

TUESDAY

The authority of Jesus is questioned and
Jesus teaches in the temple

WEDNESDAY

The plot against Jesus

THURSDAY

The Last Supper and the Upper Room Discourse
Praying in the Garden of Gethsemane

FRIDAY

Jesus' betrayal, arrest, trials, crucifixion, death, and burial

SATURDAY

Jesus remains in the tomb

SUNDAY

Jesus is risen from the dead

The Calendar

Sadly, today there is a discrepancy between the biblically ordained calendar and the calendar followed by both observant and secular Jews. How and why this discrepancy came into being is not the subject here, but I will present both calendars to you. (For further information, follow the links referenced below.)

Passover is a good example.

Today the Jewish community has merged the singular day of Passover into the seven-day Feast of Unleavened Bread. Subsequently, Passover is celebrated on the fifteenth day of Nisan, which is actually the first day of the Feast of Unleavened Bread.

Passover is celebrated on the fourteenth day of Nisan (Exodus 12:6), and the Feast of Unleavened Bread begins on the fifteenth day and lasts for seven days (Exodus 12:7). They are separate and distinct days, with the latter being the first pilgrim festival.

This change has special significance to readers of the New Testament. Consider that by moving Passover to the fifteenth day of Nisan, it falls on one of the God-ordained pilgrim Sabbath days. But God did not originally make Passover a Sabbath day. The New Testament declares that Passover is a preparation day, the day before the annual high Sabbath day. (See John 19:31; Matthew 27:62; Mark 15:42; Luke 23:54; John 19:42)

Another challenge comes from the adjustments necessitated by trying to sync the Hebrew, lunar-based calendar with the Gregorian, solar-based calendar.

Hebrew months always begin with the first sighting of the next waxing moon following a new moon. When the first tiny sliver of the next waxing moon appears, the first day of a new month is officially declared.

A solar year is 365 days long, while a lunar year of 12 months is usually 354 days, 11 days shorter. In order to remain aligned with the solar year, an extra month is added periodically to certain years—a Hebrew leap year.[3]

The problem with strictly lunar calendars is that there are approximately 12.4 lunar months in every solar year. Thus, a 12-month lunar calendar loses about 11 days every year, and a 13-month lunar calendar gains about 19 days every year. The months on such a calendar "drift" relative to the solar year.

On a 12-month lunar calendar, the month of Nisan (which is supposed to occur in the spring) would occur 11 days earlier each year. Eventually this would occur in the winter, the fall, the summer, and then (after about 33 years) the spring again. To compensate for this *drift*, an extra month is occasionally added.

The month of Nisan occurs 11 days earlier each year for two or three years, and then an extra month is added. This means that Nisan jumps forward 29 or 30 days on the calendar, balancing out the drift.[4]

Exciting? Confusing? No wonder Paul told us not to consider one day as more important than another!

For a more detailed look at the rabbinic versus biblical calendars, visit these Web sites:

- http://antipas.net/heb_cal_2008-9.htm
- http://antipas.net/heb_cal_2009-10.htm
- http://www.hebcal.com/hebcal/

For another look at New Moon:

- http://www.ou.org/chagim/roshchodesh/default.htm

Endnotes

1. *Ariel's Radio Ministry.* (1984). Tustin, CA: The Messianic Bible Study.
2. Cheney, J., & Ellisen, S. (Eds). (1999). *Jesus Christ, the Greatest Life Ever Lived.* Eugene, OR: Paradise Publishing, p. 208.
3. In every nineteen-year cycle, there is an extra month in the third, eighth, eleventh, fourteenth, seventeenth, and nineteenth years.
4. Adapted from: http://antipas.net/heb_cal_2009-10.htm.

Meet the Author

Joan Lipis

Joan Lipis is a Jewish believer living in Israel. Author of *Celebrate Passover Haggadah*, she now introduces you to all of God's ordained feasts through *Celebrate Jesus!*

Joan grew up in a reform (liberal) Jewish home. In her late twenties, she began a search for a greater knowledge of God and an understanding of what it meant to be Jewish. Her search ended at the cross of Christ.

Joan says, "Jesus is the only way to know God, and believing in Him is the most Jewish expression of my heritage." A graduate from Western Seminary in Portland, Oregon, she now directs Novea Ministries, sharing God's love through Jesus the Messiah to Israel and the nations.

Notes

Notes

Notes

Notes

Notes

Notes

Discover truths for your life through the Holy Days and Feasts

Celebrate Jesus!

Sabbath
New Moon
Passover
Unleavened Bread
Firstfruits
Feast of Weeks
Blowing of Trumpets
Day of Atonement
Feast of Tabernacles
Hanukkah
Purim